THE BARON OF LEIPERVILLE

The Life And Times Of
James F. Dougherty

By
Richard Pagano

FIRST PRINTING

Cover Photo - James "Baron" Dougherty on the right with Jack Dempsey in Atlantic City 1925. Dougherty, who refereed three of Dempsey's fights, helped Dempsey in his early days as a fighter and was a lifelong friend of the champion.

ISBN:9780692208809_19-95_ean

Published By

CHOICE ☑
Marketing
WWW.CHOICEMARKETING.NET

369 Turner Industrial Way
Aston, PA 19014 U.S.A.

Cover and Interior Design: By Daniel J. Falone

Printed in United States of America

Dedication

This one is for you, Dad. I can't think of a sport that you liked more than boxing. As I wrote this book, I couldn't help remembering all the fights I watched with you on television and in person over the years. You instilled in me the knowledge and understanding of the Sweet Science, and I thank you for that.

Joseph Pagano, Age 26,
Serving in the U.S. Army in Europe during World War II.

TABLE OF CONTENTS

Acknowledgments

Many years before I could even conceive of writing a book on the life of Jimmy "Baron" Dougherty, he had become the subject of one of my "Sports Flashback" columns. At the time, I didn't have enough material to even think about writing a biography on this legendary character.

As the years went by, all that changed as I began to collect more and more information about his life. I finally made the decision to get the project under way after I was contacted by Mariann O'Conner, who was a great granddaughter of the Baron. The material, photos, and information she provided, was the impetus for me starting the book. Also, my phone conversations with her were very helpful. I am particularly grateful for her contribution to the project.

I also received help from the Zimmerman family (John, Charles, and Patrick), who provided me with scrapbooks and photos that were essential in writing this biography. Mrs. Joan Zimmerman allowed me to conduct a series of interviews with her father, Howard Dougherty, who was the Baron's youngest son. Her brother, Jimmy Dougherty II, also contributed stories and information concerning his grandfather.

I am also grateful to Bill Stull, another of the Baron's grandchildren, for material and photos pertaining to the life of his grandfather. My interviews with Bill's mother, Margaret Stull, the youngest of the Dougherty children, were extremely helpful in my research.

I would like to express my gratitude to Mary Damico, another one of Dougherty's daughters, who I had the opportunity to interview at her home in Ocean City, New Jersey. She was extremely insightful in her recollections of her father's life.

Also, I would like to recognize the contributions of Mary's children. Joe Damico, a longtime Delaware County lawyer, for providing some really important photos and other antidotes; while his sister Nancy Soscia's phone conversations added to the project.

I want to thank George McLaughlin, another grandson, for his memories of the Baron and the hotel; and Diane Thompson, who offered her comments concerning her father, Matt, a lawyer and the son of Baron Dougherty.

A special thanks also goes to great granddaughter Anna Marie, whose lengthy phone conversation assisted me in putting together various aspects of her grandmother's life, the Baron's first and oldest child.

The gathering of photographs for this project was extremely important and many of the photos used in this book are from the Dougherty family. However, there are others that were provided by Jim Vankoski, Tom Fizzano, J.J.Johnston and Don Cogswell, who are the authors of the book, *Uncrowned Champions*.

I also would like to thank Keith Lockhart, whose knowledge of Delaware County history is unequaled, for information and photographs of Baron Dougherty and his family.

Finally, I am profoundly grateful to writer, author, and historian Chuck Hasson, whose knowledge of the history of boxing has no match. Chuck, a voting member of the International Boxing Hall of Fame, assistant editor of PhillyBoxingHistory. com, a member of the Pennsylvania Boxing Hall of Fame and widely regarded as the ultimate expert on Philadelphia boxing history, was crucial in making this book happen. I owe an enormous debt to him for all his help throughout the writing of the book.

I am extremely thankful to all these individuals who came together to make this book a reality.

INTRODUCTION

As I walked in the side entrance of Billie Richie's Hotel & Bar at 1436 Chester Pike in Crum Lynne, I couldn't believe the length of the bar. It was my first time there, and I didn't have much trouble getting in. In fact, there weren't many of us that had trouble entering the well-known watering hole on the Pike. None of us were 21, and there weren't many, if any, in Billie Richie's that night that was over 21.

At one time it was known as the liveliest spot on Chester Pike between Chester and Philadelphia. The 1950's advertisement also said that Billie Richie's had the best of everything and was lots of fun.

For me, it was a night out with friends in the summer of 1971. We were all home from college, and we were there to see a local band (The Magic Bus) and have a few beers. We were given plastic cups at the door, which allowed us to drink all the beer we could for $3.00.

The Magic Bus, whose members were guys we grew up with, played behind the bar and was a decent cover band for the time. I can also still remember a huge painting of Jack Dempsey on the wall across from the bar.

Other than what I can recall, I really don't remember much more than that. And I surely had no idea at the time how historic that hotel and bar was. Billie Richie, a former boxer, purchased the hotel and bar from the Dougherty family in 1954.

Jimmy Dougherty, known at the time as the "Baron of Leiperville", had the hotel and bar built on an old foundation of a colonial house, which was the same tract of property that the Continental Army encamped when retreating from Chadds Ford.

The building, which Dougherty called The Colonial Hotel, was completed in 1907. It consisted of fourteen rooms, three baths, a bar, and a separate dining hall. In a building adjoining the hotel was also a pool room.

The hotel, which was built on nine acres, was constructed with imported stone and had a beautiful porch where you could sit and relax.

The bar itself was 75 feet long, and at one time it was reported to be the longest bar on the east coast. The top of the bar was made of mahogany shipped in from the Philippines, and it was 2 1/2 inches thick.

In the rear of the hotel was first a gymnasium, then a ring under a tent and eventually a boxing arena which held 5,000 fans.

It was there that some of the greatest fighters in the sport either trained or fought. Boxers such as: Jack Johnson, Joe Gans, Jack Blackburn, Two-Ton Tony Galento, Johnny Kilbane, John Henry Lewis, Tony Canzoneri, Maxie Rosenbloom, Sugar Ray Robinson, Billy Conn, Benny Bass, Mickey Walker, Kid Chocolate, Vince Dundee, Fritzie Zivic, Joey Maxim, George Godfrey, and Jack Dempsey.

Dougherty's boxing establishment was famous nationwide thanks to writer Damon Runyon. It was Runyon who dubbed Dougherty "The Baron of Leiperville", and many of his nationally syndicated columns were written about the Baron and his Leiperville boxing mecca.

Runyon was quick to recognize that Baron Dougherty was a colorful personality who made good newspaper copy. He and the Baron became close, life-long friends.

It has been established that Runyon wrote, "Little Miss Marker" on one of his long stays at the hotel.

That was the tearjerker that later became a memorable 1934 movie starring Shirley Temple and Adolph Menjou.

Dougherty was very influential in the lives of some of the nation's legendary fighters. He not only developed a friendship with Jack Johnson, the controversial and first black heavyweight champion of the world, but became his manager and trusted negotiator for his early fights in the eastern part of the country.

He befriended the great world lightweight champion Joe Gans, and had him train in Leiperville for some of his bouts. Dougherty also had Gans examined by his doctor, where it was discovered that the legendary fighter had tuberculosis.

Dougherty then loaned Gans money so he could get to the west coast, where he engaged in that memorable 42-round championship fight with Battling Nelson.

He thought he finally had his heavyweight champion when he was managing George Godfrey during the 1920's. Unfortunately, Godfrey would never get a shot at Dempsey's world title because the champion drew the color line and would not fight a black boxer.

Dougherty obtained probably his greatest national attention when he was the third man in the ring for the Jack Dempsey-Tommy Gibbons heavyweight championship bout in Shelby, Montana. Having already refereed two of Dempsey's previous fights, Dougherty was handpicked by the champion's manager Doc Kearns to work this fight.

The Baron had always felt he had partially contributed to the fistic glory won by Dempsey and Joe Louis.

He had taken in a hungry and down and out Dempsey and provided him a job waiting on tables at his hotel, while he was training for his 1918 fight with Battling Levinsky. A year later, Dempsey took the world title from Jess Willard in Toledo, Ohio.

Dougherty was instrumental in getting Jack Blackburn released from Eastern Penitentiary, where he then built Joe Louis into a world champion and the most feared heavyweight puncher in modern history.

Baron Dougherty posts the $10,000 forfeit guarantee for Johnny Kilbane in his fight with Benny Leonard to Tiny Maxwell, sports editor of the Public Ledger, as Lou Jaffe looks over Maxwell's shoulder. Dougherty promoted this fight at Shibe Park on July 25, 1917.

The Baron also promoted many outstanding fights, with the most popular being the non-title bout between Johnny Kilbane and Benny Leonard on July 22, 1917, at Shibe Park in Philadelphia.

The Colonial Hotel was a real hot spot for celebrities and attracted prominent people from all parts of the country. They all loved the Baron. Individuals such as: Mickey Cochrane, Damon Runyon, H.L.Mencken, Jack Dempsey, Estelle Taylor, Anthony Drexel Biddle, Sam Riddle, owner of the great racehorse Man O' War, Connie Mack, Postmaster General Jim Farley, actress Zazu Pitts and John B. Kelly Sr., to name a few.

I also discovered much later that the Baron's home, which was a mansion on Chester Pike in Ridley Park, was just two blocks up the street from where I lived. Unfortunately, when I moved to Ridley Park in 1962, his mansion had been sold and became an apartment complex.

The Baron also established a fire company, sponsored sports teams, was a civic worker, served two terms as a Delaware County Democratic Commissioner, raised eight children, and even tried to get Sam Vauclain, President of Baldwin Locomotives, elected president of the United States.

He once met and sipped champagne with Queen Marie of Romania at an affair in New York; and had dinner with Teddy Roosevelt (who he had met when he was New York Police Commissioner) in the White House.

More importantly, Baron Dougherty was a real friend to the people who were down and out. Many times, he would give money to someone when they most needed it.

He also loved to do things for the kids. Every year, the Baron would gather hundreds of youngsters and take them on picnics to Willow Grove or some other park.

He was as big-hearted as they came and would literally give you the shirt off his back. Vincent Mallon once said, "He was always buying food for this family, or sending a ton of coal to that family. He was a promoter who never stayed on the job at the hotel. He could have been a millionaire."

When Dougherty passed on October 5, 1949, his honorary pallbearers included such names as: Jack Dempsey, Sam Riddle, Sugar Ray Robinson, and Connie Mack.

Jimmy "Baron" Dougherty was a true legend in every sense of the word and quite possibly the most colorful sports personality in the history of Delaware County.

- Chapter 1 -

Dougherty and
Boxing's Biggest Scam

"The fight that won't stay dead."

James "Body" Johnson – Chairman of the committee that brought the Dempsey/Gibbons fight to Shelby.

In April of 1923, Jack "Doc" Kearns, Jack Dempsey's manager, was notified that a group of wealthy bankers, oilmen and cattlemen from Montana wished to stage a heavyweight championship fight between Dempsey and Tommy Gibbons in Shelby.

Shelby was a small town about thirty miles south of the Canadian border. This place that evolved into a town almost by accident had a population of about 5,000 in 1913, only to have it decline when a drought ravaged the region. People began to flee as the conditions got worse. Shelby was experiencing the same economic plague that decimated the rest of the state, and the residents began a quick exodus.

Things would begin to turn around for the small Montana town when oil was discovered north of Shelby in 1921. In his book, *Shelby's Folly*, author Jason Kelly wrote, "If Montana's history has been shaped by one telltale pattern; it is the cycle of boom-bust development.

"As the closest town to the wildcat wells that started spurting oil, Shelby became the economic beneficiary of a new population spike, unique to its lubricated location.

"By the summer of 1922, as the rest of the state's economy withered with its crops, Shelby was in full bloom. An increase in population and name recognition transformed the empty prairie, miles from nowhere, into a destination for risk-taking big spenders."

That same year, the American Legion Boxing Club was formed to promote fight cards in town. Mayor James A. Johnson's son James "Body "Johnson became the chairman of the committee and he promoted a few successful shows.

It seemed that real estate sales that followed the initial oil strike had really slowed down, and Shelby's thoughts of becoming "the Tulsa of the West" were fading. That is when Johnson suggested that Shelby host Jack Dempsey's next heavyweight title defense against challenger Tommy Gibbons.

After finally contacting Doc Kearns, it took months to persuade him to sign a contract. Kearns demanded his fighter be paid $300,000 for the bout with Gibbons. He wanted $100,000 when the contract was signed, another $100,000 sixty days before the fight. The final $100,000 would have to be paid in full one week before the fight.

These were not real experienced boxing promoters in Montana, but they did love to gamble. Many fight experts around the country felt that it was an advertising scheme to give publicity to the unknown out-of-the-way town.

Even Tex Rickard, who was known as one of the greatest promoters in history, was very skeptical of this promotion. "I cannot see how the promoters can hope to get a crowd to Shelby which will make the bout a financial success," said Rickard. "And if they do attract the necessary crowd I do not see how they can handle it."

Loy J. Molumby, who was the statewide commander of the American Legion in Montana, met Kearns in Chicago on May 1st. At that meeting, the first $100,000 was given to Kearns and a contract was signed. In his book, *A Flame of Pure Fire: Jack Dempsey and the Roaring '20s*, Roger Kahn wrote, "Kearns wanted to be clear about something else. If the Shelby people missed a payment, if they missed either of the two later one hundred thousand dollar installments, then the contract would be null and void. Kearns and Dempsey would keep everything they had been paid, but the obligation for Dempsey to fight would end. Loy Molumby wanted the fight. He did not object to this overwhelmingly one-sided arrangement."

Robert Edgren of the *Great Falls Tribune* reported, "The Shelby people want to put Shelby on the map and they are willing to pay for it. They are so willing that they will put up $300,000 for Dempsey's end, the same amount Tex Rickard paid Dempsey for the match with Carpentier at Jersey City."

Eddie Kane, Gibbon's manager, was also at the meeting and he raised the issue of money for his fighter. Gibbons agreed to fight without any guarantee of any kind. On the other hand, his manager asked to have some of the rules changed for the fight. "In clinches, Dempsey delivered a fierce wallop to the back of the neck," wrote Kahn. "This so-called rabbit punch jolted the spinal cord. Kane wanted rabbit punches prohibited. He lost that argument. He also wanted kidney punches ruled fouls. Dempsey's tremendous hooks into the body were usually propelled into the ribs. Sometimes, when an opponent turned, a Dempsey hook landed flush on the kidney. A fighter thus struck would find blood in his urine for some time afterward. In the short term he might not want to fight anymore. Kearns had the champion; Kearns was in charge. Kane lost again."

Besides Dempsey's money, the most important aspect of the fight that was discussed in Chicago was the referee. Kane wanted Michael Collins of Minneapolis, a matchmaker who was a friend of Gibbons. It is important to note that if there was no knockout in the fight, the referee would then decide the winner. Having been running the show up to this point, Kearns said there would be a fight only if Jimmy Dougherty of Lieperville, Pennsylvania, got the job. Dougherty was a good friend of both Kearns and Dempsey. Kane put up an argument but lost. Delaware County's own Jimmy "Baron" Dougherty would be the referee.

In his book, *The Fight That Won't Stay Dead,* author Body Johnson said, "The terms of the contract provided that Gibbons was to receive $10,000 as advance training expenses, of which he was paid $7,500, and in addition he was to receive a percentage of the gate after the $300,000 payment to Dempsey had been paid. Of course, he never received anything on this percentage.

"Let me explain that Gibbons did not fight for nothing, as has often been said. In addition to the $7,500 cash payment that was made to him, he was furnished a free house for himself and family with all his expenses paid during the period of his training in Shelby."

Dempsey's camp was in Great Falls, and he and Doc Kearns were greeted with a parade when they arrived. Dempsey had quite a few boxers at his camp to get him ready for his fourth title defense since capturing the world heavyweight championship from Jess Willard in 1919. Included in his stable of fighters was Billy Wells, English heavyweight; Jack Burke, Pittsburgh heavyweight; Pacific Coast lightweight Joe Benjamin; English heavyweight Harry Drake; and George Godfrey, the Black Shadow of Leiperville, managed by Kearns' handpicked referee Baron Dougherty.

George Godfrey possessed every attribute (6'3", 240 lbs.) necessary to become the heavyweight champion of the world except the right skin color. Even though he beat plenty of top contenders, he never got the chance to fight for the world title.

Dougherty had a good relationship with Kearns and was able to get him to hire Godfrey as one of Dempsey's sparring partners for the fight with Gibbons. They both felt that Godfrey could really help the champion get ready for this historic bout in Shelby.

George Godfrey (r), who was managed by Baron Dougherty, was Dempsey's (L) top sparring partner as he prepared for his bout with Tommy Gibbons in Shelby, Montana in 1923. (Tony Triem Collection)

However, during the sparring matches, Godfrey discovered that he could outbox the champion and his confidence grew. At times, he gave Dempsey more than he expected and actually made him look foolish.

Sports writer Harry Newman reported, "While he was making ready for his affair with Tommy Gibbons at Shelby, Godfrey was reported to have knocked Dempsey out during one of their training bouts. The war correspondents that were there at the time got word that the affair took place during one of the private bouts between the champ and Godfrey, but they were never able to confirm it. Godfrey refused to talk about the incident and the champion made light of it and scoffed at the idea when the boys tried to get the low down."

Kearns would never admit the story was true, but he felt there was no sense in taking chances with such a powerful fighter. As a result, Kearns had "Big George" removed, and a story was created that Godfrey quit because of broken ribs that Dempsey had given him.

This canard was hardly fair to Godfrey, because, of course, the public believed it, and nobody doubted Dempsey's ability to break ribs.

Dick Kain, sports writer for the *Philadelphia Record*, wrote in 1925, "Dougherty does not hesitate to say that Dempsey is afraid of Godfrey, and he claims that Jack fired the big Negro from Mobile out of his camp where Dempsey was training to fight Tom Gibbons because Godfrey was too rough in their practice boxing."

There were plenty of things to get accomplished between May 17, and the date of the fight on July 4. A wooden arena large enough to hold 40,000 people was built on a hillside outside of town. The cost of the stadium was $82,000 and it was paid for in cash. It was in the shape of a huge octagon, and more than a million feet of lumber, all cut and milled in Montana, was used in its construction. When the fight was over, the arena would be torn down and salvaged for practically the entire cost of the lumber as the arena was designed to use the type of lumber that was readily saleable for use in oil field operations. Johnson recalled, "It was so constructed without backs to the seats so as not to injure the lumber in its building or demolition."

There was still another problem, and it had to do with the final payment to Doc Kearns. The promoters were having trouble raising the third $100,000 payment. Someone had actually asked Kearns if he would take 50,000 sheep instead of the money.

"What the hell am I going to do with 50,000 sheep in New York, "said Kearns at a Great Falls news conference. "I want these people to live up to the terms of their contract. If I don't see $100,000 on July 2, Dempsey will not fight."

Author Roger Kahn wrote, "On July 3, the Associated Press dispatched a bulletin from Great Falls: *Shelby Bout Called Off.* They told Kearns there was no money, none at all, for the final $100,000 payment. Kearns said he would settle for $50,000 now and take the final $50,000 after the fight. The promoters said there was no $50,000 now. Kearns walked out and told reporters, 'This fight is definitely off.'"

"There was a final scramble, then, including a shakeup of the promotional team," wrote Earl Gustkey of the *Los Angeles Times*. "James Johnson leased most of his cattle and his oil properties, borrowed the rest, and somehow came up with the final $100,000.

However, Kahn claimed, "Stories persisted that Dempsey and Kearns were not serious about Shelby, and that there would be no fight in the wilderness. Dempsey and Kearns simply intended to take as much Montana money as possible, leave the state without boxing and without being imprisoned, then fight the winner of the Firpo-Willard fight."

Finally, the fight was on again, and later, sports writer Grantland Rice reported that Kearns had actually called off the fight on seven different occasions. Kearns was determined to get the entire $300,000 that the original contract called for, and he got it.

During the 48 hours before the fight, there was still confusion about whether the fight would come off. Because of the stories that persisted, many trains scheduled to arrive in Shelby did not show. Many trains were canceled when reports were received that the promoters were having trouble with their finances.

The crowd at the fight was estimated at only 12,000, and most of them were last minute gate-crashers. There were even some 50 Blackfoot Indians led by Chief Curly Bear in the reserved section in feathered headgear. The Blackfeet had made Gibbons an honorary chief. Before the fight began, Chief Curly Bear, waving the U.S. flag, led his Indian group from the $20.00 seats down to the $50.00 ringside seats.

All the country's well known sportswriters were also at ringside. Some of those distinguished scribes included: Damon Runyon, Grantland Rice, Bill Corum, Westbrook Pegler, Ring Lardner, W.O. McGeehan, Heywood Broun, Jim Dawson, Hype Igoe, and Otto Floto. Floto, who had covered every heavyweight championship bout in the last forty years, said that the only fight that he could remember that was held on a hotter day was the championship fight between John L. Sullivan and Jake Kilrain in July, 1889. Some reports had the temperature at 114 degrees in the ring.

Finally at 2:30, every ticket was marked down to ten dollars. Seating then became first come first served. About a half an hour later another five thousand people crashed the gate and rushed into the arena without paying anything at all.

By now, the day had become extremely hot, and Dempsey finally entered the ring at 3:36. It was unusual for the champion to climb into the ring before the challenger, but Gibbons didn't appear in the squared circle until eight minutes later. Before the fight got started, things would get even a little more bizarre.

"There was no referee in sight," wrote author Randy Roberts in his book, *Jack Dempsey: The Manassa Mauler*. "James Dougherty, Dempsey's old friend whom Kearns had named as the referee in the contract signed in Chicago, had been guaranteed $5,000, but been paid nothing, and so refused to enter the ring until he received the money. Unlike Gibbons, Dougherty was not willing to work for free, and he knew Kearns too well to expect to be paid after the bout. So while the fighters waited under ring umbrellas, Dougherty was on strike in the locker room area. Finally, about four o'clock, Dougherty ended his holdout, climbed into the ring, and started the fight."

Some accounts of the fight had Dougherty getting paid half ($2,500) of his money before the fight and half after the bout was over. His fee for refereeing was the most any third man in the ring had ever received for a fight and stayed a record for many years.

Author Jason Kelly wrote, "At last, the referee, Jim Dougherty, summoned the boxers to the center of the ring for instructions. After only a few words, Dougherty sent them back to their corners and tugged his tweed cap down on his forehead to keep the sun out of his eyes."

Referee Dougherty stands in between Dempsey and Gibbons giving instructions before the fight began. Dougherty's fee of $5,000 was the most any third man in the ring had ever received up until that time.

The fight was a classic matchup between slugger and boxer, but it fell short of being a classic bout. Dempsey started by pounding Gibbons' body, and Gibbons, when he had the room and time, would easily outbox Dempsey and avoid being hit. In the fourth, fifth, and sixth rounds, Gibbons gave Dempsey a boxing lesson. However, when Dempsey continued to pressure the challenger, Gibbons began to clinch in the later rounds.

Montana boxing rules did not prohibit clinching as a defense, so Gibbons continued to clinch quite often. Author Jason Kelly wrote, "That left Dougherty to pry the fighters apart often and as best he could without the threat of disqualifying Gibbons, and the referee sweated gallons at the work."

"The crowd was intensely partisan and Dempsey could not hit his opponent a foot above the belt without cries of foul ringing out," wrote Heywood Broun. "On the other hand Gibbons could not be criticized for holding on. It is a triumph to last against this champion. Dempsey's short punches to the body carried no such snap as they did against Carpentier. At the moment, he is not the killing Dempsey the ring once knew. The crown has sobered him. He may yet be dethroned while playing it safe and Louis Firpo might do it."

Baron Dougherty worked really hard separating the fighters during the contest because Montana boxing rules did not prohibit clinching as a defense.

As the fight ended, Jimmy Dougherty raised Dempsey's hand in triumph after the fifteenth round. "Of course Dempsey was awarded the decision," wrote Bill Corum in his book, *Off And Running*. "It was virtually guaranteed, because he couldn't have had a better friend than the referee and sole judge of the fight. He was Jimmy Dougherty, the Baron of Leiperville. The good Baron, about whom Damon Runyon wrote so entertainingly, was an intimate friend; Jack couldn't have been safer if his own father, Hiram Dempsey, had judged the fight."

"Shocked as Damon and the other scribes at ringside were by Gibbons' staying power, there was little doubt in their minds as to who would be declared the victor," wrote Tom Clark in his book, *The World Of Damon Runyon*. "For the referee and only judge, James Dougherty, was a pal of Dempsey's and the manager of the champ's chief sparring partner, George Godfrey."

Referee Dougherty, who was hand-picked for the bout by Doc Kearns, and was also the only judge in the contest, raises Dempsey's hand in victory after the 15th round.

"From the sixth round on it was all Dempsey," wrote Kearns in his autobiography, *The Million Dollar Gate*. "Now sometimes, if you haven't been careful in your planning, you have to worry about the possibility of a decision. But with my good friend, the 'Baron', as the third man in the ring, I had no cause to worry on that score."

After Dougherty raised Dempsey's hand, both of them slipped through the ropes and down the steps. They were running up the aisle as fast as they could when the bottles and seat cushions were thrown into the ring. It was really not a protest against the decision as much as it was a comment on the entire affair.

"Within three minutes the entire Dempsey crowd, Kearns and Dougherty included, was out of sight," wrote Corum, who had covered the fight at ringside. "They headed for a railroad siding where two private cars were attached to a steam locomotive that was warmed up and ready to roll. They climbed aboard and an instant later the heavy chugging sounded as the two-car special headed for Great Falls."

There is another version of what transpired after Dempsey's bout with Gibbons and it appeared in a magazine called *Great Moments in Sports* in the February, 1958 edition. The article was entitled, "When Dempsey K.O.D. Shelby, Montana, but not Tommy Gibbons".

It seems that Dempsey, Kearns, and the Baron did not leave for Great Falls immediately following the fight. Kearns, who had paid the government men the taxes on the tickets he sold at the box office, discovered that they were coming to his hotel the following morning and taxing him again on the tickets that were sold before he took over the box office.

The article reported, "Quietly Kearns formulated a plan of retreat. He summoned his associates: Baron Dougherty, a colorful old fight character who had refereed the fight; Joe Benjamin, a former boxer known as 'Laughing Boy', who worked Dempsey's corner; and Jerry 'Nick the Greek' Lavatas, Dempsey's trainer.

"'Baron, I put most of the money in that bank on Main Street,' said Kearns, 'You've got to get over there and loosen up the guards so that they'll let you take it.'"

Kearns sent Benjamin down to the railroad yards so he could find out if there was a train to get them to Great Falls.

He sent "Nick the Greek" to let Dempsey know what they were doing, so he would be ready to leave.

Kearns was going to do his best to make the town's people think that he and his small entourage were not leaving any time soon. So he went to Shelby's biggest and most popular saloon to greet every person in the place.

At the saloon, Kearns explained, "'No matter what happened with the gate, I'm glad we came here. You people did everything you could for us. C'mon, have a drink on Dempsey and me.'"

All the business people present, the mayor, even the bankers, all began to crowd Kearns and accept his drinks.

"'You're all right Kearns,' said one man, 'but we thought you were making a mistake demanding the money in advance when we didn't have it'

"'I'm sorry, I guess I did make a mistake,' said Kearns. 'Well, let's have another drink.'"

While Kearns was taking care of the town's people, the Baron was over at the bank trying to con the men in charge.

The article reported that Dougherty said, "'You fellows must be getting thirsty just standing around here.

"'A little,' said the head guard.

"'That's the thing,' Dougherty went on. 'Kearns was worried about you; he knows you were just doing your job over here. He asked me to see what you'd have. I can go down the street and get a few bottles of whiskey.'

"'Go ahead', he was speedily advised.

"The Baron returned with enough fire water to float a battleship. Seals were ripped open in no time.

"The guzzling was equally as rapid."

As with Kearns at the bar, Dougherty witnessed a change in the attitude of the men.

"'Your friend is okay, even if he got off on the wrong foot with us,' the head guard confided.

"'You fellas are all right with us too,' said Dougherty. "He paused for a final check of their condition via their eyes. Yes, they were adequately glazed, and then he made his big pitch.

"'Chief,' said Dougherty to the head guard. 'Kearns is supposed to get this money in the morning. It wouldn't make any difference if you let me take it to him now, would it?'"

The head guard hesitated at first and then Dougherty slipped a crisp bill into his hand.

"'No, no, I guess there's nothing wrong so long as you're getting it anyway,'" said the guard.

He opened the vault and handed the money to the Baron, who tried to appear almost casual as a he left the bank quickly.

During this time, Benjamin was arranging for the group to catch a train as soon as possible. Unfortunately, there were no passenger trains out of Shelby until late afternoon the next day. However, there were freight trains running. Benjamin hoped that they could catch one of the freighters.

When they all met back at Kearns hotel room, they decided to meet at the railroad yard about 6:00 a.m. In the meantime, Mayor Johnson was at the saloon hollering at the guard that gave Dougherty the money.

The guard explained, "'I gave the money to Dougherty because I thought I was supposed to.'"

During the confrontation, Kearns entered the saloon again and said, "'What's going on here? I heard you two. You're trying to play tricks with the money that belongs to Dempsey. I'm warning you, I turned that dough over to the bank, and I expect to get it in the morning, all of it.'"

The article further explained, "The next few hours were the tensest of Kearns career, as well as of Dougherty's and Benjamin's. They sat in Kearns's hotel room with their bundle of bills, half-expecting an onrush by the Shelby crowd, which might have learned the facts.

"Just before dawn, they tip-toed downstairs, past the desk and into the street where they reached the freight yard. They attempted to jump on the first freight train they saw, but the engineer let them know that they were not permitted to carry passengers.

Kearns said, "'Is it worth $500 to you and $150 apiece to your men to take us to Great Falls?'"

The engineer took the money, and in 15 minutes, Kearns and his group were on their way. Before the town of Shelby discovered what happened, Kearns, Dougherty, Dempsey, Benjamin and "Nick the Greek" were having breakfast in Great Falls.

A week after the fight, four banks had to close. "The Stanton Trust $ Savings Bank of Great Falls went out of business," wrote Roger Kahn. "There was no federal insurance for customers in 1923; depositors lost their savings. On July 10 Mayor Jim Johnson's First State Bank of Shelby stopped payments to depositors and closed its doors. It never reopened. On July 11, the First State Bank of Joplin, Montana, an affiliate of Stanton's Great Falls Bank, closed. On August 16, the First National Bank of Shelby was shuttered. Shelby had now neither a bank nor significant assets."

When Dougherty returned home, he voiced his opinion on how Gibbons could have beaten the champion. Dempsey hit Gibbons on the head early in the fight," recalled Dougherty. "And from then on Gibbons was on the defensive. If he had opened up and forced the fighting, he could have beaten Dempsey that day for with his recognized boxing ability, a good punch and a wise boxing head, he always is a dangerous opponent. But Dempsey stung him, and the lack of a fighting heart lost him his big chance."

The *St. Paul Pioneer Press* account of the fight stated, "Referee Dougherty permitted Dempsey to hit low four or five times during the bout, and never even cautioned the champion for his foul tactics. Twice the champion hit Tommy with hard blows after the bell had ended the round, but not once was he warned. And once Dempsey pushed Tommy through the ropes and then hit him while the St. Paul fighter was trying to get back in the ring. The fans did not approve of Dempsey's tactics or Dougherty's work, and time and again they roared their disapproval."

Dougherty said that he did not witness any fouls by either fighter and didn't feel anyone else saw any either. He called Gibbons as fast as a bantamweight and felt he was the gamest fighter that he had ever had the pleasure of refereeing.

Gibbons, however, did not feel that Dougherty gave him a fair chance during the bout.

"You can tell the world that Jim Dougherty won't referee for me again," explained Gibbons. "Every time he broke us, he picked on me, and would set me back so that Dempsey would jump in and bat me. He didn't say anything about Dempsey's fouls, but when I accidently got Dempsey with a back hand, Dougherty warned me."

Delaware County's own Jimmy Dougherty had been a part of the most preposterous series of events in boxing history and probably the biggest scam in the history of boxing. However, three years later Dougherty gave the fight in Montana a few more bizarre twists when he was interviewed in Atlantic City where Dempsey was training for his bout with Gene Tunney.

Sports writer Sam Hall was covering Dempsey's training sessions when Dougherty ran into the champ and Dempsey refused to greet him very kindly. Remember, at this time, Doc Kearns was no longer Dempsey's manager. Dempsey had married actress Estelle Taylor from Wilmington, Delaware, and he no longer wanted Kearns as his manager. Kearns was very upset about his decision, and he also hated Dempsey's new wife. However, Dougherty was still friends with Kearns, and Dempsey may have felt that the Baron had sided with Kearns. In one of his columns, Hall wrote the following:

"Dempsey forgets," said Dougherty, "that I went a long ways for him that day I refereed his fight with Tom Gibbons at Shelby. The crowd was hostile that day and it took a man with some nerve to lift his hand after the fifteen rounds were over. He won the fight on his merits, but I could have called it a draw or given it to Gibbons and walked out of the place unharmed.

"I was offered $200,000 (later he said $1,000,000) to see that Dempsey did not win that fight. The money was offered by a bunch of crooked gamblers that wanted to make certain that the champion got no better than a draw. I turned down all that money for the sake of the game and my friendship for Dempsey.

"I do not say that I protected Dempsey in the fights that I refereed for him, but I did see that he was not robbed. If that is protection, then he had it from me. I refereed the bout in which he knocked out Battling Levinsky in Philadelphia and the one in which he stopped Billy Miske at Benton Harbor.

"I have befriended Dempsey at times when he was poor and fighting his way to the front. I did not deserve the treatment from him today and I can see no occasion for it."

Many years after that, Dougherty told another story of how he was almost kidnapped before the fight ever started. "I sensed that there was going to be trouble a day before the fight, so I beat it up to Great Falls, near Dempsey's training camp. I was told that all the arrangements had been made by Gibbon's friend, Spike O'Donnell of Chicago, who was rated enemy number one before Al Capone. O'Donnell knew of my friendship with Dempsey, and he sent a gang out of Chicago to kidnap me on a special train that was held up in St. Paul. Then they heard that the fight was off, which happened quite a few times, and they returned to Chicago. At one point, I really did fear for my life."

Dougherty was 55 years old when he refereed the Dempsey-Gibbons fight in Shelby, but it was not the end for him in the world of boxing .There was still more ahead for the nationally known sportsman, but more importantly, was his humble beginnings in the city of Chester, Pennsylvania.

- Chapter 2 -

The Early Years

"All my life, I felt like a naked runner facing a storm of spears."

Jimmy "Baron" Dougherty

James F. Dougherty was born on December 16, 1868, at 20th and Chestnut Streets in Chester, Pennsylvania. His boyhood home was in a poor section of the city known as "Stone Row".

"It was not much more than a hovel," Dougherty once said.

The city of Chester was first settled by the Swedes in 1643 and called Upland. Then in 1682, William Penn made his first visit to the province and renamed it Chester for the English city of Chester. It was the county seat for Delaware County until the county seat was moved to Media in 1851. Chester's naval shipyard supplied the Union during the Civil War and the United States in subsequent wars.

Today, the city that is situated on the Delaware River, between the cities of Philadelphia and Wilmington, Delaware, has a population of 36,000.

Dougherty was baptized at St. Michael's Church in Chester by Rev. A.P. Haviland. His sponsors were James Kelly and Hannah Tolano, neighbors of his parents in the Stonehouse Row area.

Owen, Dougherty's father, was born in county Donegal, Ireland, in 1824. He was educated in Ireland, and at the age of seventeen, came to the United Sates where he settled at Kerry Bank, near Leiper's Quarries, which is where he found his first employment. He continued to work there until a premature explosion caused him to lose his eyesight. Owen then learned the art of making brooms, which was a trade he engaged in until his death in 1906.

Ann McLaughlin, Dougherty's mother, was also from Donegal, where she had known her husband from their childhood. Both families claimed to descend from the Danes who invaded Ireland and settled on the Irish Coast near the present Mollinghead Light House, which stands on land once owned by the McLaughlin's. Ann, who died in 1902, gave birth to eleven children, with only three surviving childhood. Of those three, Dennis died at the age of 22, and Joseph passed at the age of 16. The only child to live a full life was James.

James Dougherty attended the public school at 18th and Chestnut Streets and the Oak Grove School, but at the age of twelve he dropped out. "School never appealed to him, so his formal education was extremely thin," wrote Orrin Evans of the *Chester Times*. "Matter of fact, and he never was ashamed to admit it, he didn't learn to read without too much difficulty until comparatively late in life. But he was compensated for this lack by an amazing craftiness which enabled him to face life's hazards."

"All my life," Dougherty once said, "I felt like a naked runner facing a storm of spears."

For the next nine years, he worked in the Chester mills during the winter months and in the brick yards during the summer time.

As a young man, Dougherty was strong and tough, and had quite a temper. He reportedly earned his first dollar as a wrestler, and often pinned laborers at the brickyard where he worked in the summer. To show people how strong he was, he used to put a big Belgian granite block on his chest and let people smash it with a sledgehammer.

At a very young age, Dougherty was very athletically inclined. Baseball was really his first love and then he got interested in boxing. When he was 17, his family moved out of Chester, and went east on Chester Pike to Leiperville, today known as Crum Lynne. Leiperville was established in 1810 and named for Thomas Leiper, a Scottish immigrant who was involved in the quarry business. The stone from Leiper's Quarries was granite and it was used for buildings up and down the East Coast. Leiper died in 1825, and by 1884, the name had changed and the Crum Lynne Post Office opened.

"Actually, Leiperville was settled by the Swedes 60 years before William Penn came up the Delaware River," explained Dougherty in an interview in the *Chester Times* in 1936. "The first governor of Pennsylvania was from the Leiperville district, and that was the Swedish Governor Printz. His old home was on the banks of Crum Creek. Then a chap named Ridley came over with Penn and was given a grant that included the settlement and the township was named after him."

Dougherty continued, "Around 1730, the Leipers, tobacco folks from Virginia, established a factory there, and Tom Leiper is said to have built the first railroad in the United States in the township.

"The Leipers had a lot of money and financed Andrew Jackson's campaign, and Jackson and Thomas Jefferson visited them. So did John Morton, one of the signers of the Declaration of Independence."

In his book entitled, *The History Of Ridley Township*, local historian Keith Lockhart wrote, "Although James Dougherty was known as the 'Baron of Leiperville' in the 1920's, the name Leiperville itself was on the way out."

It was in Leiperville that Dougherty chose the national pastime as his life vocation and began playing baseball. In one of those games playing for Leiperville against Chester, he was given the name of "Jimmy the Wrestler". The story has it that he was running from third on a squeeze play and spiked Jimmy Murray, the catcher of the Chester team, which wound up in a dugout emptying fight and the umpire had to call off the game.

Actually, the first documented professional baseball player from Delaware County was from Leiperville. Tom Berry was born in Leiperville in 1842, and after fighting for the Union Army during the Civil War, he began playing baseball. From 1868 to 1870, Berry played left field for the Athletics, leading them to the championship in 1870. After his playing days, he became the Chief of Police in Chester and later a Delaware County detective. In 1915, at the age of 72, Delaware County's first major league baseball player died of tuberculosis.

Baron Dougherty with his wife Mary Elizabeth Bryan and their second child James, who was born in 1899.

Baron Dougherty is seen sitting next to his first child Ann somewhere around the turn of the century.

In 1893, Dougherty found the time to get married to Mary Elizabeth Bryan at the St. Rose de Lima Church in Eddystone. Mary's father, William Bryan of Baltimore, fought for the north in the Civil War; and her cousin was William Jennings Bryan, who later was the Secretary of State under Woodrow Wilson. Dougherty would always refer to William Jennings Bryan as uncle.

Two years later in 1895, Anna Marie was born, the first of the Dougherty's eleven children (only eight lived into adulthood).

BARON'S 1914 COLONIAL - Throughout his long career in Leiperville, Baron Dougherty sponsored and outfitted scores of sports teams. This 1914 entry in to Delco Baseball League was a memorable one. Pictured (in back from left) are Lee Athey, Rip Millett, Bill Feeley, Rube Mahoney, Dougherty, Tippy Martin, Ollie Athey and Jack Feeley. In front (from left) are John Copple, Clarence Wright, Dan Dolan, Joe Dougherty and George Mc Commons. Vincent T. Mallon of Woodlyn, who identified the players, says Mc Commons pitched both right- and lefthanded. In one July 4 doubleheader, he pitched the morning game with one hand and the afternoon game with the other, Mallon said. Child in photo is Howard Dougherty.

During that time, Dougherty even managed that Leiperville team he played on for a few years. He had some outstanding players on his squad such as: Mattie and Mike Kilroy, Jack Clements, who had played for the Philadelphia Phillies from 1884 to 1897, Earl Latham, a major leaguer for Chicago, and Vernon Smith. Before the popularity of the major leagues, semi-pro baseball was really big and Leiperville had some outstanding competition with teams such as: Chester, Cape May, Bridgeton, Salem, Camden, Harrisburg, Carlyle, and Dover. Some of those games were the largest crowds to ever watch baseball in the city of Chester.

Dougherty was a promising first baseman, later playing with Allentown in the Pennsylvania State league, as well as other clubs in that circuit. He also played in the South Jersey League until an accident caused him to drop the sport.

Sportswriter D.F. Montgomery wrote, "In one particular game, a pitched ball crashed into Dougherty's cheek bone, shattering it as well as his confidence, which knocked him from the baseball diamond to his first connection to the boxing game."

One day he decided to walk to Darby and take the trolley into 9th and Arch Streets in Philadelphia where Billy McLean, the grand old master of the fight game, was teaching the manly art of boxing at a gym for a small fee. Dougherty decided to take advantage of this opportunity, even though he didn't make much money working at Sam Rose's Brickyard in Chester, where he was making bricks by hand. So he began walking to the gym every day to save money; and he also considered it good training for the sport.

"It was in this gymnasium that Jimmy boxed with such noted men as Charlie McKeever, Mike Coyle, and Frank Craig the Cuban Wonder and other mitt men of note," wrote H. Walter Schlichter of the *Philadelphia Inquirer*. "He soon learned to be a very good boxer and also a wrestler under the tutelage of Daff Diggins, one of the craftiest little English wrestlers ever to come to this country."

Dougherty also got McLean interested in putting on boxing shows in Leiperville, which at that time was very much prohibited by the laws of most communities throughout the state of Pennsylvania. In spite of that, they both staged several fights in a little one story shack known as Foley's Hall. Most of the fighters at these bouts were McLean's pupils, including Dougherty himself. He boxed many bouts at Foley's Hall, including a fight with one of the outstanding fighters of the day, Charlie McKeever.

"In those days, Jimmy Dougherty was matched to fight Andy Black who had won the Championship of New York and Pennsylvania for the Schuylkill Navy as a middleweight," wrote Schlichter. "While Black was training for this fight, he took sick and never recovered and they substituted a man by the name of Jack McCoy. McCoy had given Jack McAlive, undefeated, retired champ, two of the best fights that he had in his time in Philadelphia. They fought ten, hard, vicious rounds to a draw. It was the first and last fight that was ever held in Darby Borough. A Philadelphia promoter by the name of Jack McCarey ran the show, and it was a sell-out."

Dougherty made a nice sum of money for that bout. "It was the most money I ever had in my possession at one time," recalled Dougherty.

With some money in his pocket, Dougherty thought he would branch out and become a promoter. So, he and sportswriter Walter Schlichter became partners and secured a large tent and staged a number of 15-round fights in Leiperville. At that time, boxing was taboo in the city of Philadelphia, but their fight cards drew a good audience in Delaware County.

31

Schlichter wrote sports, first with the *Philadelphia Item* and then *The Inquirer* for over 65 years. He was also the co-founder and co-owner of the Philadelphia Giants of the Negro League with Sol White. He had his own stable of boxers and was a very well-known referee, working mostly in the Philadelphia area from 1898 to 1910.

Schlichter also appears as the referee in the famous Thomas Eakin's 1898 painting *Taking the Count*. The painting shows Charlie McKeever and Joe Mack at the Philadelphia Arena with McKeever standing over Mack, as referee Schlichter carries out the count.

Dougherty's good friend and promoting partner, Walter Schlichter, appears as the referee in the famous Thomas Eakins's 1898 painting, "Taking the Count". The painting shows Charlie McKeever (L), who the Baron once fought, and Joe Mack ® with Schlichter carrying out the count.

"We put on some fights that drew good money in those days or any time," remembered Schlichter. "The accommodations were not as palatial as they are today. We had an old-fashioned oil lamp hanging in the center of the ring and that was the only light. Some of the matches that we put on were really classics and how the matches were consummated I can attribute only to the persuasive eloquence of Jimmy's tongue. Of course, we saved money by my acting as the referee and Jimmy attending to the box office."

One of those early fights promoted by Dougherty and Schlichter in Leiperville was on August 18, 1905, between Jack Blackburn and Sam Langford. Langford is considered one of the greatest boxers in the history of the sport and an uncrowned champion; while Blackburn, a good fighter from Philadelphia, later became Joe Louis' trainer. Louis was quoted as saying that if it wasn't for Jack Blackburn, he would have never become champion.

In his book, *Sam Langford: Boxing's Greatest Uncrowned Champion*, author Clay Moyle described the fight in Leiperville, "Blackburn had been scheduled to fight Joe Walcott, but Sam filled in when Walcott was unavailable. This time, the two men boxed in a tent with less than one half of the available seats filled with spectators. Once again, Sam built up an early advantage as he assumed the role of aggressor carrying the fight to his lighter opponent. Each time Sam got in close he punched Jack severely about the body. A game Blackburn came on strong from the tenth to the fifteenth sessions and steadily ate away at Sam's early lead. Blackburn fought at a furious pace in the thirteenth round and had Sam on the defensive in the fourteenth. At the finish it was the opinion of those present that Sam had a shade better of the bout by a small margin, but no official decision was awarded."

Another promotion by Dougherty and his sports writing partner was the Young "Yi Yi" Erne and Harry Lewis bout which took place on June 20, 1905. Both hailed from Philadelphia, with Lewis later capturing the world welterweight championship, and *Ring Magazine* editor Nat Fleischer, also ranking him the sixth best welterweight of all-time; while Erne, a lightweight, had over 270 bouts in his career. The fight went the distance with Erne taking the decision and two months later they fought again in Leiperville with the same result, an Erne decision.

On April 1, 1901, Schlichter and Dougherty were both involved in a promotion in Leiperville that today would have been a conflict of interests for both promoters. The two fighters who were scheduled for the Main Event were Elwood McCloskey and Eddie Lenny. McCloskey was managed by Schlichter and Dougherty was Lenny's manager. McCloskey, the Old War Horse, used to give all the champions he fought the toughest fight of their career, including the legendary Terry McGovern. Lenny was an up and coming Italian featherweight fighter from South Philadelphia who had moved out to Leiperville to be managed by Dougherty. Lenny was actually the first fighter that Dougherty had ever managed, beginning in 1898.

Soon after the Leiperville promotions got off the ground and had some success, a group of men consisting of: Tom O'Rourke, Dick Kane, Billy Roucap, and Tim O'Leary built a large boxing club in Essington, Delaware County. It really hurt the Leiperville fight scene and put them out of business. However, when Judge MacDade was elected the New District Attorney, he procecded to close the boxing club in Essington. The club had several lawsuits and summonary convictions against them, and the final blow came when the promoters tried to match Bob Fitzsimmons and Tommy Burns for the world heavyweight championship at their club. MacDade appealed to Governor Pennypacker to stop the fight, and he sent in the State Police which took over possession of the club. When the special trains arrived from New York, Baltimore, and Washington for the contest, they found that the State police had taken over and the fight was cancelled.

With the closing of the Boxing Club in Essington, Dougherty was back in business again promoting. However, he was also busy managing Eddie Lenny, who would get the opportunity to fight for the world featherweight championship under Dougherty's management.

- Chapter 3 -

Eddie and Harry Lenny

"I gave President Roosevelt nerve treatments for the pains in his legs before and after his trip to the Yalta Conference in 1945."

Harry Lenny – boxer, trainer, and touch healer.

Eddie Lenny was born Eddie Serata in South Philadelphia on November 22, 1878, but his parents later moved to Chester, where he spent most of his life in and around Leiperville. Bobby Dobbs, the great black lightweight, is given credit for getting Lenny started in his ring career. Taking up the sport in 1896, he improved so rapidly that he began to attract the attention of fight managers from Philadelphia to New York. However, Lenny chose Dougherty to direct his career because the Baron had taken a liking to the 18 year old.

In 1896, at the age of 19, Lenny made his professional debut as a featherweight and with his new name. In his first fight at the East Side A.C. in Philadelphia, he lost a four round decision to Kid McGlone.

During this time, Dougherty was 30 years old and working as a clerk in Leiperville when his relationship with Lenny began in 1898. That year alone, and with the Baron as his manager, Lenny fought 24 times. He really became well known in Philadelphia where most of his fights were at the Arena A.C. at Broad and Cherry Streets. In Philadelphia, only six round bouts were permitted, so Dougherty searched for fights where bouts of longer duration were permitted. The first of his long-distance fights was with Harry Burke at the Olympic A.C. in Athens, Pennsylvania. In that contest, Lenny won by a decision in 15 rounds.

Lenny's training quarters were behind the McLaughlin Hotel on Chester Pike in Leiperville, only a short distance from where the Baron was soon to establish a boxing mecca that would be known nationwide.

Lenny's training quarters (1897) were behind the hotel run by Dr. and Mrs. Wernz (standing at the top of the steps), who bought it from the Coward family. The hotel was located on Chester Pike in Leiperville. Lenny is seen sitting on the steps and Baron Dougherty is at the far right with his daughter Ann.

Ed McLaughlin had purchased the hotel from Dr. Wernz in 1901, and he had taken it over from the Coward family before that.

"My grandparents owned the McLaughlin Hotel, which was formally the Leiperville Hotel on Chester Pike," said Charles McLaughlin, the grandson of the owners. "Dorothy, who was my mother and also Baron Dougherty's daughter, married George McLaughlin, the son of the owners."

With a record of 30-5, Lenny lost a real heartbreaker to Harry Forbes at the Crescent A.C. in Toronto, Canada. Fought on March 31, 1899, it was a real battle that went 20 rounds, with Lenny losing a close decision.

He then fought eight bouts in a row without a loss. It began with a 10-round draw with Jerry Marshall in Chester, a decision over Jack McDonald in ten rounds in Coney Island, and then another draw with Patsey Haley in 20 rounds in Brooklyn, New York. After he knocked out Jeff Smith in 17 rounds in Toronto, he drew with Joe Bernstein in 20 rounds in Brooklyn, and then boxed a 25-round draw with Harry Forbes again, this time in Coney Island.

As Lenny continued to improve his record, the Dougherty family continued to grow. Jimmy was born in 1899, just a few short years after his two brothers, William and Thomas had died in infancy. Jimmy would later become an award winning champion pool and billiard player in the late 1920's and early 1930's.

Lenny's Boxing Quarters – Chester, Pa. Standing at the far left is Baron Dougherty with his fighter Eddy Lenny (sitting). Next is Ray Coates with Young Peter Jackson in front. Beside Coates is Gus Coblens with his boxer Herman Miller and at the far right is Al Herford with the legendary Joe Gans (with dog).

Dougherty finally got Lenny a shot at the world featherweight title on November 21, 1899, at the Broadway A.C. in Brooklyn. He was scheduled to meet the champion George "Little Chocolate" Dixon. With this opportunity, he would become the first American born Italian to fight for a world championship.

Dixon was the first African American to capture a world title and had been the bantamweight champion from 1890 to 1892. He also won the featherweight championship in 1890 and held that title until 1900.

Many boxing authorities still feel that pound for pound, Dixon was the best fighter ever. He actually defended his title a record 33 times, followed by Joe Louis with 27 defenses.

That night, Lenny gave Dixon one of the toughest fights of his long career. Although Dixon won the decision after 25 rounds, the local paper stated, "Lenny fought marvelously well for a lad who had only a limited amount of experience. He fought a clean contest and gave the champion a good fight. Referee Johnny White remarked that Lenny was an excellent prospect."

In the book, *Black Dynamite*, the legendary boxing historian and writer Nat Fleischer wrote, "The fight was not a one sided affair. Although Dixon outpointed the Philadelphia star, Lenny showed a disposition to mix matters at all times.

"Lenny showed enough cleverness and skill to justify the opinion that he would be a factor in the featherweight ranks, and he was. He was tricky and resourceful

Eddie Lenny was the first boxer that Dougherty ever managed. Lenny became the first American born Italian to fight for a world title when he lost a decision to George Dixon after 25 rounds in Brooklyn, New York, in 1899.

but in the respect, he found a man at least his equal in the champion.

"At the end of the tenth round, Lenny's nose and mouth were bleeding and his eye was cut. He showed signs of distress. The punches on the ribs and stomach were beginning to tell and his speed was gradually lessened. Dixon roughed it hard in the clinches and winded his opponent.

"As the fight progressed, Lenny regained much of his confidence and with it, his strength. He fought with vim and vigor. In the last five rounds, his work was more effective than in the early part of the fight. He stood off Dixon's rush with neatness. It was a good contest, and Dixon knew that he had been through a real fight when the final bell was rung."

The following year, he lost to Terry McGovern in Philadelphia. The bout was three months before McGovern defeated Dixon for the championship. Lenny's showing was a big disappointment to the local crowd. McGovern knocked out the "Chester Champion", as he was called, in the second round.

A year later, the Dougherty's second son, Matt, was born in 1901. Matt would later attend law school at Dickinson College and have a law practice in the county.

On January 24, 1902, Lenny finally beat Dixon in nine rounds in Baltimore. Unfortunately, Dixon was no longer champion.

"Dixon was so weak that he had to be assisted to his corner when the bell rang," wrote Walter Schlichter. "The decision was given to Lenny. Generous-hearted Eddie, instead of taking all the credit for the victory, stepped to the ropes and asked the newspapermen to say that Dixon had slipped and not to give him credit for defeating the old champion.

"It is a curious fact that in the myriads of stories written about Dixon, not one writer, as far as I know, has ever mentioned this fight, but it is recorded in Tom Andrew's record book and it is true. The bout took place January 24, 1902, in Baltimore."

Six months later, he fought Dixon for the third time. This time the fight was held at the Armory Hall in Chester and was called a draw after six rounds.

The *Chester Times* reported, "The bout was clean, scientific sparring, wonderful blocking, quick foot work and demonstrated general skill in the art of self-defense, however, on points, Lenny had the best of the former champion."

Later in the fall of 1902, Lenny met Young Corbett in Philadelphia. The bout, which occurred one year after Corbett took the title from McGovern, was a no decision after six rounds.

By 1915, Lenny had developed tuberculosis of the throat and was no longer fighting. That same year, a benefit was held for him at the Fairmont Athletic Club, where there were quite a few bouts and over $150 was raised.

Unfortunately, on May 14, 1918, Eddie Lenny died at the very young age of 40.

Many years later, Schlichter of the *Inquirer* interviewed Dougherty for his column. During the interview, Dougherty mentioned that Lenny was his favorite. "When you mention Lenny it reminds me that had Eddie been fighting in these days, he would have made thousands instead of hundreds, recalled the Baron. "He was a remarkable boy in every way. He never was a champion, but he mingled with champions.

"I managed many fighters, but there were none that I thought more of than that little Italian-American. He was a great boy, honest, appreciative and considerate. He fought for the love of the game. He was a wonder."

Eddie Lenny also had a younger brother, Harry (Viotti), who was the other half of the boxing brothers. Harry, also managed by Dougherty, had 40 fights as a lightweight, featherweight, and welterweight from 1902 to 1915. He fought successfully, but never quite attained his brother's status. Harry was what the British would call a useful fighter and good enough to fight with many of the headliners of his era. His two best performances were with Willie Lewis in a pair of six-round no-decision bouts in Philadelphia and New York.

When Harry retired from the ring, he turned to handling fighters as an instructor, trainer, and manager. One of his most successful fighters was Jack Delaney, a French Canadian and one of the most popular boxers during the 1920's. Lenny, as his trainer and advisor, was largely responsible for him becoming the light-heavyweight champion of the world, when he defeated Paul Berlenbach.

Through the years, Lenny managed many more fighters, but never was lucky enough to produce another world champion. Some of his best known products were featherweight Allie Ridgeway and heavyweights "Napoleon" Jack Dorval, Paul Swiderski and Ray Impelletierre.

On the other hand, Lenny did achieve some national acclaim outside the ring. What lifted Harry to this celebrity status was a gift that linked him to the last months in the life of President Franklin D. Roosevelt.

Harry recalled, "I gave the president nerve treatments for the pains in his legs before and after his trip to the Yalta Conference in 1945."

Harry was what you might call a touch healer, not a masseur. For years, he worked on the bodies of many people with his hands. "It's a blessing I was born with,"said Lenny. "It's been in my family for many generations. The last one before me was my grandmother who died in 1908. This type of treatment isn't massage; I just have a way of touching the nerves."

Harry Lenny, Eddie's younger brother, was also managed by Baron Dougherty. Harry never quite attained his brother's status as a fighter but was a successful trainer and touch healer.

On Christmas Day, 1944, Harry was summoned by a letter to a mysterious tryst in Rhinebeck, New York, by a Miss Margaret L. Suckley.

The letter stated that Miss Suckely had a friend she wanted Harry to treat.

When he entered the huge home at Hyde Park, Miss Suckley, who Harry found out later was the President's cousin, took him to a room where President Roosevelt lay.

Remember, this was 1944, and Roosevelt was contemplating a fourth term in the White House and he was a very ill man, suffering from angina, high blood pressure, gall stones and exhaustion. His weight had dropped from 190 to 165 pounds, and he slept 10 to 12 hours a day.

Suckley would stay with him for days at a time and was really worried about his health. She had never seen the president so melancholy, restless and disinterested. That is when she suggested to the president that he meet Harry Lenny.

Carlton Spitzer wrote, "When the press raised questions about his health, they were assured the president was simply tired from overwork but physically sound and looking forward to his fourth campaign against Thomas Dewey of New York.

"When that first treatment turned out to be successful, Harry was called back six times to repeat the procedure in New York and in Washington, D.C. Roosevelt's blood pressure had dropped, his fatigue lessened, and he was able to campaign in an open car through Manhattan in the pouring rain as millions of New Yorkers lined the streets and waved from office windows."

"Lenny returned to New York, and FDR, having handily defeated Dewey, traveled 14,000 miles by plane and ship to meet at Yalta with Joseph Stalin and Winston Churchill to discuss war strategies. Stalin and Churchill were stunned by FDR's appearance."

After the President returned from the Yalta Conference, Lenny gave him nine more treatments. Again, they were very successful and Roosevelt was now able to move his toes. Roosevelt's last treatment was on March 26, 1945. Soon after that, he left Washington for the polio rehabilitation center he founded in Warm Springs, Georgia. While there, he suffered a cerebral hemorrhage and died on April 12, 1945.

As Harry recalled some years later, "Before Roosevelt went to Warm Springs, we had set another date for a treatment on April 29, but he never came back alive."

Lenny always kept the letters from Miss Suckley thanking him for the good he had done for the President while he was alive. Lenny also received a reward for his services from Basil O'Conner, Roosevelt's personal lawyer.

"I remember making a dozen trips to the Roosevelt home on the Hudson and at least four to the White House to use my method of hand healing on the President," remembered Lenny. "I even have a Photostat of a check for $245 made out to me by the Roosevelt estate. That paid for my expenses. I never charged a fee."

Suckley remembered, "The healthiest weeks FDR had known during the previous year were the ones when Harry Lenny the boxer was his private therapist."

Even after his work on the President, Lenny would still get calls from people all over the country to receive treatments.

"A rugged sort, who believed in practicing what he preached to his fighters," wrote Jersey Jones of the *Ring Magazine*. "Harry kept himself in suburb physical condition and looked at least 20 years younger than his actual age until the winter of 1960, when, during a blizzard, he slipped in the snow crossing 8th Avenue, in front of Madison Square Garden, and smashed his left hip. An operation seemed to have repaired the damage, but two years later complications set in and Harry's health gradually declined."

Harry Lenny died on April 21, 1963, in New York. As a boxer, he never achieved the international fame of his brother, but as a healer, he forged a link with one of America's greatest Presidents.

Eddie and Harry Lenny were the first of Dougherty's fighters, and his management helped the two brothers reach some success in the sport of boxing. Dougherty also thrived as a promoter in Leiperville in the early part of the century. However, during this time, he met and managed a boxer who would shortly turn the boxing world upside down.

- Chapter 4 -

Jack Johnson

"Jack Johnson would stop in at our house quite often."

Mary Damico – Baron Dougherty's daughter

Jack Johnson was born Arthur John Johnson in Galveston, Texas, on March 31, 1878. One of six children, he had his first official bout in 1897 in his home town. He fought in Texas and in California, before he got the opportunity to fight for the Colored Heavyweight Championship. On February 3, 1903, Johnson defeated Denver's Ed Martin in a 20 round fight on the west coast for the title.

He now had reached the highest level to which any black heavyweight could realistically attain. Blacks fighting in the lower weight divisions had been fighting for world titles, but black fighters in the heavyweight division never had that same opportunity.

Though not sanctioned by any governing body, the Colored Heavyweight title was publicly recognized due to the color line in pro boxing in the 19th and early 20th centuries, when white champions drew the color line and would not defend their title against a black man. In the heavyweight division, the color line was drawn by John L. Sullivan, the first modern heavyweight champion. Sullivan had fought black fighters on his way up to the title but would not defend it against a black man.

In his book, entitled, *Unforgivable Blackness: The Rise And Fall Of Jack Johnson*, author Geoffrey C. Ward writes, "Sullivan had all the prejudices of his time and class. Black people were beneath his notice. 'Any fighter who'd get into the same ring with a black man loses my respect,' he told one reporter, and he did his best simply to ignore the existence of black challengers."

Succeeding white heavyweight champions James Corbett and James Jeffries followed the same pattern. Since the white champions had fought black fighters as equals on their way up, the color line was undeniably maintained due to racial prejudice. Since black boxers were being denied a shot at the world title solely due to their race, the general public gave credence to the Colored Heavyweight title.

Later in 1903, Johnson was living in Bakersfield, California, and fought Sam McVey, where he won every round and the decision. After the McVey bout, he headed east to fight for the first time. He first fought in Boston, where he beat a local favorite, Sandy Ferguson. Then he went south where he made his Philadelphia debut at the Washington Sporting Club on May 11, 1903, against a black boxer named Joe Butler. The law in Philadelphia required bouts to go no longer than six rounds and no official decisions were rendered if the boxers went the distance. That was no problem for Johnson, because he knocked out Butler in the third round.

Johnson did not return to Los Angeles after the fight with Butler. He had already fought all of the good black heavyweight fighters on the West Coast, so he decided to stay in Philadelphia, where he made the City of Brotherly Love his unofficial headquarters. At some point living there, he met his second wife Clara Kerr from North Philadelphia.

In the early years before he became a world champion, Dougherty was one of those managers that looked out for Johnson when he was fighting in the east and Johnson trusted the Baron.

"Clara Kerr was a sporting woman working out of a North Philadelphia whorehouse when Johnson met her," wrote Geoffrey Ward. "They would live together for much of the next two years." Johnson remembered, "I was able to set up a splendidly furnished suite of rooms where we lived happily."

"During that summer living with Kerr," wrote Ward, "Johnson earned a little extra cash playing several games as a first baseman with the all-black Philadelphia Giants, backing up his friend and fellow Texan, the pitcher Andrew 'Rube' Foster."

At some point during his stay, he also met Jimmy Dougherty, and they not only developed a friendship, but Dougherty became his manager and trusted negotiator for some of his fights in the eastern part of the country.

44

"Most black fighters believed they had no choice but to defer to their managers," wrote Geoffrey Ward. "They would turn over to them the bulk of their winnings, sometimes following their orders to throw fights or pull punches or carry opponents in order to remain profitable."

As champion, Johnson always said he was his own manager, but earlier in his career, he had to put some faith in white managers who had some control in his boxing career. Dougherty was one of those managers that looked out for him in the early part of his career and Johnson trusted him.

After a few fights in California, Johnson was back in Philadelphia again, this time to take on Black Bill, whose real name was Claude Brooks. The fight was his second defense of his Colored Heavyweight title and it took place at the Lenox A.C. Johnson defended his title, winning by a decision after six rounds.

Dougherty then made arrangements for Johnson to fight Black Bill again, this time in Baltimore. The *Chester Times* reported the following story on Monday, February 8, 1904, "James F. Dougherty of Leiperville, left last week for Baltimore, accompanied by big Jack Johnson, Colored Heavyweight champion of the world, after whose management the big fellow has placed himself why he is in this part of the country. Their object in going south is to sign articles for the fifteen round contest on February 15, with Black Bill of Merchantville, New Jersey, before the Knickerbocker A.C. "

A few days later, the *Chester Times* again wrote about the fight between Johnson and Black Bill, "The men have been matched to fight in Baltimore for 15 rounds with Jimmy Dougherty arranging Johnson's end of the bargain."

Before the trip, the 26 year old Johnson talked freely of his ambition to meet the world's famous heavyweight champion, James Jefferies, in a finish fight.

It is important to note that Johnson had yet to beat a top contender, but he was already publicly challenging Jefferies for the title.

"I see by newspaper reports from the Pacific Coast today," said Johnson to the *Times* before departing with Dougherty on their trip to Baltimore, "that Jefferies has decided to withdraw the color line and this will give me the opportunity I am looking for. I only hope it is true because I was unlucky enough to be born black is no fault of mine. After my fight with Black Bill I will start out and make preparations to force Jefferies to a matchup with me in three months, or claim the heavyweight title. I would also like to meet Kid Carter, Jack O'Brien or any other man that can be produced for six rounds before any club in Philadelphia offering the best inducements."

Jack Johnson even trained in Leiperville for some of his fights in Philadelphia.

The *Times* continued, "Johnson says he only weighs 178 pounds and that is not too big for Carter or the rest of the fellows who really mean business."

In 1905, and at times using Dougherty as his manager, Johnson fought 10 out of his next 12 fights in Philadelphia. That same year, Jefferies retired his world heavyweight championship, and Marvin Hart and Tommy Burns fought for the vacant title in 1906 with Jefferies as the referee. Burns was victorious, and for the next two years Johnson stalked Burns and taunted him in the press to give him a shot at the title. Finally in 1908, Johnson got his opportunity and defeated Burns for the world heavyweight championship in Sydney, Australia.

Johnson defended his title successfully four times before he met James Jefferies who was lured out of retirement to fight him in Reno, Nevada, on July 4, 1910. The fight was stopped in the fifteenth round with Johnson being crowned the winner. After the fight, there was pandemonium and bloodshed throughout the nation. In all, thirteen blacks were killed and hundreds were wounded as angry whites retaliated the loss of their so-called Great White Hope.

Johnson was never socially accepted because whites considered him too uppity, mainly because he had a white wife. He did not fight at all in 1911 and only had one fight in 1912. That year he was also indicted for violating the Mann Act, which made it a crime to transport anyone across state lines for immoral purposes. He was eventually sentenced to a year and a day in prison and was fined a thousand dollars.

To evade jail for these ridiculous trumped up charges, Johnson fled the country, where he fought in France and Argentina before losing his title to Jess Willard in Havana, Cuba.

Six year later, Johnson returned home to serve his sentence on July 20, 1920. At Leavenworth Prison, he served only eight months of his original sentence because of good behavior.

Johnson had opened a night club in Harlem, which he later sold to a gangster, Owney Madden, who renamed it the Cotton Club.

It had been quite some time since Dougherty had seen Johnson, and one evening in the summer of 1922, the former champion stopped by to see his onetime friend and manager. He was now 44 years old and was traveling down from New York where he was tending to his nightclub. Dougherty had been in touch with Johnson about a fight between him and Jack Thompson of Chester.

"Jack Johnson would stop in at our house in Ridley Park quite often when I was young to see my father," remembered Dougherty's daughter Mary Damico. "He would always drive up in one of his cars and even stay overnight at times.

"One time, Johnson arrived with his wife, and my father let him and his wife sleep in mother and father's bed. My mother was really angry with my father over that one."

"We had stopped over at Dougherty's house at Ridley Park, just outside Philadelphia, recently for dinner," wrote Damon Runyon in his syndicated column. "And John Arthur came roaring up out of the night in a big powerful car which he was driving himself.

"We could just see the whites of John Arthur Johnson's eyes as the old ex-heavyweight champion of the world sat back in the gloom of Jim Dougherty's veranda and talked."

"He got to talking about his past, and Johnson's past is always interesting, more interesting than his future, if he has any future as far as the boxing game is concerned. Personally, we doubt it. We rather doubt if Johnson himself believes he can really fight again.

"However, he undoubtedly believes he has enough skill left to prevent such as Thompson from doing anything to him. He seems to be highly skeptical about the ability of the present day crop of fighters, especially Harry Wills."

Johnson had only been out of jail for less than a year, and Dougherty asked him if he had made any money since leaving Leavenworth.

"Yes," said Johnson, "I've always been able to make money. I've always been a lucky fellow that way. That trouble of mine in Chicago cost me $200,000 one way and another, but somehow they were never able to keep me broke. I've always been a good hustler. I've never asked anybody for anything, and I've got a little something put away right now."

Both Dougherty and Runyon were curious how old Johnson was.

"I'm about forty-two," said Johnson. "I weigh about 230 pounds now, but I'm not working. Don't I look younger than Wills?"

"He stepped out into the glow of an incandescent light to let us see," wrote Runyon. "We are not sure that Jack looks younger than Wills, but he looks as young as about forty-two anyway."

"His head is shaved to the scalp, and was suspect the shaving is to remove any evidence of frost on the old bean. His coat was buttoned so tightly over his abdomen that the buttonhole yawned. Withal old Jack is still far removed from the Uncle Tom stage."

Runyon continued, "Old Jack seemed particularly anxious to talk about his famous fight with Jeffries twelve years ago."

"I've often heard it said that Jeff called me all kinds of names in the ring," said Johnson. "Jeff never made one remark to me. I hit him on the head, and he said, 'It's a pretty tough old head isn't it?'

"He could have raised the sympathy of the crowd and made it mighty hostile to me if he wanted to, but I never fought a fairer man. Old Jeff was fine all the way through."

"The fellow who gave me the talking to was Tommy Burns," continued Johnson, his gold teeth flashing in the dim light as he smiled at the memory. "He called me everything he could lay his tongue to when I was beating him down in Australia. I never answered him except to say, 'All right, old boy!' Jim Flynn was a mighty talky kid but he was nothing to Tommy Burns. Jiminelli, how that boy talked."

"But I got even with him," continued Johnson. "I kept pulling his nose."

"Anyone who has ever conversed with Johnson will recognize that Jiminelli," wrote Runyon. "It is the strongest word he uses."

"I think Jeffries was a game fellow," Johnson went on after a brief pause. "He could have done most anything he wanted to me and got away with it at Reno. I've always had mighty kind feelings for Jeff, and although I haven't seen him since that day, I'm glad to know he's doing well.

"I think one of the gamest men I ever fought was Frank Moran. I gave him a good lacing for twenty rounds over in Paris, and he never quit."

"That's the time they thought they had me in the bag, continued Johnson. "I know all about what they intended doing to me. George Carpentier was the referee, but I didn't care who refereed. I knew I would lick Moran so far that they couldn't take it away from me. I'd have stood for Danny McKetrick, Moran's manager, refereeing.

"They thought I didn't train for that fight. That's where I fooled them. I would wait until just before dawn, then go out and do my training where no one could see me. In the afternoon and evening I showed up around where the gang hung out, and they thought I wasn't training a lick. As a matter of fact, I was in good condition, and I think Moran was a good fighter that night."

After a few hours of conversation with the former champ, Runyon and his girlfriend at the time needed a ride to their destination, so they left Dougherty's beautiful house on Chester Pike that he just had built two years prior, and Johnson gave them a lift.

"We should have known better to get in that car with Johnson," wrote Runyon. "Jack swore by the bend in the great horn spoon that he would take it easy."

"Man," said Johnson. "I been driving a car for years and years and nothing ever happened to me except the time I got in jail in San Francisco for speeding. Look at the experience I've had. Don't you remember my race with Barney Oldfield? I was supposed to win one heat, but something happened to my car.

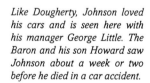
Like Dougherty, Johnson loved his cars and is seen here with his manager George Little. The Baron and his son Howard saw Johnson about a week or two before he died in a car accident.

"You know that old flyer I owned? That big gray thing? I left it in Chicago the night I was making my getaway. I told the man who was driving it for me to wait for me at the station, and maybe he's waiting there yet. Well, here's a nice hill, and I'll show you what a good car can do on a hill.

"I'm the most careful driver in the world. I never go over sixty-eight miles an hour, no time."

Dougherty would see Johnson off and on until the former champion's death in 1946.

"Johnson would stop by the hotel at times to borrow money from the Baron," recalled Dougherty's youngest son, Howard, who always referred to his father as the Baron. "In fact, the Baron and I saw Johnson about a week or two before he died. We were cleaning up at the bar when he arrived in one of his new cars. He didn't stay long, but again borrowed some money from the Baron and then left. Not too long after that, we heard that he was killed in a car accident."

"He was on his way back from Texas on the evening of June 9, when he pulled into a diner just outside Raleigh, North Carolina," wrote Ward in *Unforgivable Blackness*. "With him was a young man named Fred L. Cook whom he had hired to relieve him at the wheel when he got tired. 'They told us we could eat in the back or not at all, Cook remembered. "We were hungry and the food had already been served, so we ate. But back in the car, Jack really got angry.'

"Johnson took the wheel of his latest high-powered automobile, a Lincoln Zephyr, and roared north along Highway One at better than seventy miles an hour. Hurtling around a sharp curve near the little town of Franklinton, he didn't see the truck rushing toward him until it was too late. He lost control. The car swerved across the white line, left the road, and slammed into a telephone pole.

"Fred Cook was thrown clear and survived.

"Jack Johnson died in the hospital some three hours later."

In one of his visits to Dougherty's in 1922, Johnson introduced the Baron to a black heavyweight boxer who would finally give him hope of managing a world champion. That 6'3" 21 year old fighter from Mobile, Alabama, was George Godfrey.

However, before the saga of George Godfrey begins, the Baron's establishment of the Colonial Hotel must be told. Between his short stint of managing Jack Johnson and taking over the management of George Godfrey, Dougherty built a Hotel and Bar on Chester Pike in Leiperville that would eventually become nationally known.

George Godfrey on the left is seen sparring with Jack Johnson before Johnson introduced Big George to Dougherty in 1922.

In the 1940's, Johnson on the left and Godfrey on the right got in the ring one last time for a publicity shot.

51

- Chapter 5 -

The Colonial Hotel

"The Baron's hotel was the Sea of Fisticuffs and a camp of many noted fighters."

-Damon Runyon

In his 20's, Jimmy Dougherty worked as a bartender and manager at Coward's Hotel.

His nickname, "Jimmy the Wrestler", was again mentioned, but the origin of that moniker had a different story this time.

"He had created a bit of a reputation for himself as 'Jimmy the Wrestler,' wrote Orrin Evans of the *Chester Times*. "He gained that moniker through his prowess in throwing husky laborers at the Chester brickyard in which for a short spell, he had worked. He was ready for the rough-and-tumble life that was ahead of him."

"He learned one night at the old Fairview Hotel in Woodlyn that know-how can be very valuable," continued Evans.

In his 20's, Jimmy Dougherty had created quite a reputation for himself as "Jimmy the Wrestler" and as a bartender and manager at Coward's Hotel.

"Every Saturday night the dandies of that era escorted their bustle-adorned ladies to the Fairview Hotel to take gingerly flings at the schottise, waltz and occasionally a sprightly cake walk. And the beau brummels of that day were no foppish cookie pushers. There was brawn and derring-do under the raiment they wore.

"On one of these gala Saturday nights, someone insulted someone. That was the match that flared volatile tempers and hot blood into a blaze of screaming women, shouting men, flying fists and the quickly jerked-up knee.

"Sides were formed on the basis of residence, and the gallants from Leiperville were outnumbered."

"Two bums had me cornered," recalled Dougherty. "And they were moving in to let me have it. But it didn't last long because of my combined knowledge of boxing and wrestling got me through that tense crisis with nothing more serious than a slightly busted finger."

In 1905, Dougherty purchased a property in Leiperville, which was the site of an old colonial house along the eastern side of the Baldwin Locomotive plant on Chester Pike. He then began construction of a hotel and bar on that foundation laid in the early Colonial days.

That property and an early colonial building were originally constructed in 1846 by Judge Leiper. It was later owned by Mike Bagley, Daniel Lee, and Smith Longbotham.

Finally, the Chester National Bank came into possession of the property, and they sold it to Dougherty. The property was the same tract that the Continental Army encamped when retreating from Chadds Ford.

Dougherty established Leiperville's first fire company called the James F. Dougherty Fire Company in 1907 with eleven members. In 1919, it was renamed the Vauclain Fire Company. Pictured here are Dougherty (right) and Pat Dolan (left) with his first fire pump apparatus which was pulled by horses. (Keith Lockhart Collection)

Arden Skidmore of the *Daily Times* wrote, "Between the hotel and the Baldwin Plant was the Baltimore & Ohio Railroad spur which developed from the historic railroad Thomas Leiper built to haul stone from his quarries in Avondale.

"It stamped the Leiper railroad as the first commercial rail line in America."

While his hotel and bar were being constructed, Dougherty also found time to establish Leiperville's first fire company. It was originally called the James F. Dougherty Fire Company and was chartered on January 20, 1908, with eleven members.

In 1919, it was renamed the Vauclain Fire Company #1 in honor of Samuel M. Vauclain, who was president of Baldwin Locomotive Works and donated money and equipment to the company. Vauclain was also an engineer and the inventor of the Vauclain compound locomotive. He was awarded the Distinguished Service Medal for arming the United States during World War I and was a lifelong friend of Dougherty.

After the hotel was complete in 1906, it was not until a year later that Dougherty was able to obtain a liquor license. He actually bought beer and gave it away free to his patrons until the license was obtained.

"In launching his first big scale business operation, the Baron ran into difficulties," wrote Evans. "Opposition to granting him a liquor license for his new place developed, and the Baron had to do it the hard way.

This is the Colonial Hotel on Chester Pike in Leiperville
only a few years after it opened in 1907

"The law could not prevent him from handing out free beer, and for a long time he did just that, mean-while developing a loyal group of followers."

Actually, the first dollar Dougherty earned at his bar came from William Bradford Pierce, an employee of Baldwin's on October 21, 1907. Howard, his youngest son, still had that framed bill for many years.

Not only did Dougherty complete the building of the hotel in 1906, but that year also saw an addition to his family when Howard was born. Howard would later become very close to his father and take over his promotional duties which will be discussed more thoroughly in Chapter nine.

In 1907, the Dougherty's family increased to five with the birth of their second daughter, Dorothy, who would later marry George McLaughlin. George's father also ran a hotel up the street from the Baron on Chester Pike.

The building was appropriately called the Colonial Hotel and consisted of fourteen rooms, three baths, a bar, and a separate dining hall.

Dougherty's office was on the second floor, which consisted of a desk with wrought iron legs and a glass top and a bearskin rug on the floor.

Daily Times staff writer Arden Skidmore wrote, "Young Joe Fizzano, who fought for the Baron as a 12-year old, thought the office was one of the most impressive he'd ever seen."

Baron Dougherty, who is on the left with his pet terrier and Tippy Martin, the first bartender he ever hired, pose inside the hotel behind the 75 foot bar, which at one time was reported to be the longest bar on the east coast.

In a building adjoining the hotel was a pool room which William "Tippy" Martin operated for many years. Martin was also the first bartender that Dougherty hired and was a mainstay at the Hotel for many years.

The hotel, which was built on nine acres, was constructed with imported stone and had a beautiful porch where you could sit and relax.

The bar room was very impressive. The bar itself was 75 feet long, and at one time it was reported to be the longest bar on the east coast. The top of the bar was made of mahogany shipped in from the Philippines, and it was 2 ½ inches thick. The bar also had a brass rail and a water trough running around the bottom.

The bar room had a stone fireplace, a soup and lunch counter, and a piano. The floor was constructed of solid marble tiles, and there was a mirror worth $1,000 covering one entire wall.

Dougherty employed 20 bartenders, with Martin serving as the head bartender for many years. Many days the bar would be packed solid from the bar to the wall, with beer passed chain fashion to customers unable to get near the bar.

"The Baron had 12 bartenders around the clock," recalled Nick Hayes, an old-time Philadelphia whiskey salesman. "They hauled the whiskey up from the cellar in buckets and poured it day and night. The Baron bought whiskey five barrels at a time. I know. I was a salesman for Gibson whiskey."

Vince Mallon recalled, "Things really jumped at the bar during the noon hour, and on Friday nights after the workers at the nearby Baldwin Locomotive Works had been paid."

Howard Dougherty remembered that 100 half barrels of beer were delivered daily by the Chester Brewery.

"The Baron," as Howard would refer to his father, "would also purchase 50 to 100 barrels of straight rye whiskey at a time. Then he would have it blended at the hotel and cut to about 85 proof. It was then put into half pint, pint and quart bottles."

"There was a stock ale machine in the cellar," wrote Arden Skidmore of the *Daily Times*. "With the aid of a mirror and levers, glasses were lowered to the cellar by chute, filled and returned. The ale was kept cool by cellar temperature. No ice was used."

"Each day 20 blocks of ice weighing 300 pounds apiece and 100 half barrels of beer were delivered to the hotel daily," recalled Joe McElwain, one of Dougherty's bartenders.

Employees at the Baldwin Locomotive plant were paid in $20 gold pieces and silver dollars during that time.

"Hundreds of workers left and reentered Baltimore & Ohio Railroad trains at the stop beside the Colonial Hotel," wrote Ed Gebhart of the *Daily Times*. "Most of those workers cashed their gold pieces at Dougherty's with baskets used for the transactions."

When cash registers were finally installed, they would become so overloaded that the money had to be stacked on the bar.

Charles Price, a black man who was a porter at the hotel, described Dougherty's affluence in 1914 as follows, "On Friday nights he had 10 or 11 bartenders working. There were five cash registers along the back bar, but it wasn't long before they'd be bulging with money. Then the bartenders would stack the money up on the back bar."

"It wasn't unusual to see $20,000 to $25,000 in cash on the bar," remembered Howard.

The workers were apparently very carefree with their silver dollars.

Price, who also had to keep the brass rail polished and the water trough cleaned out, recalled, "I would find 50 to 60 silver dollars in or near the water trough every Saturday night after the bar would close."

Two years after opening the hotel, Dougherty purchased a 1909 Studebaker E.M.F. Touring Car. It was definitely one of the first cars ever seen in the area.

Two years after opening the hotel, Dougherty purchased a 1909 Studebaker E.M.F. Touring Car. Notice the man on horseback as Dougherty sits behind the wheel and his young son Howard sits in the back seat.

"The Baron owned the first auto I had ever seen in Delaware County," recalled Mallon. "It was an E.M.F., an early Studebaker model."

"The Baron was always coming up with something," remembered Vince Mallon. "Once he had his employees coat the adjoining railroad tracks with goose grease. The locomotives pulling coaches loaded with workers would then slide backward instead of negotiating the upgrade pull. With this delay, workers would leap from the train and rush into the Baron's to buy pints of whiskey."

Dougherty also built a gymnasium in the rear of the hotel for boxers to train. After the gymnasium was complete, he installed a boxing ring enclosed in a tent. Finally in 1929, a boxing arena that held 6,000 fans was constructed.

Orrin Evans of the *Daily Times* wrote, "Dougherty always had the desire to be a step ahead of the crowd. And that accounted for the fact that he was one of the first promoters in the nation to construct an open-air boxing arena."

It was there that some of the greatest fighters in the sport of boxing trained or fought. Fighters such as: Joe Gans, Jack Johnson, Johnny Kilbane, Jack Dempsey, Tony Canzoneri, Jack Blackburn, John Henry Lewis, Maxie Rosenbloom, Billy Conn, Benny Bass, Mickey Walker, Kid Chocolate, "Two-Ton" Tony Galento, Joe and Vince Dundee, Fritzie Zivic, Joey Maxim, George Godfrey, Sugar Ray Robinson, Johnny Jadick, Bobby Barrett, Pancho Villa, Joe Anderson, Alex Hart, Tiger Thomas, Harry Blitman, Pete Nebo, Leo Lomski, Jack Dorval, Steve Martin, El Ettore and Popper Stopper.

Seen here is the Dougherty family in 1917 before they moved to their new home in Ridley Park. The top row is l to r: Elizabeth, Jimmy Jr., Mrs. Dougherty, Matt, the Baron, and Jimmy's roommate at P.M.C. Bottom row l to r: Dorothy, Mary, and Howard.

Dougherty also had a movie theatre constructed which was called the Colonial Theatre. Besides showing movies and having vaudeville shows, the theatre was also used for boxing shows.

The Dougherty family continued to grow when Elizabeth was born in 1910, the same year that Halley's Comet appeared. Halley's Comet is arguably the most famous and returns to the earth's vicinity about every 75 years. The last time it was here was in 1986, and it is projected to return in 2061. Elizabeth, who worked in the office of Chester police Chief Joseph Bail, later married Jim Dwyer.

The following year, Mary, the Dougherty's fourth daughter was born. She later married Joe Damico, who had been the captain of the Chester High School football team in 1927.

Boxing historian Chuck Hasson said, "It seemed that boxing shows had stopped for a period of time in Leiperville, and then in 1915, they started up again. The Leiperville A.C. sponsored shows at Dougherty's Colonial Theatre."

"I have rented my moving picture house to Lewis Bailey of Philadelphia, who is recognized as one of the best and cleanest promoters of these boxing shows in the game," said Dougherty in the January 2, 1916, edition of the *Chester Times*. "Any show given hereafter in my theatre, the receipts will have to go to some reliable newspapermen who will have to take charge of all arrangements.

"It's not that Mr. Baily has not run the shows successfully at the Colonial. The last show given by him at this theatre was recognized by men of high position in life, who attended the show, to be one of the cleanest and most orderly conducted affairs that they ever attended. There were also several ladies in the audience who voiced their approval of the good order. No high-class theatre ever had better order than prevailed at this show."

Remember, before 1919, boxing was banned in most states as a kind of criminal activity that offended public morals and Christian values. Dougherty was very aware of how boxing was viewed by society, and he wanted to do what he could to make it more presentable to the public.

Howard, who was weaned on boxing, got to know personally most of the fighters who fought and trained at the hotel.

Each boxer had some idiosyncrasy which Howard was still able to remember many years later.

"Benny Bass was a clean living lad. Didn't drink or smoke," recalled Howard. "While Mickey Walker used to stay around the bar and kid with the customers when he wasn't training.

"George Godfrey was a playboy. You could never find him when it was time for him to train.

"Jack Johnson always loved to wear giant-sized, flashy diamond rings. He went in for big, fast cars and was a very reckless driver. He liked to take people out for rides. And scare the daylights out of them."

"John Henry Lewis, who was the light heavyweight champion of the world when he trained here, was a very religious fellow," recalled Howard. "He was always reading the Bible. Never smoked or drank."

In 1938, the *Chester Times* reported, "John Henry Lewis, the world's light-heavyweight champion who is now training at Leiperville, watched fights on Howard Dougherty's first card three weeks ago."

"Tony Galento could always be found at the bar guzzling beer when he wasn't training," Howard continued.

"Kid Chocolate, of Havana, Cuba, was a great man for clothes and sports cars. He had a custom-made Cadillac and Packard which he kept in a garage near the arena when he trained here. He weighed only 118 pounds and when he got behind the wheel of his mammoth Cadillac he looked lost."

"Kid Chocolate and Company, Inc. burst in upon the quietude of Leiperville's Open Air Arena late yesterday afternoon and opened for business," reported the *Times*.

"Everything happened suddenly. The neighborhood of the Dougherty stadium was unusually quiet, save for the low babble of voices from the sprinkling of spectators who have expected the Keed for the past several days to prepare for his July 15 title bout with Benny Bass.

"Suddenly, a burst of motors broke in the little alley way that is Main Street to fight customers every Tuesday night, and when the contents was emptied the Kid Himself, his manager, interpreters, water boys, masseurs, sparring mates and a half a dozen photographers from Philadelphia and New York eyed the humble training quarters."

That night, Kid Chocolate and Benny Bass were at ringside where they were both introduced at Howard's boxing show.

"Billy Conn kept kind of quiet," remembered Howard. "Never saw him drinking or smoking. He drew the most fans when he trained. Many Irishmen from all over the county would come down to see Conn and featherweight champ Johnny Kilbane workout.

"Sugar Ray Robinson, who was a nobody then and had come to Leiperville to train for a prelim bout at the Philadelphia Arena, was always dancing when not drilling.

"Bantam champion Pancho Villa, who died later after having a tooth pulled, was very splashy in dress and cocky in mannerisms.

"Middleweight champion Vince Dundee was a quiet guy. He had real tiny hands and always used to put a lot of cotton over them to protect them from being bruised.

"Johnny Jadick, who established a record when he sold out the Philadelphia Arena ten straight times, went in for loud, sporty clothes.

"Joey Maxim and welterweight champ Joe Dundee were strictly money fighters. It was all business with them.

"Bobby Barrett was tough as nails. He was famous for his KO sock.

"There were many fighters who trained at the Baron's at one time or another," recalled Howard. "Fighters like Jack Blackburn, who would later go on to gain fame as Joe Louis' trainer."

Jack Blackburn, also known as the "Philadelphia Comet," moved to Philadelphia in his youth and it was there that he began his pugilistic career. He had every asset of a good fighter and if he had been properly handled, he might have become a champion. He had one other problem and that was the fact that he only weighed between 132 and 140 pounds, and he was forced to fight men in all divisions to survive.

By 1908, Blackburn was recognized as one of the world's great lightweights. He fought some of the greatest boxers in every division such as: Sam Langford, Joe Gans, Jimmy Gardiner, Jack Twin Sullivan, Jimmy Barry, Dave Holly, Philadelphia Jack O'Brien, Harry Lewis, Larry Temple, and Joe Grim.

The *Police Gazette* wrote in July 24, 1909, "A lightweight who fought at his best at 138 pounds, Blackburn was powerful enough and clever enough to beat men of the middleweight and heavyweight classes, Ketchell and Papke avoided meeting him, and Battling Nelson also feared him."

His contests with the legendary Sam Langford were classics. They met five times, and all five of those battles ended in draws. As I mentioned in chapter two, one of those bouts was fought in 1905, and promoted by Dougherty at the Leiperville Athletic Club.

Unfortunately, when Blackburn was at the height of his career and close to a

title shot he got into an argument with a man named Alonzo Polk on a January night in 1909, about his common-law wife Maude Pillion. The argument escalated into a shooting in which Blackburn shot and killed Polk and also attempted to murder Polk's wife and his own wife, Maude.

Five months later, he was tried and found guilty of manslaughter in the shooting of Alonzo Polk and was sentenced to fifteen years in Moyameusing State Prison in Moyameusing, Pennsylvania. Blackburn was only 26 years old.

During his stay in prison, many friends attempted to get a pardon for Blackburn.

Jack Blackburn is seen here during his fighting career, where he won 113 fights out of 166 total bouts from 1907 to 1923, before passing in 1942 at the young age of 59.

"In the insuing years, buried in the back pages of various newspapers small accounts appeared of the efforts of friends to secure a pardon for Blackburn," wrote Harry Shaffer in his article, "The Jack Blackburn Story." "Notably, among them Jimmy Dougherty, the Baron of Leiperville, fight manager, and friend of too many black fighters. Finally, six days before Christmas 1913, Jack Blackburn was granted a full pardon. On January 14, 1914, at 8:30 A.M. he was released from Moyameusing State prison. There to meet him was Jimmy Dougherty."

"The Baron got Jack Blackburn out of jail," said Howard. "My father knew a lot of people, and he was able to get him out of jail after only four and a half years. He would have never gotten out of jail if it wasn't for the Baron."

Two months later, April 4, 1914, Blackburn, training in Leiperville, was back fighting in the ring taking on Tommy Howell at the National A.C. In 1915, he lost to Harry Greb and over the next three years, he fought about thirty times, losing ten of those bouts.

"He abandoned the ring for over two years, and then mounted another attempt," wrote Shaffer. "He had a fight against Kid Norfolk in New York City, and Norfolk knocked him out in four rounds. He fought once in 1921, three times in

1922, and finally the end of the road came in Oakland, California, March 9, 1923. Jack was battling with Ray Pelkey when suddenly he dropped to his knees, looked at the referee and said, 'I'm through; I ain't got no more wind.'"

Blackburn finally retired from the ring in 1923, with his official record showing only two losses among his 167 fights. He made his way to Chicago and began to work around the many boxing gyms in the area. However, before he made his trip, Blackburn was not set too well financially.

"Jack needed money to get to Chicago, and I gave him $50 so he could make the trip," remembered Howard. "He was doing pretty well out there training boxers, but he never paid me back. I was really upset about that because the Baron was really responsible for getting him out of jail."

In Chicago, Blackburn worked with Eddie Kane's stable of fighters and helped to make bantamweight Bud Taylor and Lightweight Sammy Mandell champions.

While working at George Trafton's gym, Blackburn was tracked down by John Boxborough and Julian Black.

Shaffer wrote, "Legend has it that when they approached Blackburn about training their young fighter Joe Louis, that upon discovering Louis was black he refused, believing no black heavyweight could make any money. Finally, Blackburn agreed to work with Louis for four weeks for thirty-five dollars a week to prepare him for his pro debut."

They both developed a genuine affection for each other and Blackburn became Louis' most trusted advisor. They grew very close and called each other "Chappie."

"Blackburn changed Louis from a box and move type to a more aggressive fighter," said Hall of Fame trainer Eddie Futch.

Louis later said, "Chappie made a fighter out of me. He was my closest friend. I could have never won the heavyweight title without him."

Howard recalled, "Without the Baron's influence in getting Blackburn out of jail, the Blackburn and Louis story could never have been told."

Howard continued to remember more of the gladiators who made stops at the well-known hotel on Chester Pike.

Pete Nebo, an Indian from Florida, who beat Benny Bass, trained in Leiperville and so did Tony Canzoneri, Harry Blitman, Tiger Thomas, Alex Hart, Joe Anderson, Leo Lomski, Jack Dorval, Steve Martin, Al Ettore and Popper Stopper.

Jack Blackburn on the left shows Joe Louis how it's done. Baron Dougherty was influential in getting Blackburn out of jail, and Louis would later say that he could have never won the world heavyweight title without Blackburn.

Howard told about the time Popper Stopper fought Slapsie Maxie Rosenbloom at the Leiperville Open Air Arena.

"On the afternoon of the day of the fight," remembered Howard, "Rosenbloom arrived at the Colonial Hotel in a taxi with two girls. He didn't have any money with which to pay his cab fare, so part of his guaranteed $1,000 purse was deducted for that purpose.

"Then Rosenbloom stayed at the bar all afternoon getting high as a kite. When it came time, he barely lasted the first two rounds, but almost murdered poor Popper in the next eight."

The one individual, who did more to put Leiperville on the map than anyone else, was the most versatile writer of his generation, Damon Runyon. Runyon, whose daily column was syndicated from coast to coast, made Leiperville his second home. Many of his columns were dedicated to the Baron, and because of his column's syndication, Dougherty and his hotel were known nationwide. Runyon would flock to the boxing mecca Dougherty had established.

In one of Runyon's columns, he wrote, "The Baron's hotel was the Seat of Fisticuffs and a camp of many noted fighters.

"The tavern and the Barony of Leiperville in those days fared the famous fighting men of the time. Joe Gans, 'The Old master', Joe Goddard, the Barrier champion, the shadowy Jack Blackburn, the lean and hungry John Arthur Johnson, the wonderful little Eddie Lenny, and many others, for the Baron's tavern was one of the noted training quarters."

It was actually Runyon who gave Jimmy Dougherty his nickname, "The Baron of Leiperville". They say it stuck because Dougherty wouldn't permit it to get away from him.

Runyon knew and recognized good copy when he saw it. Dougherty was a colorful character and it was at his Colonial Hotel where Runyon could find a world of other characters that he could fictionalize, such as: Dopey Goldberg, Nick the Greek, Jack the Beefer, and Gloomy Gus Smallwood. He also could find them at the local saloons and riverfront shacks.

Sometimes Runyon would spend six months out of the year at the Baron's hotel. He would often walk along Ridley Creek talking to people in the boathouses. He was very close to the lower class folk. Mingling with them, he was able to write with a genuine feeling of reality.

"When Runyon would frequent the Chester and Marcus Hook dives he would dress shabbily," recalled Ed Conner, a native of Leiperville who was also a professional boxer. "He was minus a tie, unshaven, and wearing baggy pants and a jacket that looked as if he had slept in it.

Conner reminisced, "Runyon was the greatest coffee drinker I had ever seen. I would sit with him for hours in a Chester diner just talking and drinking java.

"Another favorite spot of his was Darby Creek. There he would visit the decrepit shacks in the woods where moonshine was made. He would sit in the shacks for hours just listening and watching.

"When he went to the local saloons dressed as a vagrant, he would buy drinks for the poorest looking slobs and engage them in conversation. That's how he developed his Runyonese language. Damon was very close to the low people. Mingling with them he was able to write with a genuine feeling of reality."

It was a stretch for him to dress down because he was an immaculate dresser. "He would change clothes as many as three times a day," remembered Conner.

Runyon would always check into room number seven on the third floor of the hotel and spend weeks writing the stories that made him one of America's favorite humorists.

Daily Times Writer Arden Skidmore wrote, "It has been fairly well established that Runyon wrote *Little Miss Marker,* on one of his stays at the hotel. He always occupied a second floor room facing Gibbons street."

That was the tearjerker that later became a memorable 1934 motion picture starring Shirley Temple and Adolph Menjou.

Menjou was the sad-eyed bookie who accepted the dimpled, curly-haired child instead of a $2 bet.

Little Miss Marker made Shirley Temple a star and launched her career. The movie, which made its debut in 1934, actually pushed her past Greta Garbo as the country's biggest film draw of that year.

Besides looking for subjects for his column, Runyon was also very interested in developing heavyweight prospects.

"Runyon was always bringing heavyweight prospects to Leiperville," recalled Conner, who was one of Jack Dempsey's sparring partners in Atlantic City when the champion was training for his fight with Gene Tunney. "He would plunk down $50 a week in payment for room, board and training privileges for his fighters.

Damon Runyon is on the right with boxer Mickey Walker (middle) and Hollywood director Max Sennett on the left. Runyon spent a lot of time at Dougherty's hotel where he made the Baron the subject of many of his columns and even gave him his nickname, "The Baron of Leiperville".

"Many times he asked me to check his prospects and report on them to him. Most of his finds were dogs. However, he did land a husky named Jack Dorval of Emporia, Pennsylvania, who appeared as if he might make it.

"I worked with Dorval in Leiperville for a good spell. Finally, a big fight was arranged for him with Ernie Schaff in Boston. The day of the contest, we couldn't find Dorval anywhere. Runyon was frantic. He asked me to go to Emporia to try to locate the lost boxer. Well, I did find Dorval in his home town. He had a girlfriend there and was so in love that he did not want to fight. I had to talk myself blue in the face to get him to Boston, where he lost to Schaff and immediately quit fighting permanently."

Runyon never did find his heavyweight contender, but he did continue to look throughout his life for that one fighter who could win it all.

Bill Burk, an athlete, coach, and later sportswriter and sports editor of the *Chester Times*, remembered, "Damon Runyon was always in Leiperville. It was Runyon who introduced me to his world of New York. One time, he sent me four tickets for the Joe Louis – Max Baer fight, and the *Times'* managing editor Jim Glenney and I took our wives to Yankee Stadium to see them fight. The seats were $25 each but complimentary from Runyon.

"I was Runyon's protégé. He was a quiet guy and never said much. Later I worked by his side. He loved the fights but sat through all of them without changing expression. He actually wrote in long hand, one sentence to a page. He never read it or corrected it but would just hand it to his wire operator, who would then send it all over the world."

During construction, Baron Dougherty stands in front of his house that he had built on Chester Pike in Ridley Park.

In 1920, Dougherty and his family left a house they were renting in Leedom, and had a house built on the corner of Chester Pike and Stewart Lane in Ridley Park. It was a stately, four-pillared mansion that was called "Sequoia".

"My father named our estate, 'Sequoia', after the sequoia tree found in California," explained Margaret Stull, Dougherty's youngest child. "In his trips to California, he fell in love with these trees, and decided to name our home after them. Known as Redwood trees, they are the largest species of trees in the world."

During that time, he also constructed a gym for training in a garage behind the house. He even had a ring installed on the lawn, where sparring took place among his stable of fighters.

In 1920, Dougherty and his family left the house they were renting in Leedom and moved into a mansion on the corner of Chester Pike and Stewart Lane in Ridley Park. It was a stately four-pillared home that was named "Sequoia".

"As a youngster, I would spend time at the Baron's place watching some of the greatest boxers of the day train," remembered Jack Nilon, who later became Sonny Liston's manager when he captured the world heavyweight championship. "I used to see Alex Hart, Benny Bass, El Ettore, Bobby Barrett, Marty Collins, Billy Angelo and the legendary George Godfrey."

"My brother Bob and I also parked cars for the Baron for 10 cents," explained Nilon.

At public workouts and small fight shows, Bob and Jack would park cars and sell lemonade. They also would sweep out the gym and listen to the Baron's stories about boxers such as Dempsey.

Jack and Bob would get the worn-out old boxing gloves from the gym and then make up cards matching neighborhood kids. "We would charge a nickel admission from kids that had a nickel and sell lemonade at three cents," said Nilon.

Besides spending time at the hotel, Runyon would also visit the Baron's house in Ridley Park quite often. "He was always at our house," recalled Margaret Stull. He always called at Christmas time to ask me what I wanted for a gift. He would buy me whatever I wanted. One Christmas, he surprised me with a beautiful watch."

Runyon was a big coffee drinker, and after he stopped smoking, he even began drinking more coffee. "My mother kept a huge coffee cup in our kitchen for

Jack Nilon (sitting on right), who during his childhood spent time at Baron Dougherty's estate parking cars during boxing exhibitions, sits with Joe Louis as they both watch Sonny Liston train for his title fight with Floyd Patterson.

Runyon," recalled Margaret. "He would drink a lot of coffee when he was at our house. I was told that at that time, he was drinking forty cups of coffee a day."

Margaret continued, "Runyon also did a lot of hunting during his stays with us. He would travel to the swamps of Essington to shoot Reed birds. He would bring them to our house, and my mother would cook them and Runyon would eat them. I was only a young girl at the time, but I remember that he would eat the entire bird, bones and all."

In his book entitled *The World Of Damon Runyon*, Tom Clark wrote, "Dougherty had kennels in which he kept hunting dogs for his close friend Damon Runyon, to the readers of whose sporting column he became well known as the Baron."

Clark also wrote, "In late autumn, during Thanksgiving, Runyon would exercise his hunting dogs that he kept at his pal Jimmy 'Baron' Dougherty's home so he could do some duck hunting."

"Sometimes Runyon and I would drive to Virginia to hunt," remembered Howard. "He later gave me two of his dogs and a rifle to keep."

Jimmy Dougherty and Damon Runyon would develop a friendship that would last a lifetime.

And it was Jack Johnson who brought together the Baron and George Godfrey in 1922. It wouldn't be long before Runyon would tag the big heavyweight with his new nickname," The Black Shadow of Leiperville".

- Chapter 6 -

The Black Shadow of Leiperville

"I still believe George Godfrey was the most handcuffed boxer of all time."

Chuck Hasson – Boxing historian and voting member
of the International Boxing Hall of fame.

Jack Johnson brought big George Godfrey to Leiperville sometime in 1922, and asked Jimmy Dougherty if he would be interested in buying Godfrey's contract for $1,000 and managing Big George. Johnson, who was good friends with Dougherty, said this was his gift to the Baron, and that Godfrey had the makings to become the next world heavyweight champion.

However, the story of who bought Godfrey's contract gets a little confusing because of various conflicting newspaper reports taken from interviews with Dougherty himself.

Dougherty originally told the story like this, "Jack Johnson, shortly after serving his term in the federal penitentiary, took Godfrey on as a sparring partner, paying him $75 a week. Big George was a little too much boy for Johnson to handle safely in exhibition matches and was making Johnson look bad so he brought him to my hotel, and I agreed to purchase his contract for $1,000."

Another account by R. A. McNally of the *Philadelphia Bulletin* has Dougherty buying

George Godfrey was introduced to Baron Dougherty in 1922 by former heavyweight champion Jack Johnson.

Godfrey's contract from Dempsey's manager Doc Kearns for $1,000. "I had no use for Godfrey because I wasn't interested in backing fighters at that time and certainly could see no reason for handing Johnson $1,000 for him, said Dougherty. "But just at that time Kearns was looking for a good hefty sparring partner for Dempsey, who was getting ready to start training for his fight with Tommy Gibbons. So I sent Godfrey on to Kearns, and Jack bought his contract."

Later, at some point, Dougherty bought Godfrey's contract from Kearns. "That's all bunk about Kearns and Godfrey," stated Dougherty. "I'm the only boss that Godfrey recognizes, and I bought his contract from Kearns for $1,000."

The Godfrey/Dougherty/Kearns story took another twist when in February of 1925; Edgar T. Gleeson of the *San Francisco Call* interviewed Dougherty and wrote that Kearns had always been the manager of Godfrey.

"Kearns signed Godfrey for ten years at Atlantic City," said Dougherty. "And he signed him for one purpose. Every time now, that Harry Wills starts a drive for a Dempsey match, somebody pops up with the question, 'Can Wills lick George Godfrey?' If he can't, why does he set up the claim that he is the champion of his race?'"

Nat Fleischer in his book *Black Dynamite Volume V* wrote, "Ex-heavyweight champion Jack Johnson was preparing for a vaudeville tour and wanted a big sparring partner, impressive-looking, but not too clever, so that the former boss of the heavies could make a good showing on the stage in exhibitions. Godfrey was tried out by Johnson, who decided that the youth was a bit too fast for his purpose. At the same time, Jack considered George entirely too fine a future prospect to remain in obscurity.

"Back in New York, Johnson looked up his friend, Jimmy Dougherty, known in sportdom by the sobriquet of 'The Baron of Leiperville,' and advised him to take hold of Godfrey."

"I'm making you a present of the next world heavyweight titleholder," said Jack.

"Dougherty naturally had respect for Johnson's judgment in such matters and at once took Godfrey under his managerial wing," wrote Fleischer.

Fleischer, who had just published his first issue of *Ring Magazine* in 1922, was also aware of stories concerning who really managed Godfrey.

In *Black Dynamite Volume V*, Fleischer wrote, "Dougherty was Godfrey's manager by record, but about this time it was rumored that Kearns bought Godfrey's contract for $1,000, with the intention of using him as a sort of buffer between Dempsey and Wills. Jack Kearns, manager of champion Jack Dempsey, was being annoyed considerably just then by the persistent challenges hurled at the Manassa Mauler by Harry Wills. The idea was that Kearns would tell Wills to go whip Godfrey first, whenever the Black Panther got too busy on Dempsey's trail. Godfrey was then without any experience worth speaking of, yet there were many experts who thought he would prove too strong for Wills in battle.

"While Kearns used Godfrey as a sparring partner for Dempsey, he always denied that he managed Godfrey. However, that may have been, certain it is that the champion's pilot did on several occasions inform Wills that the latter must defeat Godfrey before Harry could get a shot at the heavyweight title."

"Godfrey is really the property, pugilistically speaking, of Kearns," wrote Alec X. McCausland of the *San Francisco Call*. "Sam Langford put a high recommendation on him to Kearns. Kearns at that time didn't want opposition of too serious a nature and color lines were rather severely adhered to. Kearns took Godfrey over, shipped him into pugilistic oblivion by turning him over to his pal Dougherty, and he allowed Godfrey to knock off minor fighters. In other words, Godfrey was Dempsey's buffer just as John Pesek has for years been Ed 'Strangler' Lewis' buffer in the wrestling game. You see folks; it is strictly business both in wrestling and in fighting. Pesek can throw Lewis and a great many wiseacres believe that Godfrey, a 240-pound boxing giant, whose speed, footwork, boxing and blocking are amazing, can whip Dempsey."

George Godfrey was born Feabe Smith Williams in Mobile, Alabama, on February 27, 1896. The ring name that he later adopted was chosen because of his admiration of a former great black fighter, George Godfrey.

The original Godfrey was known as "Old Chocolate," and he fought a long list of outstanding boxers such as: Peter Jackson, Joe Choynski, Peter Maher and Jake Kilrain.

For many years, the major black challenger to John L. Sullivan's title was George Godfrey. Sullivan was the first of the modern heavyweight champions to draw the "color line." Sullivan had stated that he would meet Godfrey in the ring anytime, if the purse was right, but he never came close to doing so.

Godfrey's family moved to Chicago when he was two years old, however, when he reached school age, he was sent back to his hometown and attended classes in Mobile and Tuskegee.

Later, at age 17, he was employed full time by the Alabama Dry Dock and Ship Company.

"He was too strong for older men who tried to bully him," wrote J.J. Johnston and Don Cogswell in their book *Uncrowned Champions*. "There was a big black man named Eddie Singleton who worked in the same boiler shop and was the local tough guy. The other workers made up a good-sized pot of money and matched the two big guys. Each man had his own fans. Singleton rushed out and hit young Feab with a powerful punch on the chest and Feab landed a right to Singleton's jaw and broke it in two places. He wound up with several hundred dollars. A local druggist who dabbled in the boxing game became his first manager. Dr. Frank Caffey taught Feab the basics."

When the United States entered World War I, Godfrey decided to enlist in the 131st Infantry Regiment before the draft, one of the first Negro regiments.

"One of the officers took a fancy to him, and when he found he could box, he encouraged him to exhibit his prowess against some of the other members," wrote Edgar Gleeson of the *San Francisco Call*. "In a boxing show at one of the southern towns Godfrey donned the gloves against Sam Langford. He made such a good showing that Sam said to him, 'Boy, yo ever come back from da war, hunt me up. I'd like to know you better.'"

"In one bout," explained Dougherty, "George tried to show Sam what it was all about and Sam poked him a stiff left that floored Godfrey. 'That's just to teach you a lesson,' Sam remarked to George."

Gleeson continued, "After the war, Godfrey did come back. He joined up with Sam and was used by the latter in a number of bouts, soft spots around the country that Sam worked. Eventually, he was steered into Jack Johnson. The former champion was getting ready for a vaudeville tour and wanted somebody he could slam around. He signed Godfrey up to a contract and started working out with him."

"Jack found him too good," said Dougherty. "He called on me one day, 'I've got one of the greatest boxers in the world,' said Johnson. 'But he isn't any use to me. I can't show off against him in the way I would like. But he'll make anybody a wonderful present. I'll pick up a big, strong fellow that I can display my stuff on. But it's a shame if this fellow Godfrey doesn't get a chance in the ring.'"

"I didn't have any cause to sign Godfrey," continued Dougherty. "But I thought of Kearns and mentioned the incident to him; Johnson wanted a thousand dollars for Godfrey's contract. And Kearns bought it."

When the war ended, Godfrey was transferred to the 421st Labor Battalion, stationed in Camp Sheridan in Montgomery, Alabama.

Langford had been so impressed with Godfrey; he told him if he wanted a job after the war was over, to look him up in Chicago. Knowing Langford's reputation, Big George headed to the Windy City.

In Chicago, he became a pupil of Langford's, as well as Bobby Dobbs and Jack Blackburn, who years before had trained boxers for Dougherty at Leiperville. Blackburn had also fought most of his career and resided for many years in Philadelphia and Chester. Under their expert instruction, Godfrey improved considerably in a very short period of time.

Godfrey was knocked out by Langford twice in regular bouts, and he was also stopped by Jack Thompson and Battling Norfolk.

Boxing historian Chuck Hasson explained, "I believe that the Langford knockouts of Godfrey were set-ups as Langford used Godfrey in his employment with his touring troupe."

Johnston and Cogswell wrote, "Godfrey was now living in and fighting out of Chicago. Sam Langford turned his protégé over to Johnnie Tholmer, and ex-fighter and now a good trainer. All these men imparted their knowledge to George who was becoming both skillful and a powerful puncher. He was also very fast for a big man."

Under the management of Dougherty, Godfrey had his first fight in the northeast against George Ward on October 20, 1922, at the National Club in Philadelphia. In Godfrey's first bout in the City of Brotherly Love, he was victorious, scoring a knockout in the fifth round.

The Philadelphia Bulletin reported, "It begins to look as if Philadelphia would have a heavyweight fighter of class, something that has been lacking in this city in many years. On Friday night, at the National Club, Jimmy Dougherty turned loose a giant colored man, who is sure to make boxing history if nothing happens to cut short his career. This man, George Godfrey, is the best young heavyweight boxer since the days of Jim Corbett and Jack Johnson. He is 6 feet 3 inches tall, weighing 210 pounds, hard as iron, without a pick on his bones; all hard muscle, with feet as large as ordinary canoes.

"He is going to make his home in this vicinity, and for the future will represent Philadelphia in the boxing world. From now on there will be no necessity for any heavyweight fighter looking for trouble to pass by Philadelphia. It will be a case of bring them along, first come, first served. The city of Philadelphia has long been celebrated for its boxers in various classes, but it has not had even a good third-rate heavyweight for a long while, but there was never so promising a heavyweight prospect here as this big fellow Godfrey."

After three more victories, Godfrey took part in a box-off to see if he was good enough to fight on a Madison Square Garden program.

In 1923, Leo P. Flynn, the matchmaker for Madison Square Garden, arranged a box-off at Billy Grupp's Gym in the black section of Harlem," wrote Nat Fleischer. "The bouts were to decide if any of the contestants were worthy to fight on the Garden program.

"George was one of those contestants, and in his first bout, he knocked out Clem Johnson, a promising heavyweight, in two rounds. George then took on the Canadian heavyweight, Jack Renault. They sparred four rounds, at the close of which Renault had taken such a battering that he was practically 'out on his feet.'"

It was after this performance that Flynn, who was also Renault's manager, decided to put Godfrey in a main event at Madison Square Garden. A Winnipeg syndicate had announced before the fight a proposal to match the winner of this fight with Harry Wills.

George Godfrey is pictured here training in Leiperville for his fight with Primo Carnera in 1930. During a break in training he holds up spectators Bill and Lee Garling, twins, who would later star in track and football, playing for legendary coach Phil Marion at Ridley Township High School.

The fight turned out to be a real learning experience for Godfrey. As a result, he was knocked out in the eleventh round. Nevertheless, the bout was surrounded by controversy because Big George never really threw a single hard punch the entire fight.

In *Black Dynamite Volume V*, Fleischer wrote, "Godfrey, aware of how he had handled Renault in the gym, felt confident of victory. However, before the fight, Flynn told Godfrey that he had received a warning tip that if Godfrey whipped his white opponent, the Ku Klux Klan would have him kidnapped and hanged. The consequence of Flynn's fine strategy was that Godfrey, who firmly believed the horrible tale, was so scared when the hostilities began, that he never threw a single hard wallop through the entire contest, which ended with Renault scoring a knockout in the eleventh round."

It was just the beginning of an up and down career in the ring, which at times was no fault of Godfrey's.

Dougherty got Godfrey back to Leiperville so he could start doing more roadwork and boxing at his training camp. From there, Godfrey headed to Dempsey's training camp in White Sulphur Springs, New York, where the champion was preparing for another title defense, this time against Luis Firpo, the "Wild Bull of the Pampas"at the Polo Grounds in New York. Dempsey and Godfrey would pick up where they left off during training for the Tommy Gibbons fight in Shelby, Montana.

Three days after Dempsey floored Firpo, Godfrey had his one and only bout in Delaware County when he scored a TKO in the second round over Buddy Jackson at Smedley Field in Chester on September 17, 1923.

It seemed that Big George did not like to train. "George's roadwork would consist of running from Leiperville to Springhaven Golf Course and then back again," recalled Howard. "There were days when he didn't return and I would go looking for him, and he would be sitting by the creek with a dog. He would take water from the creek and put it on his face to make it look like he was sweating. Other days, I would find him sleeping by the creek. I always had to get after him about training, especially when he had to do roadwork."

Godfrey, who was now 6 ft. 3inches tall and 235 lbs., scored knockouts in his next two fights against Big Bill Tate and Rough House Ware. However, he lost on fouls against both Battling Owens and Tom Cowler. He was beating Owens convincingly before he hit him low, and Owens was given the fight on a foul in round five. He actually knocked Cowler down with a left and followed with a right while Cowler was on one knee, fouling again to give Cowler the win in the second round.

Godfrey knocked out his next two opponents, Farmer Lodger and Jack Thompson, but unfortunately, he then went to New York and lost on another foul, this time to Jack Townsend.

"Before the 'no foul' rule went into place in most states, a low body blow would win for an opponent who wanted to take the easy way out," explained authors Johnston and Cogswell. "Or a referee who was crooked could award a fight on a foul to save or win a bet. George Godfrey was one of the hardest punchers in ring history. He learned that skill from the great Sam Langford who told him 'kill the body and the head dies'. Many times in his career Godfrey, who could give or take a punch, was accused of hitting low instead of knocking out an opponent to save or win a bet for the gamblers."

On September 8, 1924, Godfrey fought Jack Renault in a rematch before a large crowd in Philadelphia at Shibe Park.

"In the first half of the contest, Godfrey was clearly superior to the Canadian,' wrote Nat Fleischer. "Fearing lest making too good a showing would scare off other prospective opponents, he eased up and coasted in the latter rounds. Many spectators thought he was entitled to the decision. That he failed to get it was due to his own poor judgment."

Godfrey scored knockouts in his next five fights against Joe White at the Arena in Philadelphia; Black Soldier Jones in Pottsville, Pennsylvania; Tut Jackson in Madison Square Garden; Vic Alexander in Wilmington, California; and Sam Baker in Vernon, California.

Margaret, the youngest of the Baron's eight children, was very young when Godfrey was training at the Dougherty house in Ridley Park.

George Godfrey is seen here training on the back lawn of Baron Dougherty's estate in Ridley Park. Dougherty would occasionally have a ring set up for exhibitions and training for his stable of fighters.

"He trained in a ring in Daddy's garage, and he was always in our house," remembered Margaret. "He'd come in every morning for breakfast before his training run. He'd take two eggs and crack them and swallow them. It used to make me sick.

"I'd play school with him. I'd ask him to spell a word, and he would misspell it on purpose. Then I'd say, 'Now you have to stand in the corner,' and this great hulking man would do it. I just adored George.

"One day he took me to the circus, and he carried me on his shoulders, this little red-headed child on the shoulders of this huge black man. There had been a kidnapping about that time, and the police stopped us, I guess to make sure George hadn't kidnapped me.

"I really loved George. He was a real doll and very gentle."

"There were times when Damon Runyon would drive George and me down to that little island near Walber's on the Delaware River," recalled Mary Damico,

Margaret's older sister. "We would both go in the river and swim together."

The Vic Alexander fight was Godfrey's first bout in the state of California. After knocking out Alexander in six rounds, Godfrey preceded to win five more consecutive bouts on the west coast.

During this time, Howard traveled all over the country with Godfrey. He was out of school, having graduated from Ridley Park High School in 1924.

"I went to St. Rose Lima School in Eddystone," recalled Howard. "I got in fights all the time and finally was kicked out, and the Baron sent me to Penn Charter, the prep school. Later, I went to Ridley Park.

Howard Dougherty, wearing a P.M.C. college sweater, talks to an unknown fighter while in Los Angeles training his father's boxers.

"Out of high school, I went to California for two years, training the Baron's fighters and spending a lot of time with George. I traveled all over the country with George and even went to Mexico with him.

"One time we were driving through Texas, and there were some areas we went through where I told him to slide down in the seat because certain people in that area did not take kindly to blacks and whites being together. Remember, this was the 1920's. So I got stopped by the state police for speeding and George got out of the car. Remember, at this time, he was 6'3" tall and weighed about 240 pounds. The state cop said, 'That is the biggest black man I have ever seen.'"

Godfrey's second fight in California was against Sam Baker at the Arena in Vernon.

"Godfrey was matched in Los Angeles with a monstrous black fighter, Sam Baker, whose hands were so big that he had to have special gloves made," wrote

Cogswell and Johnston. "Film star Douglas Fairbanks managed him. George knocked him out in four rounds"

Baker was actually down 20 times in the contest, including eight times in the fourth round alone.

Hap Navarro, who is a boxing historian, writer and an expert on California boxing, wrote, "From the night of his power-punching display at Jack Doyle's Vernon Club, Godfrey's fame grew steadily until the magnitude of his achievements was reflected generously at the ticket windows wherever he performed.

"Godfrey was the main draw for three California outdoor promotions during the first nine months after the state's ten-round law had taken effect January 1, 1925. It was this Alabama giant who gave the heavyweight ranks in the west a much-needed jump start."

While in California, and with his popularity growing with every victory in the ring, Godfrey decided to try acting. He was a natural actor and audiences seemed to enjoy watching him on the big screen. This acting talent definitely ran in his family, because his brother was also an actor and comedian who worked under the name "Crybaby Godfrey".

Remember, the movie industry was in its infancy. After World War I, the American movie industry gradually moved to Hollywood, California. Sport's icons like Babe Ruth, Red Grange, and Jack Dempsey were all making films in Hollywood. The film studios didn't seem to be concerned with whether these athletes could act, but they were more concerned with their popularity and star power. People wanted to see these legendary sports figures on the big screen and that translated into big bucks for the heads of the film industry. However, at the time, few movies offered blacks parts with any authenticity. Most blacks generally played conventional roles as chorus girls, convicts, racetrack grooms, boxing trainers, and flippant servants.

That was not the case for Godfrey as he landed a part in James Cruze's production of *Old Ironsides*. Godfrey played a cook on board the USS Constitution. *Old Ironsides* was a real classic from the silent movie era about romance and adventure in the battles against the Barbary pirates. Besides Godfrey, the cast consisted of some really fine actors which included: Esther Ralston, Charles Farrell, George Bancroft, and the legendary Wallace Beery. Also, Boris Karloff and Olympic gold medal winner Duke Kahanamoku had bit parts as pirates.

Many years later, critic Tim Lussier wrote, "Finally, to Cruze's credit, and remember this is 1926, George Godfrey's color was not exploited for humor. Cruze

Howard Dougherty (2nd from right) with friends in California, where he spent two years training the Baron's fighters on the west coast.

uses one running joke for Godfrey's character, the bit where he spits through his fingers for good luck. Also, when the four men are captured and sold as slaves, there is no distinction between each one as they are chained together and escape to freedom."

Godfrey was definitely featured in a more significant role than black actors of the time were usually given.

"The movie was shot in and around Catalina Island," explained Howard. "I was out on the West coast at the time training George, and I got the opportunity to be an extra in the movie. If you look close enough, you can see me in some of those crowd scenes.

"George also had an embarrassing moment when he had to jump overboard to save Ralston, Bancroft's love interest in the movie, and they found out he couldn't swim."

Budd Schulberg, who is well known for his 1954 Academy- award- winning screenplay for *On The Waterfront*, wrote in his book, *Moving Pictures: Memories Of A Hollywood Prince*, "My father produced the movie *Old Ironsides*, and I spent an idyllic summer at the film's location on Catalina Island. I took swimming lessons from the Olympic champion Duke Kahanamoku and received the obligatory attention of the cast. The formidable black heavyweight George Godfrey, also aboard the USS Constitution, talked fights and sparred with me."

Godfrey was also a big hit with all the cast, hired hands, and the thousands of extras from *Old Ironsides*. Many of them would attend his fights and followed his boxing career.

In his next two movies, Godfrey was no longer in front of the camera, but wrote the screen stories for *A Sailor's Sweetheart* And *One Round Hogan*, both in 1927. *In One Round Hogan*, Godfrey and F.L. Giffen worked together on the screen story about the son of a champion boxer (played by real-life-champion James J. Jeffries). Hogan has a lot of trouble living up to his father's reputation, but wins the big fight and the love and devotion of the leading lady. *One Round Hogan* was produced by the legendary Mack Sennett.

In 1929, Godfrey was back to acting again, this time in a movie called *Sea Fury*. He finished his acting career in two movies in 1937, a western called *The Riders Of The Whistlig Skull*, where he played professor Fronc; and *Big City*, a movie where Godfrey played a character by the name of Nathan. *Big City* had a cast which included quite a few former athletes, especially boxers. Those cast members were: Man Mountain Dean, Jackie Fields, Frank Wykoff, Jim Thorpe, Maxie Rosenbloom, Jimmy McLarin, James Jeffries, and Jack Dempsey.

Godfrey was one of the first blacks to be given a respectable movie role in those early Hollywood years. He also acted with some top notch actors and even wrote two screen stories. He obviously had the ability to read and write, and besides boxing, he held his own in front of the camera.

During that time, I think it was important to white America to portray Godfrey as a big loveable buffoon, someone who was a mountain of a man without much upstairs.

In the article, *Dempsey's Favorite Sparring Partner*, the following was written, "Godfrey is illiterate and untrained, and famed reporter Willie Ratner spent endless hours teaching George how to write his name and when the loveable fighter finally learned to scratch out the letters in proper order, everybody in camp felt a glow of satisfaction and warmth; especially Dempsey."

That doesn't sound like the Godfrey who a few years later would not only be acting in Hollywood but also writing screen stories.

By late 1925, he was still fighting the best heavyweights who would fight him and challenging all the rest. Dougherty felt that he should claim the title for George since Dempsey hadn't fought in two years.

"As I feel sure that Jack Dempsey will never fight again," said Dougherty. "I claim the world's heavyweight championship for Godfrey. George will fight anybody in the world."

Godfrey would never get the opportunity to fight Dempsey for the title. A black fighter by the name of Harry Wills was always talked about at the time as Dempsey's next opponent. Wills was considered the number one contender to

Dempsey's world championship belt. However, after becoming champion in 1919, Dempsey said he would not fight a black boxer.

California sportswriter Sol Plex explained promoter Jack Doyle's offer to Wills, "Thoroughly convinced that Jack Dempsey will never again sidle through the hemp for the purpose of defending his world championship, Jack Doyle, veteran Vernon promoter, today telegraphed Paddy Mullins a flattering offer for Harry Wills to meet George Godfrey at Maier Park on the afternoon of June 6, in a bout that would determine the Manassa Mauler's successor.

"Doyle told Mullins that he would give Wills a $5,000 diamond belt emblematic of the title. All he asks is that the "Brown Panther of New Orleans' give Godfrey the first shot at the crown."

"The color line was the chief obstacle in Godfrey's path, as in the case of Wills," wrote Nat Fleischer. "The race issue was formerly much evidence where pro boxing was concerned. Also, those Negro fighters often had to take what they could get in the way of matches and frequently 'fight to order,' and carry opponents whom they could have defeated.

"Godfrey, an easy-going, good-natured chap, fought 'under wraps' many times. Not being of a worrying disposition, he seldom protested against such conditions, but did as commanded, even though he knew his reputation was bound to suffer in consequence of obeying."

"The Baron and I had to tell George at times to carry opponents or we would not be able to get him fights," recalled Howard. "We made concessions in order for George to meet high rated fighters including carry opponents, and fouling out."

Chuck Hasson, a top boxing historian and a voting member of the International Boxing Hall of Fame, wrote, "I still believe Godfrey was the most 'handcuffed' boxer of all time. His loss to Johny Risko was a case in point as some fair eyewitness scribes have noted that Godfrey easily handled Risko for the first eight rounds at Ebbetts Field, then Risko made a courageous stand in the last two rounds and they awarded him the decision.

"It was widely understood in Philly that Godfrey agreed to 'carry' Risko, that his first two matches with Jack Renault were 'smellers' and his 'foul-outs' were ordered. Today, people don't realize that one leading black challenger (Wills) was tolerated because of his 'good name' with the New York commission but two top black challengers were frowned on. Godfrey and his management (Dougherty) tried to alleviate the situation by attempting to lure Wills into the ring by any means, but of course Wills and Paddy Mullins were not about to risk their position that they earned by taking on young, and very dangerous opponent like Godfrey.

"By the way, if you look at photos of Godfrey before 1926, before his frustrations caused him to gain weight. His body was ripped with muscle and he was always in top condition."

Sportswriter Harry Newman wrote, "While all the fuss is going on about matching Harry Wills with Jack Dempsey, why wouldn't it be a good scheme to send Harry in there for a bout with that fellow George Godfrey, who is now looming up as a pretty bright prospect, and one that might make a formidable opponent for any of the boys in the heavyweight division.

"It may be that Wills will never get a chance with Dempsey, so why wait on the champion any longer? Godfrey and Wills ought to make an ideal fight. A wonderfully molded athlete is George Godfrey, possessing speed, plenty of skill as a boxer and has shown that he has plenty of sting in his punches.

"Right now it looks like Godfrey has arrived. For a while George didn't look so good, and was suspected of being chicken hearted. We saw him stopped by Jack Renault about a year ago, but we suspected at the time the bout was a Barney and that it must be thrown out of the reckoning.

"Since the queer one, we were there the night George knocked out Bill Tate in the Garden, and now his decisive victory over Tut Jackson stamps him as a logical opponent for any of the heavies."

Many of the newspaper write-ups from this time period seem to find fault in Godfrey's lack of aggressiveness in some of his bouts. Some sportswriters found him too good-natured and not vicious enough in the ring. I think they were unfair evaluations of his ability as a boxer because in many of those bouts he was handcuffed and could not give his all.

"Godfrey will beat Wills just as certainly as the Day of Judgment if they get in the ring together," said Dougherty in the *Albuquerque Morning Journal* in 1925.

Dougherty denied the stories sent out from Los Angeles that Wills and Godfrey had been matched definitely for a fight in Los Angeles on August 1, but said that a match was practically assured, although the date has not been settled. Dougherty did meet with Wills' manager Paddy Mullins in Los Angeles and Mullins promised that Wills will meet Godfrey. Dick Donald, a Los Angeles promoter, promised to promote the match and said it would probably be in September.

"Godfrey will dispose of Wills alright," said Dougherty. "He's too young, too strong, too fast and too good a boxer to let Wills beat him. That boy can box like Benny Leonard. Wills is overrated."

Actually, at one time, Wills' manager Paddy Mullins turned down a $125,000 offer from Tex Rickard to fight Godfrey in New York. The story was confirmed in a wire from a special correspondent in New York and was confirmed by a telegram from Dougherty.

"I don't believe Wills will fight Godfrey," wrote Dougherty. "Rickard today offered me a $50,000 guarantee for my end and more than twice that much to Mullins for Wills. Mullins flatly refuses to sign Wills for a Godfrey match. That means that Godfrey will stay in California. I'll go anywhere to fight Wills and the same goes for Dempsey if he means what he says in those European stories about his desire to battle."

In their third fight, Godfrey finally beat Canada's Jack Renault in San Francisco.

"Renault never had a chance with Big George," said Dougherty. "The only time the Canadian tried to stand up and fight was in the fourth round, and he hit the floor twice before the welcome sound of the gong. The rest of the time, he spent principally in trying to keep Godfrey from knocking his head off."

After the Godfrey-Renault fight on the west coast, Dougherty headed east on a train where he was going to attend the Harry Greb- Mickey Walker bout in New York. He was accompanied on the train by several coast newspapermen and by Jack Ketchell, a young Philadelphia light heavyweight who had been fighting on the coast for several months.

George Godfrey has his hand raised as he decisions Jack Renault in their third meeting in San Francisco's Ballpark on September 8, 1925.
(Tony Triem Collection)

"My father was always traveling to California," remembered daughter Mary Damico. "I would drive him to the train station in Philadelphia, and it would take him four days to get to the west coast. He would stay out there for weeks at a time."

"During a period of ten years," wrote H. Walter Schlichter of the *Philadelphia Inquirer*, "Jimmy Dougherty made sixty round trips from the Atlantic to the Pacific

Baron Dougherty, who is the referee in the center of fighters Joe Benjamin (left) and Jack Silvers (right), was the first ever imported referee for a fight in California after the ban on boxing was lifted in 1925.

coasts besides innumerable long trips of lesser mileage. With his fighters, with his promotional enterprises and with his refereeing jobs, Jimmy said that he had been in every town in the United States that had 200,000 or more inhabitants, besides many cities in Mexico and Canada."

As a referee, Dougherty was brought in from Leiperville to be the third man in the ring for a fight on Washington's Birthday in Fresno, California in 1925. It was a bout that marked the return of big-time boxing in California. Professional boxing in the state had been banned, allowing only four-round bouts. That ban was lifted in 1925.

The principals for the contest were Joe Benjamin and Jack Silvers and they were fighting for the Pacific Coast lightweight championship.

John Brannigan of the *San Francisco Call* wrote, "The bout between Benjamin and Silvers turned out to be a big success fistically and money wise. A crowd of 20,000 and receipts of $43,000 was remarkable considering prices ranged only one, two, three and five dollars."

"Benjamin became the champion, and not a murmur went up from the gathering of 20,000 when Dougherty lifted Benjamin's hand in victory. It was one of the fiercest fights ever waged in a California ring. Benjamin's aggressiveness and timely punches no doubt prompted Dougherty to raise Benjamin's hand."

"In reference to Jimmy Dougherty acting as a referee in California, he is in my 'Famous Firsts' section in 'California Boxing Scrapbook' for that very reason," wrote Hap Navarro. "He was the first ever 'imported' referee for a fight in the state after the law of 1925 took effect.

"The commission here finally decreed in 1940 or 1941, that no third man could be imported to officiate at a local fight. I guess the local guys were complaining about the payday.

"You see, refs out here are paid a fixed fee for weekly bouts, but they get a small percentage of the gate for the outdoor biggies."

Godfrey's next fight on the coast was against Sully Montgomery, who had been a former pro football player for the Cardinals and Frankford Yellow Jackets before he jumped in the ring. Over the years, many pro football players have tried to make that transition from the gridiron to the ring. Another football player, who actually played on the Frankford Yellow Jackets' 1926 NFL Championship team, was Tex Hamer. Interestingly enough, Hamer made a stop in Leiperville when he fought Pat Patterson on August 8, 1929, at Leiperville's Open Air Arena.

Against Montgomery, Godfrey had him down a couple of times before he won on a foul.

BoxRec.com wrote the following about the Olympic Auditorium bout, "In defeat, Montgomery gave one of the worst exhibitions of mucker tactics ever seen in a California ring. The only thing he didn't do was bite. Montgomery was guilty of at least a dozen fouls. Frank Holborow, the referee, over looked all of Montgomery's muckerism until Dr. Lloyd Mace examined Godfrey between the seventh and eighth rounds. He declared Godfrey had been badly fouled and Holborow then awarded the bout to Godfrey."

Still with no chance of Godfrey fighting Dempsey, Dougherty continued to challenge Harry Wills.

"From late 1923, Baron Dougherty issued challenges almost daily for Wills to take on Godfrey, who was Philadelphia's greatest drawing card," explained Hasson, boxing historian and co- author of *Philadelphia's Boxing Heritage 1876-1976*. "Promoters Herman Taylor and Bobby Gunnis figured such a match in Philadelphia would do between $250,000 to $500,000, and the winner would be the 'logical challenger' for Dempsey. Dougherty offered all kinds of perks to Wills including that Godfrey would take the match for $1.00.

"We do know that Wills would not fight him. Even the dean of the black newspapermen of that period Rollo Wilson was critical of Wills for not meeting Godfrey, claiming Godfrey would beat Wills.

"Being the 'most handcuffed boxer of all time' in my opinion doesn't necessarily mean that he was the best of his period, just the 'most feared' with the cuffs off."

Just like Harry Wills with Dempsey, no promoter was going to put up the money to see Godfrey or any black boxer get the opportunity to fight for the title. The public just wasn't interested; Jack Johnson was still fresh in white America's mind.

Godfrey fought Chuck Wiggins on June 6, 1926, one of the dirtiest fighters in ring history. Johnston and Cogswell in their book entitled *Uncrowned Champions* gave the following description of the fight, "Wiggins drove Godfrey wild by using the laces of his gloves on Godfrey and stomped on his feet. Then he went to work inside and gouged George's eye. This all happened in the first round.

"By the sixth round Godfrey's neck and waist were raw from glove-lace scraping and the giant Negro was limping from repeated stomps on his feet. Finally George started fouling back and Chuck never complained. Instead, he got in close and worked with his thumbs in George's eyes until George finally landed a hard one in Chuck's groin. The referee gave the fight to Wiggins on a foul.

"Wiggin's got away with his mayhem, and George was suspended for 30 days."

After that debacle with Wiggins, Godfrey lost a close one to Jack Sharkey in Boston, and then defeated Bob Lawson on the under card of the Dempsey-Tunney fight at the Sesquicentennial Stadium in Philadelphia (later called JFK Memorial Stadium).

George Godfrey, in striped robe, stands next to Baron Dougherty and Spain's Paulino Uzcudun, who he outpointed at Wrigley Field in Los Angeles. The fight was Godfrey's biggest payday ($22,000) of his career. Afterwards, he rented a big house in Beverly Hills. (Tony Triem Collection)

That same stadium was also used that year as the home field of the Philadelphia Quakers of the new American Football League (AFL). In 1926, the Quakers captured the AFL championship, and the Frankford Yellow Jackets brought home the NFL title. It was the first and only time in Philadelphia history that football teams from two different leagues captured championships in the same year.

Godfrey went on a tear after the Sharkey loss to register twenty-two consecutive wins, with sixteen of them coming from the knockout route. His last fight before losing to Johnny Risko at Ebbet's Field in June of 1928, was against Spain's Paulino Uzcudun at Wrigley Field in Los Angeles, California.

Godfrey was the greatest drawing card during this time in California, and it really peaked when he outpointed Uzcudun in ten rounds. A huge crowd of 40,000 paid $128,000, which set a new California record and was the first bout ever in California to draw a $100,000 gate. Uzcudun received $35,000 and Godfrey got the biggest payday of his career, $22,000.

"After the fight, Godfrey rented a big house in Beverly Hills," recalled Dougherty in a *Chester Times* interview after George's death. "He set himself up with a Chinese cook and a Japanese butler. He invited lawyers, doctors, and the cream of Negro society, to dinners and banquets. He lived high.

"Inside of 90 days, he called me. He was broke and he wanted a fight. I got him a fight for $7,500. The day he was weighing in he handed me a paper. 'Take care of this,' he said. 'It's the law. I don't know nothing about it. You take care of it.' It was a bill from the telephone company for $900. He had been calling all over the country since he didn't have to put any money in the box.

"Even after the fight he bought himself a Chrysler and a Ford. The Ford just to run around in, and hired himself a chauffeur. He even bought my son, Howard, a huge Cadillac with all the shiniest decorations and trimmings. And he was broke again in less than two months."

"My father was really upset about how he spent all his money and the fact that he bought me a car," remembered Howard. "George and I drove all the way home across the country in that Cadillac. Boy, the Baron was really angry at George."

During this time, Godfrey was being called the "savior of the fight promoters" because everywhere he fought, he sold out the arena. He was the biggest draw in California, selling out the Olympic in Los Angeles twice, and he also was a big draw in Philadelphia.

"Promoters Gunnis and Taylor, of Philadelphia, were in the red to the tune of $15, 000," recalled Nat Fleischer. "They called upon the services of Godfrey and set a new indoor record for the City of Brotherly Love. The Arena Corporation in

Philadelphia was in financial straits when Godfrey was matched to fight Jack Gross and once again, the towering charge of Baron Dougherty sold out a house and shoved the club into the money-making brackets."

Fleischer continued to explain Godfrey's blight, "Instead of the fight convincing the fistic powers the Godfrey was the outstanding challenger in the division, and it only caused contenders to duck the issue all the more. They too were convinced that he was tops, or very close to it, in the heavyweight class, and they wanted no part of him. They knew when to leave well enough alone, and once more George had to content himself with fighting in the smaller clubs for very little money."

Having been in the top ten of the world heavyweight rankings since 1924, when he was ranked eighth, Godfrey had now moved up to second in 1928. Dempsey had been beaten by Gene Tunney and boxing had a new world heavyweight champion. Now, like he did with challenges to Wills and Dempsey, Dougherty was concentrating on challenging Tunney.

However, Dougherty and Tex Rickard's friendship really turned sour when Rickard said, "Godfrey is one of the worst fighters I ever saw. Fought three times here in the Garden and never showed anything. Besides Tunney wouldn't meet a Negro, even if Godfrey knocked out a few more setups."

"This talk of Rickard is ridiculous," explained Dougherty. "Rickard should be the last man to draw the color line, inasmuch as the first money he made out of boxing came through Joe Gans, a Negro.

"When Tex first came east to secure Jack Johnson, he ate, drank and slept in the same room with Johnson."

Dougherty then sent a telegram to Rickard that said, "George Godfrey is a clean living fellow and the heavyweight champion today.

"You would be glad to enter Godfrey in your so-called elimination tournament if you thought he could be beat."

Dougherty also charged that the heavyweight boxing situation was controlled by gamblers and called Rickard the chief of the gang.

Hap Navarro also wrote about the strained relationship between Dougherty and Rickard, "One of the early reasons Godfrey was bypassed as a titular contender was because of the strained relationship between promoter Tex Rickard and George's manager, Jim Dougherty, who was quoted as telling Tex to 'go hang himself' for not using Godfrey in any of his important fistic extravaganzas. It seems Rickard repeatedly snubbed the big man in favor of lesser lights."

Dougherty was in Portland, Oregon, in late 1927, to see one of his boxers, Tiger Thomas, fight at the Armory Arena. While there, he saw and was able to talk to Tunney, who was acting at a local theatre, but there was no talk about fighting Big George.

The local newspaper reported, "He enjoyed Gene and got a real kick out of the one-round slow motion picture work staged between Tunney and a sparring partner in which the champ shows his famous punch to the solar plexus and chin. It is the big riot of the act.

"When Jimmy walked into the champion's dressing room, he was given a rousing welcome by the king of the heavies. The two quickly got their tongues to wagging about the past and present.

"As Jimmy left the room for a minute, Gene whispered to several of the writers about the time that he first met the Baron and how Dougherty could have been his manager only that six years ago the name Tunney was never heard of outside of the ham and egg class."

"Jimmy, bet you can't remember when you first met the champion," asked Don Skene, local dramatic critic and famous French sports writer.

"Yep, twas at Vincent Treanor's desk, sports editor of the *Evening World* in New York," said Dougherty.

"Correct," said Tunney. "Jimmy didn't give me much of a tumble, but told me to see so and so and that Vincent would treat me right. He was great to me. I never forgot the Baron for the few minutes we talked. Jimmy told me a few things about the game and shot me into a few chiefs of publicity, and he did it because he has a big heart and everybody that knows Jimmy Dougherty always speaks the name. Jimmy could have been my manager, only he didn't want to butt into some other fellow's business. You don't find many Dougherty's in the fight racket. They come few and far between," explained Tunney.

Now that Dempsey was out of the picture, Dougherty was hoping to get Godfrey a shot at the new champion, Gene Tunney. The challenging of Tunney did not last that long because on July 31, 1928, Tunney surprised everyone when he announced that he was retiring from boxing. With the announcement, Tunney stunned promoter Tex Rickard and even his manager Billy Gibson.

With a vacant heavyweight crown, Frank Wiener, chairman of the Pennsylvania State Athletic Commission, stated that Godfrey should be a foremost contender for the title.

"To my way of thinking, Godfrey is just as much a contender for the heavyweight title as Jack Sharkey, Max Schmeling or Primo Carnera," explained Wiener.

"I certainly am glad Wiener is giving Godfrey the support George deserves," said Dougherty. "What the Pennsylvania chairman says about Godfrey's right to be in the championship picture ought to make other commissions throughout the country come to their senses."

In 1928, Dougherty took his complaint about Big George being ignored to T. Von Ziekursch, the sports editor of the *Philadelphia Daily News*. Ziekursch, who wrote a column entitled, "In the Groove", allowed Dougherty to be a guest columnist for a day. Dougherty wrote the following,

"On my last trip around the country, it occurred to me that it would be a good idea to find out what the sports writer thought of the situation. Well, I decided to see what men who really know the boxing game, the sports writers, would say about Godfrey privately and about the heavyweight situation as a whole. Now I am going to pass it along to you. I'm only picking some of the most famous of the writers I talked to.

"Mark Kelly of the *Los Angeles Examiner* thought Godfrey was a great fighter, even before I did, and said so in his paper. Jim Woods, chairman of the California boxing commission, who isn't a newspaperman, by the way, told me Godfrey is bigger and stronger than Jack Johnson ever was.

"'Johnson was a waiting fighter,' said Woods. 'If he was fighting in these ten-round fights today, they'd throw him out of the ring the same as they would Jeffries. Godfrey is bigger and stronger than Jeffries was, too.'

"Now to get back to the writers, Bob Cronin of the *Los Angeles News*, and Jack James of the *Herald*, both told me there is nobody in the heavyweight division to give Godfrey a fight. Paul Lowry of the *Los Angeles Times* said Godfrey can call the round when he's really trying to knock any of them out, and isn't playing with them, like he did with Neill Clisbie. Did I ever tell you about that? You know Clisbie was a sensation in the west, a big colored boy who weighed over two hundred pounds, and was knocking them all cold. They thought they had Godfrey at last. Godfrey stuck out his chin and let Clisbie hit it four or five rounds. Then he knocked Clisbie cold.

"Now, to get back to the writers, Harry Bullion of the *Detroit Free Press*; Frank O'Donnell of the *Detroit Times*; and Sam Greene of the *Detroit News*, all told me there isn't a man living that can beat Godfrey.

"Scoop Gleason of the *San Francisco Call* said there is no fighter in the ring who has a chance with him. Tom Laird of the *San Francisco News* said that too, and told me Jack Renault has never gotten over the beating Godfrey gave him. Laird refereed that Renault fight and another of Godfrey's fights.

"Dick Kain and Gordon Mackay of the *Philadelphia Record* and you, yourself, have all told me Godfrey could take this bunch of second-rate tramps that are being lined up as heavyweight contenders and make monkeys of them, if they aren't already monkeys.

"Frank Wiener, chairman of the Pennsylvania commission, told me he didn't think there were any two men in the ring who could lick Godfrey.

"But to get back to the writers, Ed Frayne of the *New York American*, and Grantland Rice, Sid Mercer, Vince Treanor, Sam Taub, Murray Lewin and Jackie Farrell, all of them New York experts, have told me the same thing.

"Now if anybody is going to have the picking of a champion, why shouldn't it be somebody who knows something about fighters and fighting? If it was left up to the sports writers with their reputations at stake in the public mind they would be picking a fighter like George."

Nat Fleischer, the editor of *Ring Magazine*, always felt that Godfrey was the leader in the field of heavyweights after Tunney vacated the title.

"Leaving the race question out of my discussion, for I don't believe it should enter, Godfrey is the outstanding heavyweight now before the public," wrote Fleischer. "Were he permitted to fight as he can, were the color line not drawn, the next world's heavyweight champion would be George Godfrey.

"Were Godfrey to obtain the recognition he deserves, he, and not Schmeling, would now be in line for a crack at Jack Sharkey to determine Tunney's successor."

Unfortunately, that did not happen, and after almost two years of elimination bouts, Jack Sharkey met Max Schmeling on June 12, 1930, at Yankee Stadium in New York to fill Tunney's vacant title. Schmeling won the contest on a foul and the world heavyweight championship was now held for the first time by a citizen of Germany.

Eleven days later, Godfrey fought the gigantic (6'6", 260 pound) Primo Carnera from Italy on June 23, at the Baker Bowl in Philadelphia, the home of the Philadelphia Phillies. Carnera was not only known as the biggest heavyweight champion ever, but was also known to be backed by the mob. That mob was a gang headed by mobster Owney Madden. Most of his fights were fixed with some victims falling without taking a punch, but now and then they took a chance with more willing competitors like Godfrey.

George Godfrey squares off with Primo Carnera before their fight at the Baker Bowl on June 23, 1930. Howard Dougherty, who worked Godfrey's corner that night, stands next to Big George.

Owney "The Killer" Madden, who was a leading underworld figure in Manhattan during prohibition, bought the Club De Luxe in Harlem from former heavyweight boxing champion Jack Johnson in 1923 and reopened it a year later, renaming it the Cotton Club.

In 1931, shortly before the end of prohibition, Madden got out of bootlegging and became partners with boxing promoters "Broadway Bill Duffy and George Jean "Big Frenchie" DeMange. Between them, they controlled the careers of several boxing champions including Max Baer and Primo Carnera. His arranged fixed fights for Carnera eventually led to Carnera capturing the World Heavyweight title in 1933.

Before the bout began, Howard Dougherty was in the dressing room with Godfrey as he made the final preparations before heading into the ring.

"I was in the dressing room with George, and these two racketeers came in and grabbed and started to slap and push around the boxing commissioner," recalled Howard. "They said they especially needed a cup for Carnera in the fight with Godfrey. During that era, the cups were air filled and they couldn't get one to fit Carnera. They said he would have to fight without one, and we didn't want that because it would be easier for them to cry foul for any of George's low blows. The referee was on the side of the gangsters.

"I was in George's corner for the whole fight, and I jumped in the ring when they called a foul for a low blow on George."

In the fight, Johnston and Cogswell, authors of *Uncrowned Champions*, wrote, "Godfrey went to the body for most of the fight, and he and Primo put on a pleasing fight. But George did not go for Primo's chin with anything hard and made just enough action to make it look good. In the fifth round, he hit Carnera with a left hook that landed in the groin and lost the fight on a foul."

George Godfrey went to the body for most of the fight, and he and Primo put on a pleasing fight. But George did not go for Primo's chin with anything hard and made just enough action to make it look good.

"There is not the slightest doubt that Carnera's fight with Godfrey was fixed for the former to win," wrote Fleischer. "The Italian's foxy handlers would not have spoiled their racket by permitting him to tackle Godfrey otherwise. They knew what Godfrey could do to their mammoth charge, if allowed to fight in his real form.

"Knowing what instructions he had to carry out, Godfrey still with his heavy punches weakened Carnera and on several occasions it looked as though the huge Italian must go down. When that happened, Godfrey eased up and clinched to aid Primo. But at the half-way mark George was so far ahead on points, it seemed impossible that he could lose.

"There was but one way for George to execute his orders, by earning disqualification. So he began hitting low. He was warned by referee Tom Reilly to keep up his punches, but in the fifth round Godfrey deliberately struck his opponent below the belt. Carnera dropped as if he had been shot. The bout was stopped and Primo declared winner on a foul, thus saving the day for the mob that controlled him."

In the fifth round, Godfrey (who is standing in the corner) hit Carnera (on the canvas) with a left hook that landed in the groin and lost the fight on a foul. Ring magazine publisher Nat Fleischer wrote, "There is not the slightest doubt that Carnera's fight with Godfrey was fixed."

As Godfrey left the ring and headed towards the dressing room, there was a lot of booing, profanity and catcalling from the fans. They even started throwing soda bottles, old newspapers, and cuds of chewing tobacco, cigar butts and cushions into the ring.

Sports writer Bill Corum, who was one of the first to talk to Godfrey in the dressing room, wrote in his book *Off And Running*, "I took quick advantage of the situation. 'George,' I said, 'I want you to tell me just one thing and I want you to tell me the truth. Can this fellow Carnera fight?'"

"Mr. Corum," he replied promptly and earnestly, "the man can't hurt you. He's big as a house an' he kin box a little, but he can't punch, he can't punch."

"At this juncture, Godfrey's manager, Jim 'The Baron' Dougherty, rushed in and dragged the sweating fighter off into a corner where they conferred briefly," wrote Corum. "By the time the rest of the sports scribes had got inside, Godfrey was rolling his eyes and saying, "Most terrible man I ever did see; man can knock your head right off; man's dangerous, going to be champion.

"I held to the belief that Godfrey, alone and free to speak, had told me the truth."

In the February, 1948 issue of *Sport Magazine*, Jack Sher wrote that Godfrey "had a terrible time losing to Primo. It was almost impossible for this boy to fight badly enough for the huge Italian even to hit him. He finally solved the dilemma by fouling Primo in the fifth round."

That Godfrey and Carnera bout has the fifth highest attendance total in Philadelphia boxing history. The fight brought in 35,000 fans paying a total of $180,175.

Hap Navarro wrote, "It seems that the gate was tremendous, up in the hundred thousands, and Primo's camp got the larger share, many times over Godfrey's end, which supposedly came to $10,000, a pittance. George's purse was held up by the Commission, and he didn't get all of it back, but rather something like one-half and only after a year had gone by. Meantime, he was banned from boxing in the state."

"Predictably Godfrey was made the fall guy and his license was suspended in Pennsylvania for a year," said noted boxing historian Chuck Hasson. "He engaged in pro wrestling contests in the Camden, New Jersey, area while on suspension." He also had a wrestling match at Borchert Field in Milwaukee, Wisconsin, against 6'4', 230 pound Ernst "Ernie" Scharpegge, who a year earlier fought Gus Sonnenberg for the world heavyweight championship.

Godfrey was suspended after the Carnera bout and started wrestling. He is seen here in the ring with Kid Porphy at Berkshire Arena on Decoration Day in 1931. (Chuck Hasson Collection)

After ten minutes of wrestling, Scharpegge won the first fall with a crotch hold and body slam.

What followed was what the *Wisconsin News* called "one of the worst, and yet one of the most exciting, grin and grunt affairs in Milwaukee history."

Pete Ehrmann wrote, "When the best two-out-of-three falls match resumed, it was Scharpegge who resorted to fisticuffs after Godfrey got him in a strangle hold, punching George in the stomach and chin. Godfrey retaliated with a right that sent Scharpegge to the mat.

"At that point, more than 12 uniformed policemen rushed into the ring and surrounded Godfrey. As the bell rang and the crowd started to boo, It looked like the start of a riot," reported Ronald McIntyre of the *Milwaukee Sentinel.*

"But then Scharpegge and Godfrey shook hands and the match resumed, and within moments, Scharpegge took another swing at Godfrey, and when the referee objected, he took a swing at him. The cops rushed into the ring, and Scharpegge took a few of them too. The result was a win by disqualification for Godfrey."

"When the punching started," wrote McIntyre, "Godfrey might just as well have quit for he realized that if he started slugging, a race riot might have ensued."

With Godfrey being banned from fighting in Pennsylvania, he and Dougherty traveled to Mexico in late December of 1930. While in Mexico City, Godfrey engaged in two bouts. One contest was with Salvatore Ruggirello on New Years Day, with Big George knocking out the Italian in the first round. His other bout was in late February against Ricardo Rosel, which was also a first round knockout for Godfrey.

While in Mexico City, Dougherty and Godfrey also attended a bullfight, where the greatest bullfighter in Mexico performed and killed a bull for the Baron and George.

Gordon Mackay of the *Philadelphia Record* wrote, "Mr. James F. Dougherty sent me a letter from a far-distant land, and its contents told me that the biggest bullfighter in Mexico killed a bull for Dougherty and Godfrey, which was something of a treat for Jimmy, as he usually had to kill all the bull for George before this."

After the Carnera debacle, Dougherty had become so disgusted with Godfrey's inability to get a fair shake in the boxing world that he decided to leave the country for a short time. His letter to sportswriter Mackay indicates his displeasure with Godfrey's blight.

Dougherty wrote, "I write to let you know that I am still the Wandering Jew, and I'm in a new country, but I want to say that in all my travels I never struck a more freer and prosperous country than Mexico, where all men and women are equal. After all, it's a great trip for American citizens to be able in their lives to visit some place on this earth where they can enjoy the freedom and liberties that they are deprived of in their country, and where their fore parents bled and laid down their lives for it.

"I've been here now three days, and all cafes and places of amusement are wide open, and I've got the first time to see a man or woman under the influence of liquor. In my home town of Leiperville, you would see more drunken men than in all of Mexico City."

As the letter continued, the Baron talked about Godfrey's reputation as an outstanding boxer, "Godfrey and I attended the bullfight on Sunday as the guests of honor of 'El Matador Liceaga', who threw his caps into our box seat, and we were honored by the fact that Liceaga killed a bull for George Godfrey and Dougherty. I understand that this is the greatest honor that can be bestowed upon any guest, whether he is a native of Mexico or of a foreign country. The only other American ever given this honor here in the last 25 years was Colonel Lindbergh, although Mexico City has had some of the most prominent men in America visiting here. Only a few months ago, one of the most prominent men in Philadelphia visited here for the purpose of helping to finance their government. Samuel Vauclain, Senator Morrow, who was Ambassador here, never had that honor bestowed on him. That goes to show that Godfrey is honored and respected for no other reason than that he has always been honest in his contests of sports and is recognized as the champion of all champions.

"A funny thing happened at the bull ring. Someone got up in the audience and hollered out, 'Hello Baron how's Leiperville?' It happened to be a boy Alfonso Perez, who years ago his parents moved up to Leiperville, and he was one of the small kiddies that I used to take out on my annual free picnics for the children in Leiperville, and believe me, I was glad to see him, and he also to see me."

Dougherty continued to show his dissatisfaction with the treatment of Godfrey when he wrote, "Get me a buyer for the barn sheds of Leiperville, as I think I will settle here and make this country my permanent home, as I love liberty, of which the country of my birth has none.

"Any man that has the courage to fight Godfrey, and with some reputation, can come into his country and get himself a lot more money by fighting Godfrey here than he can in the States. The promoter here will give Sharkey or Schmeling $100,000 in American money to fight Godfrey. They say they will give Carnera $50,000. They do not think Ruggirello is any match for Godfrey, and neither do I, but it's not our fault. We don't pick opponents; we take whatever the club offers. This year, Godfrey has had 12 fights, one draw and 11 knockouts."

The Carnera bout was the last big fight of Godfrey's career, but in 1931, when he returned to the ring, he was still ranked third in the world. He was fighting regularly that year, and in 1932, he reeled off eleven consecutive knockouts, including a win over Ace Clark for the Negro heavyweight championship.

By 1933, Godfrey was back doing some more wrestling but was also boxing and lost his Colored Heavyweight Championship to Obie Walker at the Arena in Philadelphia. Godfrey had held that title for seven years, from 1926 to 1933. Later, Walker was beaten by Larry Gaines, and finally it was Joe Louis' long reign as world champion that would put an end to the World Colored heavyweight title.

That loss to Walker just about finished Godfrey off as far as big time U.S. boxing was concerned. However, he was still wrestling, and this time it was against some really big names like Strangler Lewis, Sandor Szabo and Jim Londos.

In late 1934, Godfrey was offered to have a series of bouts throughout Europe. Fighting in Belgium, Sweden, France and Romania, Big George chalked up eight victories. On October 2, 1935, Godfrey captured the International Boxing Union (IBU) World Heavyweight title by decisioning Pierre Charles in fifteen rounds in Brussels, Belgium. It was really a title that no one outside of Europe recognized.

It seems that in late 1934, the IBU had ordered world champion Max Baer to defend his title against the reigning European champion, Pierre Charles of Belgium. When Baer instead opted to fight James J. Braddock, they withdrew recognition of him as champion.

Subsequently, the IBU matched Charles with Godfrey for their version of the title. After his victory, Godfrey did not press any claim to the championship and it was inactive for the next two years. Then the IBU recognized Baer's successor, James J. Braddock, as their champion.

"George was treated like royalty overseas, and he indulged himself in wine, women and food," wrote authors Johnston and Cogswell. "He was soon up to 300 lbs. again and wrestling in Europe and the United States.

"Finally in 1937, George, managed by the colorful Baron von Stumme and Frank Garbut, was granted a California boxing license. He took off a lot of weight and knocked out a couple of sparring partners getting in shape for Hank Hankinson who wouldn't have lasted a round with the old Godfrey. They drew a decent house and Hankinson had a good night and finished George off in round eight."

The Hankinson bout was Godfrey's last fight, and he finished out his life living in a one room apartment. It was reported that he worked as a bouncer and doorman at various nightclubs. *Knockout Magazine* reported that he was working as a doorman and bouncer at the LaConga Nightclub in Long Beach for $10 a night. During this time, he was one of the most popular figures along Central Avenue.

"I got to see and hear George Godfrey after he had retired and set up a small business at the entrance of the original Main Street Gym back in the early 1940's," recalled Hap Navarro. "I was just a kid, but I stood by and watched him cut up with Jack Johnson, who was also around the gym in those days. I will never forget his klieg-light smile nor his feet, which were always swollen so badly he could not lace up his shoes."

His health was not good during his retirement years, and he suffered from heart and kidney problems. On August 13, 1947, Godfrey was found dead of a heart attack in his apartment at the young age of 51.

When Dougherty got word of Godfrey's passing, he said, "George was one of the nicest fellows who ever lived. He wouldn't get mad. He was just like a big kid. He would spar ten rounds with Benny Bass, a featherweight, and never hurt him.

"He could knock them all dead. When he was right, he could have taken on Louis, Tunney, and Dempsey, all of them in a Battle Royal and cleaned them up. Godfrey was never knocked down. He was never on the floor. I toured all over with George; he never had to extend himself. In most of his matches, he had to carry the fellows for a couple of rounds. We couldn't get the topnotchers to fight.

"As IBU champion, George cabled me and asked me to get him a fight with a young newcomer, Joe Louis. I tried through Damon Runyon, but Damon told me that Roxborough, Black, and Blackburn, Louis' managers, had barred only one fighter for Louis. That was Godfrey.

"I wish I could fly out to the funeral. I would, too, if I weren't in the middle of my political campaign. Yes, I'd like to go. George was one of the nicest fellows I ever knew."

Godfrey was extremely popular and there was a large turnout at his wake and funeral. There were reports that Jack Dempsey gave the eulogy at his funeral, but others said it was his close friend Dr. Darrington Weaver. Dempsey did attend his funeral, and some said he even offered to foot the bill, but it seems that the Southern California Boxers and Wrestlers Fund paid for the funeral.

In the book *Uncrown Champions*, Johnston and Cogswell wrote about Jack Roper, a local heavyweight who had fought Louis, Dempsey and Godfrey, and Roper said, "When Godfrey hit you solid it was all over."

Also, Primo Carnera, who fought both Godfrey and Louis, said, "Louis had to hit me many times to do what Godfrey did with one punch. There was no comparison with their power."

Even though the Baron could never get Big George a title shot, Godfrey did win close to a half million dollars in the ring. In his 18 year boxing career, he won 100 bouts and scored an amazing 83 knockouts.

Godfrey lived to see another black heavyweight champion when Louis took the title from James J. Braddock in 1937. He also lived just long enough to see baseball integrated when Jackie Robinson was signed by the Brooklyn Dodgers in 1947. Unfortunately, Godfrey was never given the opportunity that was given Louis or even Jack Johnson. Many historians feel that Johnson ruined it for Godfrey and other black fighters because after he won the title, he easily bowled over the White Hopes sent up against him, plus his very public fondness for fast cars and white women brought hatred from white America. The people running boxing weren't about to go through that again.

It is such a shame that Godfrey is so overlooked in the history of boxing. Unfortunately, when people look strictly at his record, those handcuffed fights damage his reputation. But pound for pound, he was one of the most dangerous fighters of his era.

Interestingly enough, six years before Dougherty took on the management of Godfrey, he had the opportunity to manage another fighter, who would become one of the greatest heavyweight champions in the history of the sport. His name was Jack Dempsey, and he would spend time in Leiperville like so many other fighters of that era.

- Chapter 7 -

The Manassa Mauler

"Jack Dempsey was the one who I let get away."

Jimmy "Baron" Dougherty

William Harrison Dempsey, the ninth of eleven children, was born in Manassa, Colorado, on June 24, 1895. His oldest brother Bernie was a fairly good professional middleweight boxer and the young Harry, his name during his childhood, was in awe of him. Harry had already made up his mind that he wanted to become a professional fighter. With the name Kid Blackie, they say he had his first professional fight in 1913. However, the record books have him fighting his first professional bout as Jack Dempsey in 1915, the same year that Jack Johnson lost his title to Jesse Willard in Havana, Cuba. Brother Bernie gave him the name Jack Dempsey, which was taken from the old Nonpareil Jack Dempsey.

Most of Dempsey's fights were in Colorado, Nevada and Utah, but in 1916, after winning nine straight bouts, even by knockout, Dempsey suggested to his manager Jack Price that they travel to New York to make some real money fighting. Dempsey was used to riding the rods, but this time they both bought train tickets to New York. Riding the rods was a very dangerous way to travel where you would cling to the brake beams under a freight car.

In the spring of 1916, the 20 year old Dempsey and his manager Jack Price arrived in New York.

"Dempsey and Price rented a room near the Polo Grounds at 155th Street," wrote Roger Kahn in his book *A Flame Of Pure Fire: Jack Dempsey And The Roaring 20'S.* "Price made the rounds of the promoters with the press clippings. Dempsey did roadwork in Central Park and punched bags and sparred at Grupp's Gymnasium on 116th Street. Money was short. Dempsey took to buying nickel beers, which entitled him to a free lunch, pickles, crackers, and cheese. He ate what he could. To save money, he and Price gave up the room. They showered at the gym. They slept on benches in Central Park."

In his second fight in the Big Apple, Dempsey again won and sportswriters such as Damon Runyon started to pay attention. Also paying attention was John "The Barber" Reisler who became Dempsey's next manager and set Dempsey up with a bout against John Lester Johnson. The fight took place at the Harlem Sporting Club on July 14, 1916, and after ten rounds the consensus of sportswriters gave a narrow decision to Johnson. To make things worse for Dempsey, Johnson broke three of his ribs in the second round.

During this time in New York, there were no official decisions. The Frawley Law was passed in 1911, which permitted fights of up to ten rounds, but prohibited official decisions. Under this bizarre legislation, people who bet on fights had to rely on newspapers for verdicts.

"Finally on May 24, 1920, the Walker Law went into effect," wrote Roger Kahn in *A Flame Of Pure Fire*. "It allowed for bouts of up to fifteen rounds, provided for decisions rendered by a referee and judges, mandated the licensing of boxers, managers, trainers, physicians, and promoters, and provided for over-all supervision by a state commission. The Walker Law became the model for boxing legislation throughout the United States."

Dempsey, who had slept in Central Park the night before the fight, was given an unfair cut of the purse by John the Barber, and he decided to catch a freight train heading west. It took him a week riding the boxcars to finally get back to Salt Lake City.

Throughout his lifetime, Dougherty mentioned numerous times that he had the opportunity to manage Jack Dempsey. He said that Dempsey was down and out and he tried unsuccessfully to get him on a fight card in Philadelphia.

Writer H. Walter Schlichter of the *Philadelphia Inquirer* explained, "In 1916, Johnny Spatola, one of the brothers of the Spatola Wine and Fruit dealers of the Reading Terminal Market, who had a penchant for managing fighters, approached Dougherty stating that he had a big fellow in tow for which he could not get any matches. He knew that Dougherty was a great friend of Jack McGuigan, who was running the National A.C. and importuned him to induce Jack to give his big fellow a chance. He told Dougherty that his man came to Philadelphia and applied at Baldwin's and the Pennsylvania Railroad to get a job. He was down and out but could do some fighting. Dougherty proposed to McGuigan to put this boy on in a preliminary to Jack Blackburn for five or ten dollars. McGuigan was cold to the proposition of matching the unknown. Spatola's protégé was the famous Jack Dempsey."

Schlichter continued, "Dougherty then took Dempsey to Leiperville and had him doing odd jobs around the hotel. All at once he disappeared. Dougherty learned that he had hocked his overcoat and went to New York where he placed himself under the management of John the Barber. Here he was not successful and returned to his home in Salt Lake City."

It would almost be two years before Dougherty would hear the name Dempsey again. He had read in the newspaper that Fred Fulton was fighting a Jack Dempsey in Harrison, New Jersey. Curious to know if it was the same Dempsey, Dougherty and Tiny Maxwell, the sports editor of the *Philadelphia Public Ledger*, attended the fight and saw Dempsey knock out Fulton in one round.

At the time, Dougherty was getting ready to promote a fight at the ball park in Philadelphia, and he wanted to sign Fulton for the show, however, after seeing Dempsey, he decided to offer Dempsey the match. Dougherty put up a $15,000 purse for a bout between Dempsey and Billy Miske. Unfortunately, the fight fell through and never happened.

When Dempsey returned to Salt Lake City, he got married to a girl named Maxine Cates, who was a piano player at Maxim's Saloon in the city. The marriage took place on October 9, 1916. He was twenty and owned one shirt, one pair of pants and one beat-up pair of boots; while Maxine was much older at thirty-five.

In 1917, Dempsey traveled to San Francisco for more fights, and it was there that he met John Leo McKernan, who went by the name of Doc Kearns. Kearns had been a welterweight boxer, a minor league baseball player, a bouncer and bartender and had hunted for gold in Klondike. He claimed to have been managed by Wyatt Earp and he traveled extensively with legendary writer Jack London. With Dempsey fighting for him, he was soon to become one of the greatest fight managers of all time.

Kearns told writer John Lardner, "When I found Dempsey in San Francisco in 1917, he was a moral, physical, and financial wreck. He wasn't eating steady. He couldn't hold a job. I taught him boxing tricks. I showed him how to throw that good left hand. Hook off the jab, the double hook. I got him going."

Kearns definitely got Dempsey fights and starting in the spring of 1917, three weeks before America entered World War I, Dempsey won nine straight bouts. The following year, he won twenty-one of twenty-two fights all over the country. In eleven of those fights, he knocked out his opponent in the first round.

When Dempsey and Kearns traveled east, they didn't venture into New York because John the Barber still claimed to be Dempsey's manager and was demanding half the money Dempsey was winning.

Baron Dougherty (center) was involved in the promotion and refereed Jack Dempsey's (right) fight with Battling Levinsky (left) at the Olympia A.C. on November 6, 1918. (Chuck Hasson Collection)

After the Fulton bout in New Jersey, where Dougherty rekindled his friendship with Dempsey and befriended Kearns, Dougherty had Dempsey train in Leiperville for a fight he co-promoted at the Olympia A.C. between Dempsey and Battling Levinsky. The fight took place on November 6, 1918, and not only was Dougherty involved in the promotion but he also refereed the bout.

It was a right hand to the jaw by Dempsey that knocked out Levinsky in the third round. *The Philadelphia Public Ledger* reported, "Jack Dempsey conclusively proved last night at the Olympia that he is one of the best heavyweights in the country by stopping Battling Levinsky of New York in the third round."

Levinsky estimated he had about 250 bouts up until this point in his career, including about 60 under the name of Barney Williams. He also claimed that although he had been knocked down about 25 times, he had never taken a ten-count prior to this bout.

While training at Dougherty's boxing establishment in Leiperville, Dempsey picked up a few dollars waiting on tables at the hotel.

"When not training, Dempsey tended at the Colonial and also waited on tables," remembered Ed Conner, a local boxer who had many bouts at the Leiperville ring as a professional. "Dempsey used

Jack Dempsey plays the piano at Baron Dougherty's Colonial Hotel in Leiperville during a break in training in 1918. Joining him in song are some of his sparring partners, including Big Bill Tate who is standing on the far right.

to serve Sam Vauclain, president of Baldwin's, his meals every day."

Dempsey was knocking them dead in the ring, but outside the ring, America was entering World War I, the war to end all wars. The draft had become law in 1917, and it was time for Dempsey to register for the draft.

Author Roger Kahn wrote, "Babe Ruth, a Boston Red Sox pitcher who hit with power, enlisted in the Massachusetts home guard. He never missed an inning. Bill Tilden, the great tennis star, joined the Signal Corps and spent two years stationed in Pittsburgh giving tennis lessons to army men, including his own commanding officer. Benny Leonard, the great lightweight champion, enlisted in the army and taught doughboys, the World War I term for GIs, to box."

When it was time for Dempsey to register for the draft, he filled out his draft questionnaire and applied for an exemption. He claimed that his father, mother, widowed sister, and her three children relied on him for support. He also listed as a dependent his wife Maxine. At that time, if you were the principal supporter of your family, and if your induction would impose hardship on your family, you did not have to serve in the military.

Late in 1918, while Dempsey was training and living at the Colonial Hotel in Leiperville, Dougherty and Kearns put out stories that Dempsey was doing his part for defense by working in the Sun Ship Yard in Chester, the world's largest drydock. With Dougherty's connections, he was able to get Tiny Maxwell, Kearns, and Dempsey to visit the ship yard and even had photographs taken and circulated showing Dempsey in work clothes. A series of photos were taken and one particular photograph had Dempsey dressed in a leather apron, like the other laborers. The only problem was that the photo also showed Dempsey's high-gloss patent leather shoes.

Jack Dempsey is seen walking out of the Sun Shipyard in Chester with his overalls and patent leather shoes. On the far left is baron Dougherty and next to Dempsey are Tiny Maxwell and Doc Kearns.

Doc Kearns, in his book, *The Million Dollar Gate*, explained it this way, "When we arrived in Philadelphia, with the end of the war only a week away, a representative from some government agency asked to have Dempsey pose in the Sun Ship Yard. It was their theory that it might influence more workers to go into war work.

"I had details of the Levinsky match to iron out, so I sent Dempsey with the government men. When the picture appeared it was a bombshell. They had slipped a pair of overalls over his regular clothing, and the picture clearly showed Jack was wearing patent leather shoes.

Jack Dempsey is pictured at the Sun Shipyard in Chester with a pair of overalls that were slipped over his regular clothing. The picture clearly showed that Dempsey was wearing patent leather shoes.

"When that picture appeared, you might have thought we had planted a bomb under the White House. Even after Dempsey had been cleared in a federal trial, he was for years unjustly accused of being a slacker."

In the *Chester Times*, the headline appeared, "Jack Dempsey as a Ship Worker". The column said, "Dempsey appeared at the Sun plant and signed up during the morning. After that, he didn't waste much time, but got to work immediately, donning a suit of overalls and going over to Shipway No. 1, where he grabbed one of the pneumatic hammers and started to drive rivets in the side of a steel leviathan.

"Although Dempsey showed that he is an expert when it comes to handling the riveting machine, he will not work in that capacity. He learned the trade in a Seattle shipyard where he had three years experience prior to the time he decided to

enter the fight game. Dempsey will be a labor agent for the Sun Company and his task will be to secure workers from all parts of the country.

"After he signed up yesterday, he came to Philadelphia and started for Chicago with Jack Kearns, his manager. From there, he will travel through Illinois, Iowa, Nebraska and Colorado, appearing at army recruiting stations and issuing calls for workers to come to Chester and help build ships."

Jack Dempsey (center) and Doc Kearns (right) talk with an employer at the Sun Shipyard employment office.

After two more fights at the Olympia, where Dempsey knocked out Porky Dan Flynn and decisioned Billy Miske, Dougherty traveled to Louisiana with Doc Kearns and Dempsey for his bout with Carl Morris.

On December 12, 1918, the *Chester Times* reported, "James F. Dougherty, Jack Dempsey, the heavyweight, and Jack Kearns, his manager, left yesterday for New Orleans, where Dempsey will go a twenty-round bout with Carl Morris. The Baron will look Dempsey over after the battle, and it is possible he will make a real business proposition to Willard."

The fight, held at the Louisiana Auditorium in New Orleans on December 16, 1918, did not last very long. Dempsey landed only one blow, a left hook to the solar plexus and Morris went down. It was a first round knockout for Dempsey.

Again, the *Chester Times* stated, "Fight fans in the vicinity will be interested to know that a letter has been received by Thomas Murray of the Colonial Hotel from James F. Dougherty, who went south to see the fistic tournament between Jack Dempsey and Carl Morris. Among other things, the Baron stated that he was in the company of Dempsey and Jack Kearns, his manager, and that the trio would hit Leiperville about Thursday if all went well."

When they returned home, Dempsey and Kearns stayed in Leiperville for a few days to get ready for Dempsey's next fight against Gunboat Smith in Buffalo, New York.

Doc Kearns (left), Tiny Maxwell (2nd from left), Jack Dempsey (2nd from right), and Baron Dougherty (right) all pose outside of the Sun Shipyard in Chester in 1918, where Dempsey supposedly had signed up to work.

"Looking as fresh as a daisy, and keyed up like a boy just let loose from school, James F. Dougherty, the Baron of Leiperville, blew back into town Friday night," wrote the *Chester Times*. "His guardians were Jack Dempsey and his manager, Jack Kearns. They came back, Dempsey with fresh laurels and faith and courage he can go the limit with Willard.

"Jim says Dempsey has the goods and as he has carefully watched the course of this young shipbuilder, this youngster with awful wallop, he is in a position to know.

"Dempsey, it will be noted, is at the Washburn Theatre this week. He is doing a special stunt, but he is offering $1,000 to any and all comers who can knock him out in three rounds."

"New Orleans is a good town," said Dougherty. "It reminds me of New York. It is prosperous, liberal and everything was in full swing from the Red Cross to the peanut man. There was no disorder. Those who wanted to go to church could do so, play baseball in the afternoon if so inclined, or go to the movies in the evening."

Up in Buffalo, Dempsey put Gunboat Smith down on the canvas nine times before hitting him with a right hand to the head for the full count in the second round.

Sportswriter V. Freanor's column stated, "Jimmy Dougherty of Leiperville, Pennsylvania, is very much interested in making Jack Dempsey champion of the world. Jimmy went all the way to New Orleans to see Dempsey fight Carl Morris.

He is involved in a scheme to make Jess Willard come out of his shell hole and train his guns on an honest to goodness challenger.

"Jimmy, in conjunction with some other sportsmen, wants to make Willard fight or retire. If he fights, Dougherty thinks Dempsey is the man to oppose him. Up to a day or two ago Willard was in retirement, but he ran into some newspaper folk in Chicago. He intimated that he wasn't sidestepping anybody. He figured, however, that his logical opponent was Georges Carpentier of France."

Dougherty was very determined to get Willard to fight Dempsey. Willard had captured the title in 1915, when he defeated Jack Johnson in Cuba. In three years, he had only defended his title once, against Frank Moran in 1916, in Madison Square Garden, a fight which Dougherty had attended. Since that fight, he had turned down all challengers, and Dempsey believed it was not because of any lack of courage, but simply because he really didn't like fighting. He was a made fighter, not a natural born one.

Walter Schlichter of the *Philadelphia Inquirer* wrote, "Dougherty was working with Kearns and put up a purse of $30,000 in a certified check, certified by the Cambridge Trust Company of Chester, to get Jesse Willard to fight Dempsey six rounds in the Philadelphia Ball Park and offered Dempsey's services free. He had so much confidence in Dempsey's ability that when our Philadelphia sportswriters like Billy Rocap thought Dempsey did not have a chance with Willard, Dougherty put up in a brokerage house on 16th and Walnut, $10,000 and advertised in the papers that anyone wanting to lay a 5 to 1 bet against this $10,000 that Dempsey would knock Willard out in less than four rounds was welcome. No one came to accept this bet."

Robert "Tiny" Maxwell, who was an All-American football player at Swarthmore College and an outstanding college football official, was a great friend of the Baron's. Dougherty asked Maxwell to take a trip to Denver where Willard was at the time and try to clinch the bout. Unfortunately, through the advice of sportswriter and referee Ed Smith of Chicago,

In 1922, Robert "Tiny" Maxwell (left), the sports editor of the Philadelphia Public ledger, posed with Baron Dougherty and his daughter Mary in front of his mansion, Sequoia.

Willard refused to sign for the fight. Eventually the match fell through, but Dougherty did his best to try and bring the fight to Delaware County. That was one of the Baron's greatest ambitions.

Schlichter explained, "When the New York Athletic Commission refused to sanction the fight in New York on account of the expensive $50.00 seats, Jim Farley (commissioner) and William Muldoon, a champion wrestler and the first chairman of the New York Athletic Commission, couldn't see where the public could afford to pay such prices. It was then that Tex Rickard, Kearns and Dougherty started to look for new battle grounds. Dougherty sold the idea to one of the outstanding financiers of Philadelphia who agreed to build the building in Leiperville along the Pennsylvania Railroad providing the Pennsylvania House of representatives and the Senate would pass the bill. All plans and agreements were signed.

"Now, Dougherty took it upon himself to have the bill put through. Four years previous to that, the House and Senate had passed a boxing bill and Governor Brumbaugh vetoed it. Now his friend, William Sproul, being Governor, he thought there would be no trouble. Senator Crowe had the bill and couldn't move it in the senate. Then Dougherty took it out of Crowe's hands and put it in the hands of Senator Vare. He sent it over to the House where it was pickled and died and never came out of the committee. Dougherty blamed Judge Harry McDevitt and William I. Schaeffer for advising Sproul."

Finally, without a site for the fight, Rickard offered Willard a guarantee of $100,000 if he would sign to fight Dempsey. Willard, after all the public demand for the bout encouraged by Kearns and Dougherty, accepted the offer and on February 11, 1919, Dempsey and Willard met in, Weehawken, New Jersey, to sign the contract.

The New York Times reported the signing and explained that there was no site but some locations were offered. Fred Dyer, an Australian welterweight and boxing instructor at Camp Grant in Rockford, Illinois, proposed that the fight be held at the huge stadium at the camp, which held 40,000. Also, mentioned in the article was Baron Dougherty who was proposing that the bout be held in the town of Eddystone in Delaware County, where 20 round bouts are permitted.

Finally, Rickard found support and financial backing in Toledo, Ohio, and that was where the fight would take place on July 4, 1919.

Even though both fighters signed a contract and the site was picked, Dougherty was still concerned about the bout being called off.

The V. Frenor's column stated, "Jimmy Dougherty is very much alarmed lest something happen to interfere with the coming Willard-Dempsey fight. The

Leiperville, Pennsylvania sporting man has heard somewhere that Dempsey has not yet posted his $10,000 forfeit with Tex Rickard as per agreement and that in consequence the match is to be called off. Yes, Jimmy is very much excited. From Hot Springs, Virginia, he telegraphs us something like this:

"'See by *Philadelphia Ledger* here that Dempsey's forfeit is not up and that match is likely to fall through. See Rickard. Tell him I will post Dempsey's forfeit and back him for any amount. Cannot get in touch with Kearns. No danger of match not coming off on account of Dempsey's forfeit. Will leave here tonight for New York.'"

"Dempsey has no greater admirer in the country than Dougherty. Jimmy thinks that all that separates Jack from the heavyweight championship is the mere formality of meeting Willard in the ring. Dempsey is very fond of Dougherty too and whenever it is possible, does his training at Dougherty's Leiperville Hotel where his chief associates are Dougherty's young son and the boy's pals.

"We can ease Jimmy's mind on the possibility of the Willard fight being called off. There isn't a chance of such a happening. Dempsey's forfeit will be put up in due time, if it isn't already up. Dempsey and his manager, Jack Kearns, wouldn't let any such detail spoil their chances at the championship, even if they had to go in pawn for a year. But there doesn't seem to be any necessity for this. Dempsey is at present on the road with a theatrical troupe and at last accounts was packing them in and knocking out ambitious heavyweights every night."

The *Chester Times* stated on February 10, 1919, "Jack Kearns, manager for Jack Dempsey, the heavyweight pugilist who will meet Jess Willard on the Fourth of July to decide where the ring honors should really rest, was an over-Sunday visitor at the home of James F. Dougherty of Ridley Park. They both discussed the $5,000 forfeit that will be part of the articles of agreement, should either of the big gladiators back out or the terms of the contract not be complied with."

Before Dempsey's bout with Willard, the challenger had some barnstorming appearances in Trenton, New Jersey, Harrisburg, Reading, and Altoona before putting on an exhibition in Chester.

On April 1, 1919, the *Chester Times* reported, "Jack Dempsey, of Salt Lake City, contender for the world's heavyweight title, made his debut in the Chester Armory last night before 1,000 Chesterites. He boxed four lightning rounds with Andre Anderson, the big Chicago heavyweight, and showed plainly his excellent fighting ability by showering lefts and rights on Anderson. He knocked Anderson out of the ring during the second round, but the Chicagoan, who lacked training, came back.

"The appearance of Dempsey in Chester was his only public exhibition in the ring prior to meeting Jess Willard. Seated at ringside were Chester's Mayor McDowell, District Attorney Hannum, County Commissioner Powel and other officials. A short distance away were seated well-known men of the boxing world, which included Jack Kearns, manager of Dempsey, Barney Gerard of New York, Bill Rocap, Tex Rickard and Joe Stetcher, the contender for the world's heavyweight wrestling honors and others. Jimmy McDevitt, an old time figure in Chester sports, was the third man in the ring.

"Advance ticket sales for the exhibition could be bought at Bris and Bill Lord's billiard parlor in Chester."

Bris Lord, who was born and raised in Upland, played eight years in the major leagues. Six of those years were with the Philadelphia Athletics, where he played in three World Series. With his steady hitting, he helped the Athletics capture both the 1910 and 1911 World Series championships.

On June 25, 1919, Dougherty had to take a break from all the fight hoopla, because his oldest daughter, Anna Marie, was about to get married. Anna, a 1914 graduate of Villa Maria Academy, was the Baron's first child (born in 1895). At the age of 18, her father had given her a horse as a birthday gift.

"My father gave my oldest sister a horse named July," remembered Margaret Stull, the youngest Dougherty child. "I was very young, but I can remember my father bringing the horse right into the living room when he presented the animal

The Baron's oldest daughter Anna is seen here on July, a horse her father gave to her in the living room of their house on her 18th birthday.

to my sister. We weren't real surprised because that was the way my father was. He would do the unusual."

On that hot June day, the Baron and his wife Mary were extremely proud parents as their daughter Anna married Bill Diamond at St. Madeline's Church in Ridley Park.

Besides attending the wedding, the Baron also spent some time attending Jimmy's (his oldest son) graduation from the Pennsylvania Military School (PMC) before heading off to see Dempsey try and take the world title away from Big Jess Willard.

After graduation, Jimmy would become an award-winning champion pool and billiard player in the late 1920's and early 1930's.

"I never shot pool for a living though I did play for money," recalled Jimmy. "I worked in the US Marshal's office as a deputy marshal and later worked as a court crier for Judge Sweeney in Delaware County Courthouse. But I always loved the Game."

During that time, Jimmy developed a life-long friendship with world champion Ralph Greenleaf. He and Greenleaf played exhibitions throughout the tri-state area.

"You had to be an excellent player to even compete with Greenleaf in those days, as Jimmy proved game after game." wrote Floyd Murray who had interviewed Dougherty in 1985. "His own run was 99 balls before miscuing on the hundredth."

Jimmy also played the legendary Jimmy Caras and had a brush with future great Willie Mosconi.

As the fight date drew near, Dougherty and the people of Leiperville couldn't wait to see if their adopted son, Jack Dempsey, could slay the Pottawatomie Giant.

I am sure that Dougherty and his crew were hoping Dempsey would not end up like Sam Riddle's legendary horse Man O' War. Owned by Sam Riddle, who lived in Delaware County and was a good friend of the Baron's, Man O' War lost its only race in 1919 to a horse by the name of Upset. It was the only loss in Man O' War's brilliant career, and the meaning of the word upset is sometimes erroneously attributed to that surprising defeat of Man O' War. However, the term upset actually pre-dates that famous race by several decades.

Conner recalled, "Sam Vauclain had a chartered Pullman train car pull in at a siding near Baldwin's and loaded it with 100 of his friends, then shoved off for the fight site in Toledo, Ohio, to root for Jack."

115

Actually, the day that Vauclain's party departed for Toledo, the eighteenth Amendment, which had been passed on December 18, 1917, became law on July 1, 1919, just three days before the fight. From that date until December 5, 1933, almost fourteen years, prohibition was in full swing. The manufacture, sale or transportation of liquor for beverage purposes was outlawed in America.

Dougherty had left much earlier than the Vauclain party, and when he arrived in Toledo, he stayed at Dempsey's camp at Maumee Bay, on the shore of Lake Erie, a few miles outside of Toledo.

It was the first time that the public was charged to watch a boxer train. Willard charged 50 cents for his workouts, and Dempsey charged a quarter.

James C. Isaminger of the *Philadelphia North American* wrote, "Willard had heard of Dougherty without knowing that he was such a strong Dempsey booster, and asked Tex Rickard to invite him over to his headquarters for a talk.

"So one night Jim went to the home that Willard had leased in Toledo for living quarters. It was the night before the fight, and Dougherty found Willard in a very optimistic mind."

"He told me," said Dougherty, "that he had reserved a stateroom on a train for New York to leave Toledo two days after the fight, when he would release his film and personally attend a large theatre where the picture would be shown at top prices. He added that his victory over Dempsey would make the thing go big.

"Then you feel sure that you are going to win? I put to him.

"Jess is a slow, careful talker and has a drawl. So he waited a second and then sat back and told me why.

"'I figure it this way,' said Jess. 'I base my ability to beat Dempsey on one fight. That was my scrap with Johnson. Now, I claim that Johnson was a better man than Dempsey is. He knew more about the science of the game than Dempsey and was a bigger man and could hit harder.'

'Now, what happened in this fight? Johnson hit me a hundred times in this fight and never hurt me once. I really believe that I could whip Johnson with my hands tied behind my back. He could hit me all day, and instead of hurting me, would only wear himself out. I believe he would become so weak from his own exertions that I could knock him out by merely pushing my head back at him.'

'Now what right then has Dempsey, who is not as good a man as Johnson, to beat me?'"

"I didn't try to argue with him, but when I saw how cheaply he had estimated Dempsey, I knew that he was in for the surprise of his life," said Dougherty.

"Willard did not know that I knew Johnson better than he did. He lived in Philadelphia for three or four years, and his style was as well known to me as any fighter's in the ring.

"Johnson was good enough to win a world's championship at a time when the heavyweights were a poor lot. Johnson was never rated as a one punch man. Anybody could stay six rounds with him without trouble. Johnson was a punishing hitter, but not a heavy hitter. I knew, then, that Willard had no idea of the terrific wallop carried by Dempsey when he ranked Johnson as the heaviest hitter."

As everyone would soon see, Willard would never take that triumphant trip to New York and make any money on film of his title defense.

Dougherty and the Vauclain party arrived at the fight about twelve noon on an extremely hot day, on July 4. Some accounts of the weather conditions the day of the fight had the temperature as high as 114 degrees.

At the entrance to the stadium were the self-appointed keepers of the peace, Bat Masterson and Wyatt Earp. Roger Kahn wrote that Masterson was there as a sportswriter for the *New York Morning Telegraph*, but Colleen Aycock and Mark Scott wrote in their book *Tex Rickard: Boxing's Greatest Promoter*," Masterson and Earp posted themselves at the entrance to the stadium and disarmed men and women, taking their knives and guns."

Fortunately, Dougherty and the Vauclain party had no knives or guns to hand over to these legendary figures.

Wyatt Earp, who Kearns claimed had been his manager when he was fighting, had also been a saloon owner in Nome, Alaska, with Tex Rickard before he became a federal marshal.

Bat Masterson, who had gained fame as a gunslinger in his younger days, was also an army scout, an Indian fighter and a buffalo hunter before he became deputy sheriff of Dodge City, Kansas. Later, he moved to New York City and became a sportswriter.

Besides being one of the greatest promoters in history and the architect of the million dollar gate in boxing, Rickard was also the founder of the New York Rangers Hockey League (NHL) franchise and the builder of the third Madison Square Garden in New York City. His hockey team was initially Tex's Rangers named after him and the nickname stuck. They were an immediate success, winning the Stanley Cup in their second season.

A key business partner and match-maker of Rickard's during his time at Madison Square Garden was a concert and boxing promoter named Jess McMahon, who was the grandfather of current World Wrestling Entertainment (WWE) promoter Vincent K. McMahon. In 1935, McMahon's father, Vincent J. McMahon, would begin promoting wrestling through his Capitol Wrestling Corporation.

In 1928, Rickard opened Boston Madison Square Garden, better known today as the Boston Garden. He had plans to establish another Garden in Miami and altogether establish seven Gardens throughout the country. He had unbelievable vision, and at the time, thought southern Florida would be the newest thing in the winter sport-entertainment business.

He had planned an outdoor arena in Miami, and was planning to host the first big outdoor boxing event of the year. His business partner was Dempsey and they both were negotiating a match between Jack Sharkey and Young Stribling in Miami Beach in February.

Unfortunately, Rickard developed an overwhelming infection following acute appendicitis and died on January 6, 1929, at the young age of 59. One of the greatest promoters in history, Rickard has been compared to the legendary P.T. Barnum.

Joe Mulvihill, who was a sportswriter for the *Bridgeport Herald*, covered the fight in Toledo and wrote about how Baron Dougherty was praised by promoter Tex Rickard. It seems that Rickard had mentioned Dougherty as a serious candidate to referee the Dempsey-Willard bout. There was also a write-up about Dougherty, with his photograph, in the Souvenir program that was sold at the fight.

The flattering tribute written by Rickard said, "Few men in their lives ever reach a pinnacle of esteem in the feelings of their friends as has been attained by the popular Jim Dougherty, of Philadelphia, a man whose lofty ideals and high principles has gained for him a reputation enjoyed by the small minority.

"Those in the boxing game who have had the rare pleasure of knowing him say his word is even better than gold; many would rather have it than the medal itself.

"Mr. Dougherty is with us among the great throngs of notables who are gathered about the ringside. There is no one whom it would give us greater pleasure to tell the world of than our friend Jim".

"He is a promoter of boxing exhibitions; the game to him is a hobby. Many things, such as automobiling, he takes as a pleasure, but to promote a boxing contest is the greatest of all his joys."

"Not owning any club, but being a free-lance promoter, handling most championship affairs every venture having been successful to the public, the boxers and to himself.

"Long before the referee question of the Willard/Dempsey go was settled, a certain prominent newspaper man approached Jim to see how he stood on the question knowing that he had been named among the greatest third men in the ring in the country. His reply was, 'Not for a ton of gold would I consider the place.' Thus he disposed of himself as possible referee when the job was seeking him, not he the job.

"It must be a source of satisfaction and joy for a man to know his popularity and standing in the game, and with all James F. Dougherty remains unchanged."

Sitting at ringside, Dougherty was able to witness the horrible beating that Willard suffered. One minute into round one, the challenger landed a series of blows to the champion's body followed by a left hook that all but caved in the right side of Willard's face.

"Nearly all of the knockouts scored by Dempsey have been made with short punches while getting out of a clinch," said Dougherty. "That's the way he scored his first knockdown at Toledo, and that blow really decided the fight.

"The men were together near the ropes, when Dempsey got loose and rammed a terrific left to the jaw, a blow that didn't travel more than seven inches. Jess thought that Jack was shoving away to set himself, and was whipped by the latter when he was half doubled up.

"It must have been a great surprise to Willard all the more so because in the first thirty seconds of the scrap Dempsey looked awkward and scared and twice ran away and turned his back to Willard. Jess then thought he would be easier than he had expected, but he didn't know until it was too late that Jack was fighting under instructions and completely deluded the champion."

In 1919, a fighter who knocked an opponent down could stand over him and attack as soon as his opponent's knee left the canvas to standup, and that is what Dempsey continued to do in that first round.

After the first knockdown, Willard got up quickly, but Dempsey was right there and hit and knocked him down again. Willard struggled to get up, but was knocked down again for the third time. Somehow, he got up again, but Dempsey smashed him to the canvas for the fourth time. Each time Willard got to his feet, Dempsey was right there to put him back on the canvas. There was a fifth knockdown, and then a sixth, and then a left spun the champion around and a right hand to the side of the head dropped him for a seventh time. The champion just sat there near the ropes and didn't try to lift himself up this time.

Referee Ollie Pecord counted to ten, and Willard seemed to be knocked out. Kearns jumped in the ring and yelled to Pecord that the fight was over and Dempsey had won. However, timekeeper Warren Barbour said that the bout wasn't over because the bell ending the round had sounded at the count of seven and no one heard it.

Kearns left the ring to get Dempsey because Pecord said if he did not get back into the ring, he would be disqualified. The fight continued for two more rounds, but the damage was already done, and Willard's corner threw in the towel before the start of the fourth round.

Jack Dempsey, the fighter that Dougherty always said "he let get away," was the new world heavyweight champion. At the age of 24, Dempsey, with the help of Kearns, was at the top of the boxing world.

The devastation of the giant Jess Willard was so complete and unexpected, that rumors of foul play persisted for years. The rumor was that Dempsey's gloves were loaded, and Willard long insisted, bitterly, that the rumor was true. Dempsey always denied it.

Damon Runyon, who was at ringside, wrote the following the next day in the *Hearst Newspapers*, "The right side of Willard's face was a pulp. The right eye of the fallen champion was completely hidden behind that bloody smear. His left eye peered over a lump of flesh in grotesque fashion.

"The great body of the giant was splotched with red patches. They were the aftermath of Dempsey's gloves thumping there and giving back a hollow sound as they thumped. At the feet of the Gargantuan pugilist was a dark spot which was slowly widening on the brown canvas as it was replenished by the drip-drip-drip of blood from the man's wounds. He was flecked with blood from head to foot."

In the rest of his career, Dempsey never again inflicted such damage on any of his opponents. And he had done it to Willard in the very first round.

Thomas Hauser in an article entitled *Jack Dempsey Revisited* wrote, "Willard suffered a horrible beating. After three rounds, his jaw and nose were broken. Six teeth had been knocked out, and there cuts above and below both eyes."

"The right side of his face looked like a peach that had been repeatedly dropped onto concrete," wrote Randy Roberts in *Jack Dempsey: The Manassa Mauler.*

That classic left hook that Dempsey called "an ideal whirl-powered shovel hook," that dropped Willard and fractured his cheekbone in thirteen places bewildered sportswriter Grantland Rice when he wrote, "Willard wore a dazed and foolish look, a simple half-smile crowning a mouth that was twitching in pain and bewilderment. Has there ever, before or since, been such a punch as the single left hook that destroyed half of Willard's face?"

Bat Masterson was one of the first to raise a question about the fight that has been an issue of controversy among ring historians since that extremely hot day in Toledo. Masterson, who spent the first half of his adult life out in the Old West, came to New York in 1903, where he became a columnist and sports editor of the *New York Morning telegraph*.

After covering the historic fight for his newspaper, he came to the conclusion that there was something wrong somewhere.

Robert K. DeArment in his book, *Gunfighter In Gotham: Bat Masterson's New York City Years*, wrote, "In that brutal first round Dempsey not only knocked Willard down repeatedly, but 'slashed and bruised his face as if he were using an ax.' Perhaps, he suggested, Dempsey's hands had been wrapped with electric tape laced with cement. The 'loaded glove,' 'mailed fist,' or 'big mitt,' as it had variously been called, was not new to the fight game, he reminded his readers. It could be traced all the way back to the Romans, who called a leather strip loaded with metal on a boxer's hand a 'cestus.' Bat had seen it used before, and now suspected he had seen it again in Toledo.

"In later years, Masterson's suspicion became conviction. Dempsey's left fist, he declared, had been 'loaded for bear.' That first left hook to the jaw landed by Dempsey dropped Willard 'like a ton of brick,' and all the later damage came from that hand. 'The battered condition of the right side of Willard's face proved this conclusively. Dempsey failed to bruise or even blacken Willard's face with all the punches he landed with his right and you could hang your hat on the lumps raised on Willard's face with Dempsey's left.' A two-handed puncher who hit equally hard with either hand, Dempsey 'didn't even bark Willard's face with his right, while he cut him to the bone in several places with his left.'"

Just before he died in 1963, Doc Kearns and author Oscar Fraley finished a book on his memoirs entitled, *The Million Dollar Gate*. The account of the Willard fight, taken from the book, was part of a feature story in a 1964 issue of *Sports Illustrated*. In that account, Kearns told the story of how he loaded Dempsey's gloves without him knowing it. He claimed that he had secretly added plaster of Paris to the mix that he and the second put on the gauze that covered Dempsey's hands. The usual mix was powder and in extraordinary heat, water was used as a cooling agent, and then the gloves. The plaster of Paris would then dry into a solid as hard as cement.

"Willard's second was in there while I did it," explained Kearns in his memoir, "and when he asked me what it was, I said it was talcum powder. After I got it on, I told Dempsey to close his fists and keep them closed. I'll never forget this. While we were standing in the ring, waiting for the start, Dempsey turned to me and said, 'Doc, something must be wrong, I can't open my hands.' I said, "Forget it, Jack, go in and fight."

When the story appeared in *Sports Illustrated*, Kearns had already passed, and Dempsey sued the magazine and won. That section of Kearns memoir was removed, and when the book was released in 1966, no such story appeared.

In a series of interviews I conducted with Howard in 1990, Dougherty's youngest son, he told me quite a few times that the Baron maintained that Kearns told him that he had played some tricks with Dempsey's hands that day. Howard was very adamant about that. Remember, Dougherty died fifteen years before Kearns's account was published by *Sports Illustrated*. As many writers had pointed out in their columns, Kearns and Dougherty were extremely good friends, even during those turbulent times Doc was having with Dempsey when they were in and out of court. Dougherty always stood on the side of Doc Kearns, which put a strain on his friendship with Dempsey.

"I know dam right well that the gloves were loaded," said Howard. "The Baron told me and Willard's face was cut up so bad. They tried to get Dempsey out of the ring fast. When they finally did, they got him in the dressing room with no one else there to take off the rappings."

Also, Kearns had allegedly bet $10,000 with 10 to 1 odds that Dempsey would knock out Willard in the first round. If that happened, Kearns would collect $100,000. With a wager like that, why did it appear that he was so sure that Dempsey would knock out the 6'6", 245 pound Willard.

We may never know the real truth of what happened that day in Toledo, Ohio, but one thing is certain, a 24 year old Jack Dempsey gave 37 year old Jess Willard a horrible beating, and created such awful damage to Willard, damage that he would never inflict on another opponent the rest of his career.

That same year, and just a few months after that controversial bout in Toledo that left some fight fans wondering, major league baseball would have their own kind of scandal. At the end of the World Series, it was discovered that eight members of the Chicago White Sox intentionally lost games, which allowed the Cincinnati Reds to win the Series. Those eight players were banned for life from baseball and the fiasco became known as the Black Sox Scandal. The fix was actually the brainchild of White Sox first baseman Arnold "Chick" Gandil, with New York gangster Arnold Rothstein supplying the money through his lieutenant

Abe Attell, a former featherweight champion of the world.

Attell, who was the featherweight champion for twelve years, had a bout at the Olympic Club in Essington, Delaware County that Dougherty attended ten years before the scandal that nearly ruined baseball. On March 3, 1909, Attell fought Young Pierce of Germantown in what the *Philadelphia Ledger* called, "for five rounds it was one of the greatest exhibitions of boxing ever seen in the area." It ended shortly after that when in the sixth round Attell knocked out Pierce."

After the fight, Dempsey headed back to the Secor Hotel at 10:00, where Dougherty paid him a visit before he went to sleep.

The *Chester Times* reported, "Jimmy Dougherty called at Dempsey's hotel after the fight to congratulate the new champion. Dempsey inquired about the welfare of the Leiperville party, which was chaperoned by Dougherty.

"Dougherty said they were all well except Commander Payne, of the Philadelphia Navy Yard, who was taken ill during the fight and with difficulty, remained throughout the contest.

"When Dempsey heard this, he insisted on seeing the Commander and was taken to Mr. Vauclain's car in a moter. It was then Mr. Vauclain, who said to Dempsey,

'If you ever come to Philadelphia, I will see that you are given a reception that will do you good. I will have the Baldwin band to meet you at the railroad station and from there we will go to the country and have a good time.'

"Mr. Vauclain had planned to take the champion to the farm of Colonel Harry C. Trexler, near Allentown. The trip to Allentown will be in a motor car."

Dempsey had a vaudeville engagement in Cincinnati after the fight and then went to visit his mother in Salt Lake City before he finally arrived in Leiperville on September 15. And true to his word, Vauclain did give Dempsey a nice reception, which included a baseball game.

The *Chester Times* reported, "Jack Dempsey, world's heavyweight champion, was an interested spectator at yesterday's game between Leiperville and the Hanley Fire Company. Leiperville won by a score of 7 to 0."

Playing for Leiperville that day was Hack Wilson, who had two hits in the game and was just a few years away from the big leagues.

"I bought Hack Wilson his first suit and bat," recalled Dougherty. "When he was a youngster, I gave him the name 'Stouts' because he was buggy. He was just like a son to me."

Dougherty bought Hack Wilson, who was raised in Leiperville, his first suit and bat when he was a youngster. Wilson played baseball for Dougherty's Leiperville team before leaving for the big leagues in 1921 at the age of 21.

Stouts was a nickname used among his close friends for the rest of his life. Hack, which he got tagged with during his rookie year with the Giants, would later become his professional name.

Wilson and his family had moved to Chester from Ellwood City near Pittsburgh when he was ten years old. They eventually settled in a boardinghouse at 1321 Chester Pike in Eddystone. It was while living in Delaware County that he began playing baseball.

Interviewed by a sportswriter one day, Wilson remembered, "I recall those days along in 1915, 1916 and 1917 when Bris Lord, a star on the Philadelphia Athletics, used to drive through my hometown, Eddystone, going between Philadelphia and his home at Chester in his big automobile. I used to watch for him closely and say to myself, 'Keep on trying Lewis and you too will be a big league ballplayer and own your own automobile. Lord was a big inspiration to me.'"

Wilson quit school at the age of 16 and for a period of time worked at the Sun Ship Yard in Chester. He was actually working there when Dempsey had those pictures taken of himself as a riveter, which is what Wilson's job was at the yard.

On February 10, 1919, the *Chester Times* printed a column of brief items, and one read, "Stout Wilson, a riveter employed by the Sun Shipbuilding Company, has now beaten his former record. On Thursday, Stout put in the shell bottom of the ship, on which he is working, 1,142 rivets in eight hours. Can you beat it?"

In 1921, at the age of 21, Wilson left Delaware County and reported to Martinsburg for his first professional baseball tryout. He made his major league debut on September 29, 1923, and for the next 12 seasons; he was one of the most accomplished power hitters in the game. His 1930 season with the Chicago Cubs is widely considered one of the most memorable individual single-season hitting performances in baseball history. That season, he had 56 home runs, the National League record for 68 years; and 191 runs batted in, a mark yet to be surpassed. For a time, he actually rivaled the legendary Babe Ruth.

Delaware County, and especially Leiperville, liked the idea that their so-called adopted son or at least the fact that Dempsey had spent some time living and training in the county was now the heavyweight champion of the world. The war was over and Dempsey was becoming well known nationwide. He even traveled to Hollywood, where he received an advance plus $1,000 a week to appear in several films.

Unfortunately, things took a turn for the worse when after the Willard fight, Grantland Rice wrote in the *New York Herald Tribune*, "Dempsey is the champion boxer but not the champion fighter. It would be an insult to every doughboy that took his heavy pack to front-line trenches to refer to Dempsey as a fighting man. If he had been a fighting man, he would have been in khaki. So let us have no illusions about out new heavyweight champion. He is a marvel in the ring, the greatest hitting machine even the old-timers have ever seen. But he isn't the world's greatest fighting man. Not by a margin of fifty million men who stood or were ready to stand the test of cold steel and exploding shell. It would be an insult to every young American who sleeps today from the Somme to the Argonne to crown Dempsey with any laurels built fighting courage."

"On January 23, 1920, the *San Francisco Chronicle* published a letter written by Maxine Cates stating that Dempsey had fraudulently evaded the draft," wrote Hauser. "Cates claimed that she had supported Dempsey with her work earnings rather than the other way around. She further claimed that she had letters from Dempsey in which he'd elaborated on how he'd evaded the draft. A heated public debate fueled by more statements from Maxine, rebuttals from Dempsey and Doc Kearns, and extensive newspaper commentary followed."

To makes things worse, the newspapers began rerunning those pictures that Dougherty had arranged of Dempsey supposedly working in the Sun Shipyard in Chester with patent leather shoes peeping out from under his overalls.

Dempsey recalled, ""I was given a pair of striped overalls and told to slip them on over my street clothes. Snap. Then I was handed a riveter's machine. Snap. Snap. Snap. And that was that. The next morning, I unfolded the newspaper and there I was, dressed in those crisp overalls with my shiny patent leather suede-topped shoes sticking out like sore thumbs."

As always, Dougherty came to Dempsey's rescue and wrote a letter to Mr. Jack Skelly of the *Yonkers Herald Newspaper*. The letter appeared in many newspapers and was entitled, "Jack Dempsey is not a Slacker". The contents of Dougherty's letter read:

"Dear Friend-Colonel Frank D'Olier, National Commander of the American Legion was here last night at the Chamber of Commerce, and I had an interview with him regarding this propaganda about Dempsey.

"He informed me that the National Body of the American legion did not intend to pay any attention to these reports, as Dempsey in his opinion was no slacker; that he was drafted and rated by the United States Government, and ready, and at the command of their call to serve his country. The head of the national Body gave nobody authority for using that honorable body for such a purpose to benefit some disgruntled promoters, and therefore, he did not want to hear from Dempsey, or anything concerning the affair.

"I think it is unfair for Mr. Smith, boxing commissioner of New Jersey, to take advantage of his position because he has a grievance against Dempsey's manager because he could not secure Dempsey's services to box in Atlantic City. Smith having told me himself that Dempsey and Kearns owed him a favor because he (Smith) was responsible for Dempsey becoming champion by helping to stage the match between him and Fulton in Jersey City.

"I do not think that Mr. Smith's opinion represents the sentiment of opinion of the authorities of New Jersey. These men who are circulating this propaganda under the pretense of patriotism for the purpose of satisfying their own personal grievances in my opinion, are parasites of sport, and I think it is a shame that they should be let go unchallenged when they are trying to discredit the greatest boxing champion in the history of the world, and a real American for the purpose of elevating third rate foreigners who are not in his class at all.

"Taking it all in all, if our new champion is a slacker, I fail to see the proof."

On January 28, 1920, the *New York Times* editorialized, "Dempsey, whose profession is fighting, whose living is combat, and whose fame is battle, is six-feet-one of strength in the glowing splendor of youth, a man fashioned by nature as an athlete and a warrior. Dempsey did not go to war, while weak-armed strong-hearted clerks reeled under the pack and rifle; while middle-aged men with families volunteered; while America asked for its manhood. There rests the reason for the Dempsey chorus of dispraise."

Maxine tried to recant her charges, but it was too late. On February 24, 1920, Dempsey was indicted on a charge of conspiracy to evade the draft.

The trial began on June 8, 1920, and lasted five days. The defense established that Dempsey had in fact sent money to Maxine and his parents during the war and that he also helped raise $330,000 for the government by participating in several fund-raising bouts. After deliberating for less than ten minutes, the jury returned with a verdict of "not guilty". However, even after being cleared in a federal court, Dempsey was for years accused of being a slacker.

Two-and-a-half months after the trial ended, Dempsey made his first defense of the title on September 6, 1920, against Billy Miske in Benton Harbor, Michigan. The referee would be Dougherty for the second time in Dempsey's career, but there would be problems.

Clay Moyle in his book, entitled, *Billy Miske: The St. Paul Thunderbolt*, wrote, "Kearns wanted Jimmy Dougherty of Leiperville, Pennsylvania, a friend of his and Dempsey's to referee the fight. Dougherty, an Irish sporting man who was later tagged the 'Baron of Leiperville' by sportswriter Damon Runyon, was a part-time boxing promoter, trainer and official who owned the Colonial Hotel in Leiperville. Kearns allegedly felt an obligation to Dougherty for arranging the hire of Dempsey in 1917 by the Sun Shipbuilding Company in Chester, Pennsylvania to help keep the youngster out of the war.

"Dougherty was acceptable to Billy and manager Reddy, but Chairman Bigger said it was out of the question because Dougherty was not licensed to referee bouts in the state of Michigan, and he wasn't going to issue him a license. Kearns told the chairman unless Dougherty was the referee there would be no fight."

Even though the issue of who would referee the fight was not resolved, fight fans and over 100 sportswriters were arriving every day in Benton Harbor.

"On September 5, the day before the fight, the issue over who would serve as the referee for the contest was finally resolved," wrote Moyle. "Following his manager's lead the night before, Dempsey had told a representative of Chairman Bigger that Jimmy Dougherty was the only man they would accept as the referee for the bout. The Chairman refused to give in, and named Al Daly of Detroit as the referee.

"At that point, Fitzsimmons, who stood to lose a lot of money if the fight was cancelled, went into action. He met with a Detroit sportswriter and asked him to intercede with the chairman, and help explain that if the fight were called off he would be financially ruined.

"The sportswriter and Fitzsimmons first met with Al Day, the man Chairman Bigger had appointed for the match, and explained the situation to him. Day then accompanied the pair to the home of E. A. McCauley, Secretary of the Commission, where Bigger was staying, and after a long discussion between the parties, Day agreed to step aside. The chairman finally consented to quickly issue Dougherty a license and let him officiate.

"Reddy felt Dempsey's manager had been unreasonable but he didn't want to do anything which would prevent the fight from taking place. He felt Dougherty was a competent official and expressed the hope he would give Billy fair play.

"The story concerning the selection of the referee was the topic of conversation in local drinking establishments, and the handling of the matter by the champion and his manager was severely criticized."

For Dougherty, it was a fairly easy fight for him to referee. Dempsey knocked out Miske in one minute and thirteen seconds into the third round. The champion was successful in the first defense of his title.

Referee Baron Dougherty counts out Bill Miske in the third round of Dempsey's first defense of his title in Benton Harbor, Michigan, on September 6, 1920.

Three months later, Dempsey would successfully defend his title for the second time when he knocked out Bill Brennan in 12 rounds at Madison Square Garden, his only fight ever in the Garden. Dougherty was at ringside for the contest and so was his son Howard, who was only fourteen at the time.

"I was pretty young for that fight, around fourteen," remembered Howard. "There were rules about children that young attending fights, so because of the Baron's friendship with Dempsey, they were able to sneak me in. Dempsey actually hid me inside his coat and got me into the arena."

Besides refereeing Dempsey's bout and attending his fights, Dougherty also welcomed his fifth daughter and eighth child into the world, when Margaret was born in 1920. She would later attend Ridley Park High School and marry William Stull.

Besides having so many brothers and sisters spread out over a twenty-five year period, Margaret actually became an aunt two weeks after she was born.

Next up for the champion was Georges Carpentier, the French sensation that many felt was the best boxer in the world. Both had signed a contract binding them to meet either in March or between May 20 and July 4 of 1921. The agreement, which had twenty-seven clauses, called for the bout to be from ten to fifteen rounds and to be fought in either the United States, Canada, Mexico or Cuba.

Since no venue had been announced by promoter Tex Rickard, Herman Taylor and Dougherty were interested in staging the contest.

The *Philadelphia Record* reported, "It was announced definitely today that Herman Taylor of this city, and James F. Dougherty of Leiperville, were the promoters representing a Philadelphia syndicate in the field for the Dempsey-Carpentier heavyweight battle which may be staged at Atlantic City this summer."

"We can put our hands on that $400,000 at a moment's notice," said Dougherty as Taylor nodded, "and we expect to have an important statement to issue in a few days."

The *Record's* report continued, "Dougherty is to spend the weekend in New York City, where he says he will go into conference with Jack Kearns, Dempsey's manager. Dougherty is a close friend to Kearns."

Taylor added, "Commissioner John Smith already has informed me that he would sanction a Dempsey-Carpentier bout at the shore."

Unfortunately, things never came to fruition for Taylor and Dougherty, and the bout, which became known as "The Battle of the Century", was staged on a site known as "Boyle's Thirty Acres."

Even though they couldn't stage the fight, Dougherty was still being mentioned as possibly the referee for the bout.

The *Philadelphia Record's* headline read, "J. Dougherty May Referee Big Bout: Baron Mentioned as Third Man for Dempsey-Carpentier World's Battle."

The article went on to report, "James F. Dougherty of Leiperville is one of the six celebrities of the sporting world mentioned as eligible to referee the championship for the Jack Dempsey-Georges Carpentier fight, articles for which were signed yesterday in New York.

"The 'Baron' officiated in the ring in Dempsey's last bout at Benton Harbor, Michigan, Labor Day, when the champion knocked out Billy Miske in the third round.

"James J. Corbett, former heavyweight champion; James J. Jeffries, who lost the heavyweight title to Jack Johnson; Otto Floto of Kansas City; Robert Edgren and Bill Brown of New York, are all included in the list of eligible."

Finally, J. Harry Ertle, who worked as the third man in the ring for 15 years and over 1,000 bouts, was chosen to referee the fight. Supposedly, the decision was made over the bitter objections of Doc Kearns who wanted Dougherty.

So, with Dougherty in attendance, Dempsey knocked out Carpentier in four rounds at Boyle's Thirty Acres in Jersey City, New Jersey. Besides seeing Dempsey successfully defend his title for a third time, Dougherty was also part of an aristocracy well represented at ringside.

Thomas Hauser in *Jack Dempsey Revisited*, wrote, "The aristocracy was represented at ringside by the Vanderbilts, Rockefellers, Whitneys, Fords, Harrimans, Biddles, and Astors. Three of Teddy Roosevelt's children were there. The United States Senate and House of Representatives adjourned in anticipation of the event because twelve senators and ninety congressmen held tickets.

 Many historians have said that the fight was the biggest event in the history of sports up until that time. It was America's first experience with show business, high society, politics and the underworld, all at a single sporting event.

"The fight was also attended by a significant number of women. Ladies had been present at Willard-Dempsey but were confined to a special section. At Dempsey-Carpentier, they mingled freely with the men."

Selling the rights to the fight films of a bout of this magnitude was very popular at the time. Dougherty, Tex Rickard and three others were charged with conspiring to illegally transport films of the Dempsey-Carpentier contest. In 1925, Dougherty, Rickard and the others were acquitted in a hectic trial in Trenton, New Jersey.

It was almost two years to the day that Dempsey would have his next title defense. That was the 15 round decision over Tommy Gibbons on July 4, 1923, which was the subject of Chapter one.

Two months later, Dempsey appeared on the cover of *Time Magazine*, but not before his Leiperville friend Sam Vauclain. Vauclain, a national celebrity in his own right, made the front cover on the April 21, 1923, issue.

Four days after the issue hit the newsstand; Dempsey defended his title again when he knocked out Luis Firpo in two rounds on September 14, 1923, in one of the wildest fights in boxing history. The bout, which was held at the Polo Grounds, was the most savage two rounds in boxing history.

In round one, Dempsey, who went to the canvas twice, knocked Firpo down seven times, but The Wild Bull kept getting up and eventually knocked Dempsey out of the ring before the first round ended. The second round only lasted 57 seconds before Dempsey floored Firpo for the count.

A month before the Dempsey-Firpo bout, Firpo won on a T.K.O. in the second round over Charley Weinert at Shibe Park on August 13, 1923. Leading up to that bout, Firpo trained in Leiperville at Dougherty's training quarters. A few sports writers were concerned and mentioned in their column that Dougherty might relay Firpo's strategy in fighting the champion to his good friend Kearns. If he did, I'm sure his description of Firpo's strategy couldn't compare to what he demonstrated in the ring that night.

In 1924, Dempsey decided to move to Hollywood, where he appeared in ten movies and became one of Hollywood's most sought-after guests. Since separating from his first wife Maxine Cates, Dempsey avoided any lasting involvement with women. Although, it was rumored that he had been intimate with a long line of stars, including Clara Bow and Barbara Stanwyck.

That all ended when he met actress Estelle Taylor, who was born in Wilmington, Delaware, but had left home at age fourteen to marry a banker. After getting divorced, she had affairs with Charlie Chaplin and Wallace Beery, who would later star with George Godfrey in the movie *Old Ironsides*. Dempsey fell in love with her, and they began dating, with Taylor hoping she could eventually marry the champion.

"Before Jack married Estelle, my girlfriend and I double dated with them both down in Delaware a few times," recalled Howard. "Her parents, friends and other family members still lived in the Wilmington area, and she and Jack would visit at times while they were dating. He would always stop by to see us in Leiperville."

A picture of Dempsey and Taylor appeared on the front of the *Chester Times* on September 2, 1924. The headline read, "Dempsey Visits In Ridley Park: Champion and Screen Star Are Guests at Dougherty's Home."

The brief front page article read, "Jack Dempsey and Miss Estelle Taylor, a screen star, whose home is in Wilmington, Delaware, were guests last evening at the home of James F. Dougherty, Chester Pike, Ridley Park.

"Dempsey arrived from the coast yesterday to visit Miss Taylor at her mother's home in Wilmington. He will go to Atlantic City for the pageant and return later in the week. A new Rolls-Royce car will be delivered to him today. Dempsey denied that he and Miss Taylor were engaged. They are simply good friends, he said.

JACK DEMPSEY AND MISS ESTELLE TAYLOR

DEMPSEY VISITS IN RIDLEY PARK

Champion and Screen Star Are Guests at Dougherty's Home

Jack Dempsey and Hollywood actress Estelle Taylor are the subject of a Chester times article about their visit to Dougherty's home in Ridley Park.

"Dempsey looks much different than on his last visit to Ridley Park. An operation in which a portion of his ear was grafted onto his nose has been performed.

"Dempsey plans to be in this vicinity for several days. He will go to Atlantic City this week."

After Taylor had her nose fixed by a plastic surgeon, she talked Dempsey into going to the same surgeon. So, on August 18, 1924, the champion had his nose remodeled. His visit to Dougherty's on September 2, was only two weeks after the surgery. Also, not to be outdone, Doc Kearns went to the same surgeon and had his nose fixed too.

During this time, Dempsey truly went Hollywood. He didn't care about fighting anymore, and really only cared about Estelle. He dropped Doc Kearns as his manager, who incidentally detested Taylor. Many claimed it was Taylor who caused his break with Kearns, but Dempsey felt it was the right thing to do because Kearns was taking an exorbitant share of his income, both in and out of the ring.

Finally, on February 7, 1925, Dempsey and Taylor were married in San Diego. Kearns was not invited, but Dougherty did attend the champion's ceremony.

Damon Runyon wrote about the wedding and printed a letter he received from Alex Hart, one of Jimmy Dougherty's fighters. Hart's letter said, "I'm out here in the great open spaces where men are men, etc. But the great open spaces of Los Angeles are so crowded they fine you $5.00 if you are caught jaywalking.

"Mr. Dougherty and myself are spending the day in San Diego. We were part of the few who were fortunate enough to get a bid to the champ's wedding.

"A very beautiful wedding it was, short, but sweet. I would describe the bride's attire, but I am color blind. I do know that she looked stunning.

"And that great champion (the greatest champion we ever had excepting Kilbane), standing there smiling, it is a great feeling to know that you are being married, is it not? Mendelssohn's Wedding March, and everything!

"We spent the rest of the day at the track in Tia Juana. Those horses never could run. The weather is wonderful. Everybody is happy. Adios!"

After three years of inactivity, Dempsey finally agreed to defend his crown. James Farley, a good friend of Dougherty's and one of the first Irish Catholic politicians in American history to achieve success on a national level, was Chairman of the New York State Athletic Commission. He threatened to resign his post as Athletic Commissioner if Dempsey did not fight African-American fighter Harry Wills, who went be the name of "the Black Panther". Farley banned Dempsey from fighting Gene Tunney and publicly threatened to revoke Tex Rickard's Madison Square Garden license if he ignored the ruling of the commission.

This public stand by Farley for Negro rights would prove to be a valuable asset to the Democratic Party for generations, and would sow the seeds of the Negro bloc of the New Deal.

Farley had been appointed to the New York Athletic Commission by James J. Walker in 1923, and served as a delegate at the 1924 Democratic National Convention, where he befriended a young Franklin D. Roosevelt. He served as Chairman of the New York State Democratic Committee, Chairman of the Democratic National Committee and as Postmaster General simultaneously under the first two administrations of President Roosevelt. Farley was commonly referred to as a politician kingmaker, and was responsible for Roosevelt's rise to the presidency.

Every year, the Boxing Writers Association of America presents the James Farley Award for honesty and integrity in boxing.

Tex Rickard had been planning a Dempsey-Tunney bout to be held in Yankee Stadium, but in August of 1926, the New York State Boxing Licensing Commission announced that Dempsey would not be licensed to fight in New York until he took on Harry Wills. So, the fight was off for New York, but Rickard was also doing parallel negotiations with officials in Philadelphia. He said goodbye to the Big Apple, and Dempsey would now defend his title in Philadelphia at Sesquicentennial Stadium. The big concrete horseshoe of a stadium was built and named after the Sesquicentennial, the 150th anniversary of the Declaration of Independence.

The fight was scheduled for ten rounds, and the rich and famous were tripping over one another to get ringside seats. Kearns was sitting in the first row with a sportswriter and so was Dougherty, who was with his newspaper friends. The rest of the ringside seats were full of high society, high politics and high Wall Street people.

Vice President Charles Dawes was there, along with three members of the cabinet, six state governors, and the mayors of New York and Philadelphia. Bernard Gimbel, William Randolph Hearst, Otto Kahn, W. Averill Harriman, Babe Ruth, Vincent Astor and Charlie Chaplin were all at ringside. The heads of most of the big brokerage houses were also in attendance.

As the fight began, it started to rain, which developed into a downpour as Dempsey was suffering a terrible beating. By most accounts, he landed only one good punch, and the judges gave Tunney all ten rounds.

It was a sad night for Dougherty who was quoted in many newspapers saying that he never thought Dempsey would ever fight again after he married Estelle Taylor and moved to Hollywood. Well, he did get in the ring again, and he was not the same Dempsey that Dougherty had seen from inside the ring during three of the champ's bouts.

Doc Kearns felt even worse, even though he had hit Dempsey with three lawsuits in the months leading up to the title defense.

In *A Flame Of Pure Fire*, Roger Kahn wrote, "Los Angeles sportswriter Mark Kelly looked at Kearns,'Doc. You're crying.'

"'I am not,' said Kearns. 'It's the rain on my face.'

"'Kelly seized Kearn's arm. 'You're not kidding me, you bum. You're crying. Get up in the corner and help the champion.' "Kearns would not. He watched Dempsey take a beating and cried into his right hand through the last four rounds. When the fight was over, Kearns dried his eyes. Then he found a speakeasy and drank himself into oblivion."

The following year, Dempsey and Tunney would fight again, this time at Soldier Field in Chicago. Kearns and Dougherty would both be at ringside with a long list of celebrities which included: Alfred Sloan of General Motors; Walter Chrysler, the auto magnate; Charles Schwab, president of Bethlehem Steel; and the usual people from Wall Street and Hollywood.

Tex Rickard told writer Hype Igoe, "Kid, if the earth came up and the sky came down and wiped out my first ten rows, it would be the end of everything. Because I've got in those ten rows all the world's wealth, all the world's brains and production talent. Just in them ten rows, kid. And you and me never seed nothing like it."

Dempsey again lost on points, but in round seven, he knocked Tunney down but refused to go to a neutral corner. Referee Dave Barry would not start the count until Dempsey went to a neutral corner, which gave Tunney more time to recuperate from the knockdown. He was actually on the canvas for at least fifteen seconds but got up in time to defeat the challenger. The famous "Long Count" is still talked about today and will most likely be debated forever.

Four months before the fight, America and the world were thrilled by Charles Lindbergh's heroic flight across the Atlantic, but there was no thrill for the fans who were hoping Dempsey could recapture his heavyweight title at Soldier Field.

"I forgot the rules," said Dempsey many years after. "I lost my head and couldn't move as the referee shouted, 'Get to a neutral corner.' I was the jungle fighter so completely set in my ways that I couldn't accept new conditions."

Eight days after the Long Count fight, Babe Ruth hit his sixtieth home run, but some reports had the Bambino unhappy that Dempsey was richer and more famous than he was.

Dempsey retired from the ring and headed back to Hollywood, where two years later he lost almost everything in the Stock Market Crash of 1929. In 1930, he and Estelle got divorced, and Dempsey began to make money boxing in exhibitions and refereeing.

In 1933, the former champion married a beautiful singer named Hannah Williams who was from Taylor, Pennsylvania. "Dempsey's wife was beautiful," remembered Margaret, the Baron's youngest daughter. "After their honeymoon, Dempsey and Hannah came to visit my father at our house in Ridley Park."

A year later, Dempsey made a trip to Leiperville to referee a fight for Dougherty. It was the Vince Dundee-Tom Rios fight, and it was held at the Leiperville Arena, which was located in the back of the hotel.

Jack Dempsey (left) and Baron Dougherty pose for the camera in Leiperville before the Dundee-Rios bout which Dempsey refereed.

Jack Dempsey and Baron Dougherty on the far left, are seen at the weigh in for the Vince Dundee (on the scale)- Tom Rios bout on August 9, 1934, in Leiperville.

The *Chester Times* reported, "The Manassa Mauler was given a great ovation at Leiperville last night where he refereed the Dundee-Rios fight.

"Rain almost ruined Howard Dougherty's entertainment, but his attraction brought a mob of 2,500. The crowd would have more than doubled had the weather been clear."

The Leiperville Arena, which was sometimes called the Delaware County Arena and the Open Air Arena, held 5,000 for bouts.

"During the preliminary bouts," wrote the *Times*. "Dempsey autographed enough cards to paper a house. He's a great guy and meets all comers on the autograph book or handshake. A personality like his is worth a crowd of six thousand any day, but rain cut this to less than half."

The *Times* continued, "Tommy Rios came out of Wilmington last night on his way into a contending spot for the middleweight championship by gaining a decision over the current titleholder in ten hectic rounds at the Leiperville Arena.

"Tommy also had to take the mind of the crowd from the most popular figure that ever climbed into the ring, the one and only Jack Dempsey."

Dempsey thought that Dundee won the fight, but the judges picked Rios. The former champion felt that Dundee hit much harder and was more accurate, while Rios threw a lot of punches that were wild.

Maxie Waxman, the manager of Dundee, was crying after the fight and went to see Dempsey up in the dressing room. "He won all the way. It wasn't even close," cried Waxman.

"You're wrong there," said Dempsey. "It was too darn close and that decision wasn't robbery. After all, in a fight like that, it can be called either way without taking anything from either boy."

Just before Dempsey made his trip to the Baron's hotel on Chester Pike, his wife gave birth to his first child, a girl which they named Joan.

"Jack tells us that he wanted a girl baby," said Howard. "His wife also wanted a girl, and they were both happy that it was a girl."

"Jack made a hurried exit shortly after the bout," reported the *Times*. "His wife was anxious for his return as was Jack. He likes the people around here and is a close friend of the Dougherty's."

For the next fifteen years or so, Dempsey would stop at times to see the Baron and Howard at the hotel, and they would also spend time with the former champion at his restaurant which he opened in New York in 1935.

Besides his management of George Godfrey and his friendship with Dempsey, who he always referred to as the one who got away, Dougherty had a large stable of boxers during that period of time. In fact, one of those boxers, Bobby Barrett, a lightweight from Clifton Heights, even got a chance to fight for the world title, the Baron's second boxer to get that opportunity.

- Chapter 8 -

The Baron's Stable of Boxers

"I'll never forget that little redhead from Clifton Heights. He hit me with one of the hardest punches I've ever received in my entire career."

Mickey Walker

After 1920, Baron Dougherty's stable of boxers grew quite considerably. Besides George Godfrey, the nationally known manager, referee and promoter, had no less than a dozen well known fighters under his wing. Boxers such as: Marty Collins, Leonard Dixon, Tiger Thomas, Billy Adams, Billie Ritchie, Al Miller, Billy Angelo, Alex Hart, Joe Anderson, Leo Duncan, Billy Washington, Eddie "Kid" Dorsey, Jack Ketchell, Sid Barrett and Bobby Barrett.

Bobby Barrett, the second of the Baron's boxers to fight for a world title, was born in England in 1899. One of eight children, four boys and four girls, Barrett's father, Frank, was a carpenter and also a professional boxer. As a welterweight, Frank Barrett fought some of the best British boxers of the late 1800's. He lost a real close fight with Tom "Pedlar" Palmer, who later captured the British bantamweight championship in 1895.

Before Bobby Barrett was born, his parents traveled to South Africa, where Frank found plenty of work as a carpenter. They only stayed a few years in South Africa, but it was long enough for two of Bobby's sisters to be born in the land of apartheid.

In 1903, when Bobby was only four years old, the Barrett family decided to move to America, where they lived in New York for a short time before settling in Clifton Heights, Delaware County.

With eight children, Frank kept very busy as a carpenter, while Bobby and his younger brother Sid both attended school in Clifton Heights.

After Bobby graduated from high school, he began working at the Shipyard in Chester. It was during this time that he began boxing, and his father became his trainer and manager.

"At lunch time, boxing was staged on the shipyard grounds for the entertainment of the workers," remembered Barrett. "I started fighting in these bouts."

He had a brief four month amateur career in which he outclassed all of his opposition. His father was then able to get his son some professional bouts in Chester through a man named Frank Johnson, who ran the Princess Theatre.

"One particular bout my brother had was with a guy who fought under the name of 'The Russian Bear'," remembered Sid Barrett, Bobby's brother. "It was one of the bloodiest fights in the history of Delaware County."

At the age of nineteen, Bobby was discovered by Baron Dougherty, and he signed him to a boxing contract. At the time, the boxing laws of Pennsylvania stated that if a fighter was under the age of 21, then the parents' signature was required on the contract. For a period of two years, Bobby's parents got a percent of every purse he received.

Barrett always stayed busy, sometimes fighting twice a month. Once, he had three bouts in eight days, and won all three by knockouts. He fought at the Cambria in Philadelphia on a Friday night, had a bout in Camden on the following Wednesday and was back in Chester fighting on Friday. For all three bouts, he received a total of $31.00.

"Every once in a while a fighter springs from obscurity to fame almost overnight," wrote Vincent Treanor, a Philadelphia sportswriter. Stanley Ketchel was of that kind, being an unknown until he fought Joe Thomas, then the best welterweight in the country.

"Philadelphia is now boasting of another such fistic phenomenon. He is Bobby Barrett, a lightweight, and already Quaker experts on pugilism are picturing him as the conqueror of Benny Leonard.

"Barrett is only nineteen years old and has had only seven real fights. He has won them all, too, with a right-hand knockout.

"Baron Dougherty has seen him in all his fights. The Baron always has been strong for hitters, and he says Barrett is just another Bob Fitzsimmons on a smaller scale. He looks like Fitz, acts like him in the ring, and like old Bob is most dangerous when on the verge of defeat."

Bobby Barrett had over 20 fights before he met Lew Tendler in 1922. Tendler was one of the hardest hitting lightweights in the world. He has always been

Bobby Barrett (left) faces off with Lew Tendler (right) in a lightweight contest at the Baker Bowl on June 6, 1922. Baron Dougherty, Barrett's manager, is on the far left, while promoter and referee Herman Taylor stands between the fighters.

referred to as the great Philadelphia lightweight who tossed away a championship when he permitted champion Benny Leonard, on the verge of being knocked out, to induce him to pause long enough so he could recover and save his crown.

Herman Taylor, one of the promoters of the Barrett-Tendler bout, had problems securing an acceptable referee for the contest, so he drafted himself to officiate.

The fight was held at the Baker Bowl on June 6, 1922, and Tendler beat Barrett by what many called a questionable kayo. The bout was stopped in the sixth round, and many at the fight felt Tendler's punch was a low blow. Barrett's father was so enraged that he leaped into the ring after Tendler.

In later years, Tendler frequently mentioned the fact that he was one of probably the only two boxers ever to meet in a bout referred by the show's promoter. He felt he was also the only fighter in history ever to have to fight father and son in the same evening.

That bout with Tendler actually broke an attendance record at the Baker Bowl.

Barrett got another chance at Tendler two years later on July 21, 1924. Again, the bout was at the Baker Bowl, but the result was the same, only this time the Clifton redhead lost a ten round decision. Again, attendance records were broken, when 38,000 people turned out for a gate just shy of $60,000; which represented the largest gate ever in Philadelphia up until that time.

A crowd pleaser of the Rocky Graziano type, Barrett packed them in anytime and anywhere he fought. In 1922, *Ring Magazine*, a new publication that year started by Nat Fleischer, stated that Barrett drew larger crowds than any fighter appearing in Philadelphia.

On November 30, 1922, Barrett opened Philadelphia's new arena with a seating capacity of 8,000 and they had to turn away another 10,000 that Thanksgiving afternoon in his fight with Pal Moran.

This advertisement for Bobby Barrett appeared in Ring Magazine. Barrett, who was world ranked and was known as a real hard hitter, was an extremely popular fighter in the Philadelphia area.

Jimmy Toppi, the well-known Philadelphia promoter, said, "Barrett in his prime could knock a man out with one punch. You don't find fighters around today like Barrett."

"Barrett hits harder than Lew Tendler," said Jack "Doc" Kearns after watching him knockout Hyman Gold from California in the third round at the Olympia A.C. "He packs a meaner wallop than Benny Leonard."

"Barrett is the most feared 147-pounder in the world," wrote Ed Frayne, the sports editor of the *Philadelphia Record*.

In an interview with Walter Eckersall, the great University of Chicago quarterback turned sportswriter, Dougherty made the statement that Barrett was the hardest puncher that he had ever seen, not excluding Jack Dempsey.

On October 1, 1924, Barrett finally got his opportunity to fight for the National Boxing Association World Welterweight Championship against Mickey Walker at the Baker Bowl in Philadelphia. The Baron would now have his second boxer (Eddie Lenny was his first in 1899) fighting for a world title.

Walker was one of the toughest and most courageous boxers ever to step into the ring. During his career, he fought in four different weight classes. He began his fighting career in 1919, and by 1922, he had defeated Jack Britton for the world welterweight title.

In 1926, he moved up and won a ten round decision over Tiger Flowers to become the world middleweight champion.

During that time, Walker also challenged Mike McTigue, Harry Greb and Tommy Loughran for the light-heavyweight title. However, he lost decisions to all three men.

Finally, he moved up to the heavyweight division in 1930, and in 1931, he fought future heavyweight champion Jack Sharkey to a fifteen round draw. The referee, Arthur Donavan, scored the bout 11-4 in favor of Walker.

In 1932, Walker was stopped in the eighth round by Max Schmeling. Later, he made another unsuccessful bid for the light-heavyweight title when he lost a decision to Maxie Rosenbloom.

Walker had 163 fights during his sixteen year career. He fought the world's best in four different weight classes, but as Walker stated years later on Ralph Edward's television show, *This Is Your Life*, "I'll never forget that little redhead from Clifton Heights," recalled Walker. "He hit me with one of the hardest punches I've ever received in my entire career."

Walker explained, "It landed high on my hard head, if it had been lower, I know it would have knocked me out. I couldn't wear a hat for two weeks after that fight."

Barrett's brother Sid, who attended the fight, spent most of the time in the dressing room. "I didn't want to see my brother get beat up," recalled Sid.

The bout was held on a bitter cold night, and Barrett put up a good fight, but in the sixth round Walker knocked him out.

In reference to the money that Walker received for the bout, Sid said, "Walker's purse was set at $25,000. Herman Taylor, the promoter, put up $5,000, the Baron contributed $10,000. For Bobby, it wasn't easy. He had to remortgage his house just to get the money for the fight."

At the conclusion of the bout, Walker found out that Barrett had remortgaged his house so the fight could take place. Upon hearing this, Walker told Barrett to keep his $10,000 and he would accept $15,000 for fighting the hard hitting welterweight.

Even after his bout with Walker, Barrett still got the respect of many boxing writers and managers. In 1925, he was ranked fifth in the world as a lightweight and among the contenders for champion Benny Leonard's crown.

Frayne of the *Record* wrote, "To illustrate the respect in which Barrett is held, the writer will cite the case of Mickey Walker, the king of all the welters. Walker knocked out Barrett in five rounds, but he would never box him again. Joe Degnan, who manages Mickey, said, 'Barrett is pure poison, in my opinion. He'd knock out Dempsey if he got a solid shot at him.'"

Many people thought that Barrett was being rushed by Dougherty, but Barrett didn't feel that way. He said, "I started at the same time Tommy Loughran did and was taking home windup purses while Tommy was still in the prelims."

Even *Ring Magazine* voiced its opinion when it stated, "Bobby Barrett is being pushed forward so rapidly that he cannot stand the pace. Meeting such men as Tendler and Mitchell, is more harmful than not fighting at all, because it destroys all the natural confidence that he may have had in himself, and might have a very bad effect on his future battles."

That same year, Barrett's parents and two of their children, moved from Clifton Heights to California, where his father found plenty of work and even built his own home in Pasadena.

During that same time, Barrett and a few other fighters from Dougherty's stable traveled to California for bouts arranged by the Baron.

On the way to the west coast, Dougherty arranged a fight for him in Chicago.

"The Baron told me personally of the time he took Barrett to Chicago for a contest," recalled sportswriter Philip Heron. "Prize fighting was prohibited in the Midwest at the time and the bout had to be staged in secret. A goodly crowd of Chicago's notorious characters were on hand in the barn converted into an arena. Several of these cold bargainers entered the dressing room, as the Baron was taping Barrett's fists with black tire tape; produced their business hardware, said they had bet heavily on Barrett, and he had better win! In the early rounds, the Clifton Red head got his 'Mary Ann' over. 'The referee didn't have to count,' declared the Baron, 'He called for a doctor.'"

Barrett had five bouts on the west coast and then returned to Clifton Heights where his own family had grown and eventually consisted of ten children, five boys and five girls.

Barrett continued fighting in the east against some of the best boxers in the world. They included such fighters as: Sailor Friedman, Dave Shade, Nate Goldman, Ray Mitchell, Billy Ryan, Charley White and Pete Latzo.

After a career that lasted from 1918 to 1931, Barrett had close to 100 bouts, twenty-one which he had won by knockouts. He took his lumps from the world's best, and when it appeared he was not going to be a champion, he was cited as a boy who had been "brought along too fast".

"I remember many of Barrett's fights very vividly," recalled Delaware County sportsman John "Smoker" Gallagher. "I saw him in action in all of his Philadelphia bouts. He was the hardest hitter of his time.

"Bobby always entered the ring with one thought in mind, to flatten his opponent as quickly as possible.

"I remember his bout with Hymie Gold, who was a sensation on the West Coast.

"Gold came east to fight Barrett and entered the ring a 10-1 favorite.

"Well, Bobby caught Gold in the first or second round, I just forgot exactly which one it was, and Hymie was out cold.

"Bobby's name then became known all over the United States.

Bobby Barrett, seen here in the driveway at Baron Dougherty's home in Ridley Park, had over 100 bouts in a career that lasted from 1918 to 1931.

"I read an article in the *Police Gazette* publication, about a year ago, written by Mickey Walker, in which Walker called Barrett the hardest hitter he ever met.

"Mickey said Barrett hit him on the head so hard that a lump appeared thereon, as big as a baseball.

"I don't like to speculate on what might have been, but if Bobby Barrett, with his devastating punch, had been blessed with the boxing skill of say Benny Leonard or Johnny Kilbane, he would easily have emerged as the greatest little boxer in history."

Besides Barrett, the Baron had another outstanding lightweight who made a name for himself during the same time as the redhead from Clifton Heights. His name was Alex Hart, and he was from Lorain, Ohio. He had his first pro fight in the Ohio area in 1917, but Dougherty didn't latch on to him until he had his first bout in Philadelphia in 1921, at the Ice Palace, which remained in use for many years, known simply as the Arena.

Hart never fought for a world title, but he defeated three opponents who held world titles at one time. Those champions included: Johnny Dundee, Joe Dundee, and Jimmy Goodrich.

In 1923, two years after arriving in Leiperville, Hart fought one of the greatest lightweights of all time, Benny Leonard. The fight, which broke attendance records, was held at the Phillies Ball Park in Philadelphia and attracted over 35,000 fans. Hart gave the champion everything he had, but it wasn't enough.

The *Chester Times* reported, "Alex had speed, cleverness and unlimited courage, but Benny had more. He had the punch that Alex lacked."

Alex also had three bouts with the devastating puncher known as George K.O. Chaney. Chaney was known as the hardest hitter ever in his weight class up until that time.

"Chaney failed to knock the little fellow out," wrote the *Times*. "It was the rapier against the heavy broadsword, and the rapier flicked and darted in and out of the Chaney defense. The famous K.O. King hung up more than 100 knockouts. Many of them had come in succession, but Alex stopped this streak. He butchered Chaney with his famous in and out attack."

Two weeks before attending Dempsey's wedding while out on the west coast with Dougherty and a few of his other fighters, Hart had a bout with Dode Bercot at the Arena in Vernon, California. The lightweight from Leiperville won the ten round decision, but it was an unpopular one. The judges had Hart taking six rounds, while Bercot won three, and one round was called even.

Originally, Barrett was supposed to fight Bercot, but he fell sick, and Dougherty substituted Hart for him. Hart put on quite a show, and the west coast fans liked him.

Fane Norton of the *Los Angeles Herald* wrote, "Many of the boxing fans who saw Alex Hart take a decision over Dode Bercot at Vernon may not be strong for the eastern boy, but Alex is going to make them like him before he has been here many weeks.

"For a boy to travel 2,000 miles, train three days and then take the measure of as sturdy a boy as Bercot is no small feat.

"Hart outsmarted Bercot all the way. He was up against a tough boy who was willing to fight at all times."

On January 15, 1925, Benny Leonard, the reigning world lightweight champion, retired from the ring, because he claimed that his mother wanted him to stop fighting. Shortly after, the New York State Athletic Commission put on an elimination tournament to determine a successor to Leonard's crown.

A little more than a month later, on February 27, 1925, Hart fought Benny Valger at Rink S. C. in Brooklyn in one of the elimination bouts. Unfortunately, Hart dropped a ten round decision to Valger and was eliminated from the tournament.

Hart continued fighting some of the best fighters in the world, including the dangerous Lew Tendler. However, by 1930, he was ready to hang up his gloves and retire from the ring.

The *Chester Times* reported, "Hart lost several close ones and decided to hang up his mitts. He said goodbye to his pals of this area, parted with the Baron of Leiperville and set out for New York."

Alex hart was another outstanding lightweight who fought for Baron Dougherty. He had over 150 bouts from 1917 to 1931, finishing with an 84-42-19 record.

He seemed destined to return and in 1931, he came back to fight on a card promoted by Howard Dougherty at the Leiperville Arena. It was there that Hart defeated Frankie Hayes, but he realized that he had lost a lot of his ring savvy. He knew it was time, and he left the ring for good and returned to New York. He had fought from 1917 until 1931 and had over 150 bouts, finishing with a record of 84-42-19.

In New York and at the height of the Depression, he landed a job that provided him with steady work as a special detective for the Loew's Theatre Company.

Unfortunately, on July 4, 1934, tragedy struck Hart on a Friday afternoon on the streets of New York.

The *Chester Times* reported, "A Negro lad about five or six years old tossed a firecracker at Alex and it exploded, searing his pants and leg. He gave chase to the boy and an older Negro shot at him with a revolver. The bullet entered his leg and Alex was removed to a hospital. The leg was slow in healing and complications set in. The wound eventually became worse and blood poisoning set in. It was then that the doctor had advised Alex that the leg would have to be amputated."

However, instead of losing the leg, Hart decided on taking the easy way out by taking his own life on August 25, 1934.

His obituary read the following, "Fate and despondency teamed up to floor Alex Hart for the long count over in New York City last Saturday night. These two grim warriors of this grind known as life worked the former great lightweight boxer into a weakened state, where he couldn't assemble the will to go on, to fight against a continued succession of bad breaks. So, the bell rang, and old Alex failed to respond.

"It must have been a grim ending for the former whirlwind of the squared circle. Brooding over an operation that was to amputate one of his legs, Alex just couldn't take it any longer. He took the easier way out, turned on the gas jet and sat there while the deadly fumes finished the task that misfortune had begun several years ago.

"Perhaps Alex thought it was better to go that way. Perhaps he saw his glory of the past and it hurt him too much to think that the two legs that were once so fast would now be reduced to one that was no longer sturdy. Perhaps the beatings absorbed in the ring had sapped that old courage. Anyway, he didn't answer the bell, and took the count from the corner."

Alex Hart, at the young age of 35, left a wife and nine year old son when he committed suicide. At one time, he spent some of his early years in Delaware County, living in Ridley Park and also in Chester where he was the proprietor of the Morton House Hotel.

Dougherty paid a nice tribute to his fighter and friend when he said, "Alex was a clean, honest fighter. He was the most scientific fighter of his day. Like Tommy Loughran, he could beat any of them by his superior boxing, but the difference between Alex and greatness was his punch, or lack of one."

Joe Anderson, a middleweight, was another one of Dougherty's boxers who fought and became well known on the west coast. Anderson was born in Ohio, but Covington, Kentucky, eventually be-

Joe Anderson, a middleweight and another Dougherty boxer who was world ranked from 1926 to 1928, had 93 bouts in his career, finishing with a 50-19-14 record.

came his hometown. While he was fighting, he was frequently billed as Kentucky Joe Anderson.

Anderson's professional boxing career began in 1922 in Cincinnati, Ohio, and it wasn't long before he met and was fighting under the managerial wing of Baron Dougherty. By 1926, Anderson was fighting all over the country and had become the seventh ranked middleweight in the world. Dougherty took him out to Oregon and California for bouts, and he was a popular attraction on the west coast.

In Los Angeles, the Baron moved Anderson into his good friend Jack Dempsey's old California training headquarters. Howard was training Anderson for a bout with Leo Lomski at the L.A. Olympic Auditorium.

"During the bout, the fans knew they were seeing a great fight," wrote Sportswriter Heron. "Both men fought furiously, there were several knock-downs, but Anderson couldn't stop the ever surging Lomski. Now, the whole Dougherty stable including Anderson had backed themselves heavily. Anderson came back to his corner in pain and grimaced as he told Howard he believed he broke his right hand. He did, all right! The bone was protruding, making a slight bulge on the face of the leather mit.

"A hypodermic needle of novacaine was shot into the gladiator's painful hand, and he answered the bell. This was repeated again and again. It would last until the rounds' near end then 'Kentucky Joe' would fall into his corner stool, his gloved hand moist and sapping with blood. The fight went to the end and a decision."

He was ranked eighth in the world in 1927 and became the logical challenger to middleweight champion Mickey Walker after he won a ten round decision over Ace Hudkins, the Nebraska Wildcat, at the Olympic Auditorium in Los Angeles on October 2, 1928.

"It was one of the best fights ever staged at the Olympic Auditorium," reported the *Chester Times*. "The battlers stood toe to toe and slugged it out. At the end of the grueling encounter, Anderson's right eye was closed and Hudkin's left optic was in deep mourning.

"Joe's victory last night bears out the predictions of Dougherty that the Covington, Kentucky, lad would soon be in a position to challenge for the crown held by Walker. The Baron is happy today over Anderson's victory."

"I got my first squint at Joe when I brought him on to box Bobby Barrett," recalled Dougherty. "The courage of the Covington lad appealed. I saw that he had it in a goodly measure. Possibilities were sticking out all over him. I arranged for him to come under my wing. Promoters on the Pacific coast wrote to me for a likely-looking lad, and I recommended Joe. They took my word. I tell you it pays

149

to take a boy away from his home town and put him more or less on his own. It brings out the best that is in him.

"Joe made good all the good things I had predicted for him when he defeated Eddie Roberts in Portland, Oregon. Eddie struck Anderson low in the second round. The latter then was given the decision. Then there transpired one of the oddest incidents ever witnessed in the ring. Joe made a speech in which he said that he did not want to win in such a way. He asked the referee and the judges for a three-minute rest so that he could go back at Roberts. This was allowed. The boy then gave Roberts a boxing lesson. Afterwards, Roberts knocked out Joe Dundee in one round."

Anderson was moving along fine as a fighter in Dougherty's stable but did have some bad luck with injuries.

"There has been a jinx pursuing Joe when and after we teamed up," said Dougherty. "When I got him he had a dislocated shoulder, and then came a broken hand and his recent stabbing."

On October 10, 1927, Anderson was critically stabbed below the heart in Covington, Kentucky, by Herbert Davis of Danville. Davis, an African-American motorist, was fleeing after colliding with a fire truck when Anderson tried to stop him. Davis was charged with intent to kill and reckless driving.

Dougherty continued to praise Anderson after his victory, "When I took hold of Anderson, I saw that he was not aggressive enough, although he was keen on the defense. His punches rolled. Now he shoots them in straight, fast, snappy and with a lot of power behind them. He is hitting much better and there is room for still further improvement. We are now on the trail of the middleweight title, and I want to say that Mickey Walker has a lot of respect for him. That I take it is a pretty fair acknowledgement of the boy's ability."

A few days after the Hudkins bout, Dougherty filed a challenge with the New York and Pennsylvania commissions seeking a bout with Mickey Walker, who was now being managed by the Baron's good friend, Doc Kearns.

"If Walker wants to mingle in fast company, he should fight Anderson," said Dougherty.

Unfortunately, Anderson did not fare well in his next few fights. In nine outings, he only registered two victories with three draws. His tenth bout was a rematch with Hudkins in which he lost by a TKO in the sixth round. He was knocked down twice in the fourth round, and once in the sixth round, before retiring in his corner with a broken nose.

Joe Anderson (center) is pictured here with his manager Baron Dougherty (left) and stable mate George Godfrey (right) as they prepare for fights out on the west coast.

Anderson never did get that opportunity to challenge Walker for the middleweight crown, but he did continue to fight until 1931 when he had his last bout at the Olympic Auditorium. World ranked from roughly 1926 to 1928, Anderson had 93 bouts in his career and finished with a record of 50-29-14.

After leaving the ring, Anderson returned to Covington, where he and his wife operated the Bluegrass Gym. In 1935, they opened the Joe Anderson Café until 1947, when they sold the restaurant and bought a Wiedemann Beer distributorship, which they operated for about twenty-five years.

Joe Anderson died of a cerebral hemorrhage on May 8, 1975 in Covington.

Another middleweight fighter who gained some fame under the management of the Baron was a black boxer from Williamsport, Pennsylvania, by the name of Arthur "Tiger" Thomas. Thomas began his professional career in 1925 in Williamsport and later hooked up with Dougherty. By 1927, the Baron had Thomas fighting in Oregon, Washington and California, where his popularity grew.

In his second bout on the western tour the Baron arranged, Thomas knocked out Del Adams in La Grande, Oregon on March 19, 1927.

Sports Editor Billy Stepp of the *Portland News* wrote, "Tiger Thomas, the colored sensation of Baron James Dougherty's fistic stable, proved his worth before a record house of eastern Oregon leather-pushing fans here Saturday night when he sent Del Adams, the kayo terror of the Idaho sage-brush, to the land of dreams in the fourth round of their scheduled 10-round contest."

"The colored Tiger was master of the situation from the tap of the bell. He quickly took his giant opponent and cut him to his own size and in the second round, had the sage-brush mauler taking the count of nine in a neutral corner.

"Adams outweighed the Tiger by 12 pounds. Was easy six inches taller and had a reach of twice that of Thomas, but he has yet to reach the Tiger's whiskers or lay a glove upon the elusive pugilistic sensation that is the talk of La Grande and way points.

"In the fourth and final round of the battle the fans were treated to some fast work on the part of Baron Jim's battler. The Tiger measured Adams and sank a left hook to the solar plexus, followed with a right behind the ear and referee Gruman tolled off the fatal count of ten for the first time on the giant Delmar Adams."

Thomas fared pretty well on the west coast, winning eight bouts with four losses and three draws. The fans and sportswriters liked him too, as witnessed by the following description in the *Portland News*, "Tiger Thomas, the sensational colored boy from Philadelphia, who is making his second start at the armory arena Tuesday night against Oakland Billy Harms in a 10-round contest.

Tiger Thomas (left) is seen here with George Godfrey (right) on the Dougherty estate. Thomas, a middleweight, had 67 fights, with a record of 38-20-9, which ended in 1932.

"The Tiger is a whirlwind. He throws the leather mitts from all angles and carries a stick of T.N.T. in each paw.

"Thomas is built on the lines of Sam Langford. Strong and stout with long arms, he weaves in and out with his lefts and rights popping from all directions.

"Baron Jimmy Dougherty, his manager, predicts the boy will step into the championship path of middleweights left by the great colored fighter, Tiger Flowers.

"Thomas has yet to cast a vote, having passed his twenty-first birthday in Portland late last month.

"Within a few months of fighting under his belt, the Tiger will be on the high road to championships if the champions will ever give him a chance at their thrones."

On June 19, 1931, Mickey Walker decided to give away his middleweight crown to take a shot at the heavyweight division. With his title vacant, an elimination tournament was set up by the National Boxing Association, and Tiger Thomas was one of the middleweight fighters included in the tournament.

Unfortunately, Thomas was eliminated in the first round of the tournament when he lost a ten round decision to Gorilla Jones on August 25, 1931, at Borchert Field in Milwaukee, Wisconsin.

He only had a few more fights, with his boxing career ending on August 1, 1932, when he lost to Wally Sears at Lakewood Park in Mahanoy City, Pennsylvania. Thomas had a total of 67 bouts during his career, with a record of 38-20-9.

Another welterweight, Billy Angelo, was world rated under Dougherty's tutelage, fighting from 1927 to 1933. Angelo, a southpaw, who was born in Italy, fought some of the best boxers in the world such as: Benny Leonard, Vince and Joe Dundee and Gorilla Jones.

In 1928, Dougherty took Angelo, like he did with so many of his boxers, out to California, where he lost via the TKO route to Eddie Gill at Wrigley Field in Los Angeles.

Angelo is best known for the grudge matches he had with local Chester boxer Johnny Ketchell. From 1927 to 1932, Angelo and Ketchell fought every year, a total of seven times. Ketchell got the best of the Leiperville Italian, winning four times on decisions at

Billy Angelo, who was another world ranked welterweight under Dougherty's tutelage from 1927 to 1930, fought some of the best boxers in the world.

venues such as the Fair Grounds in Elsmere, Delaware, the Arena in Philadelphia, and the Open Air Arena in Leiperville.

On March 28, 1930, Angelo looked outstanding in one of his best bouts at the Chester Armory against a boxer from Arizona.

The *Chester Times* reported, "Billy Angelo of Leiperville gained one of the most notable victories of his career last night, when he handed the veteran Billy Algers, the Phoenix Arizona Cowboy, a lacing in the feature bout of a great fighting card at the Armory.

"The local Latin, weighing 150, and tanned to a deep brown, was on the go from the start to the finish, and with the exception of one round, the sixth kept well ahead of the iron-jawed westerner. The battle was, however, by no means one-sided, despite the apparent wide margin of Angelo, for Algers, no matter how badly he was faring, was ever dangerous and on several occasions drew the capacity audience to their feet when he flashed a two-fisted attack which had the Pride of the Pike on the defense.

"The Angelo of today is a greatly improved fighter. His victory over Alger last night boosted his standing in the welterweight ranks for the Arizona boy has long been regarded as a trial horse for the boys of that division. Jimmy Dougherty, the 'Baron of Leiperville', was in Angelo's corner and was tickled over the way Billy performed. The fight was easily Billy's best in this section. He emerged unmarked. Angelo did not loaf a second during the melee and was as fresh at the end of the festivities as when the opening gong brought the boys into action."

Angelo's last two fights were only three weeks apart in February of 1933 against Vincent Forgione, where he lost at the New Broadway A.C. and won a ten round decision at the Cambria A.C. He finished his career with a 50-17-5 record in 72 bouts.

Angelo later settled in Fresno, California, where he married Lucia Pamela, who was a one-of-a-kind entertainer. Pamela, a former Miss St. Louis, was a singer and dancer who performed in the St. Louis theatre circuit. Later, after moving to Fresno, she managed the Fresno Storyland Amusement Park.

In 1960, she married Angelo, who became her third husband. He also became the stepfather of her daughter from one of her previous marriages, Georgia. Pamela and her daughter had become a vocal duo called the Pamela Sisters and performed together on radio and television.

In 1966, Georgia married Carroll Rosenbloom, who she had been living with since 1958. At the time of their marriage, she was 38 years old and he was 55 and the owner of the Baltimore Colts. With the marriage, Angelo now became the father-in-law of Carroll Rosenbloom, one of the most powerful owners in professional sports.

Rosenbloom had met Georgia in 1957 at a party hosted by Joseph Kennedy at his Palm Beach estate.

In 1972, after capturing two NFL Championships and a Super Bowl, Rosenbloom traded ownership of the Colts for ownership of the Los Angeles Rams. Seven years later, Rosenbloom drowned while swimming off a Florida beach from an apparent heart attack. Some people suspected foul play, although medical examiners found no evidence that his death was not due to natural causes.

Upon her husband's passing, Georgia inherited 70% ownership of the Rams. In 1995, she moved the team to St. Louis and four years later, with head coach Dick Vermeil, Georgia's team won the Super Bowl. Unfortunately, Billy Angelo was not around for his stepdaughter's triumph, having passed away in 1987.

Marty Collins, whose real name was Ettore Collocchi, was another welterweight managed by the Baron from 1926 to 1933.

Marty Collins was another welterweight who was managed by the Baron. Collins, whose real name was Ettore Collocchi, fought from 1926 to 1933. He had a total of 57 bouts and finished with a career record of 27 wins, 23 losses and 7 draws.

Dougherty also managed another black heavyweight by the name of Leonard Dixon. Dixon fought from 1929 to 1939 and met some outstanding heavyweights of the day such as: George Godfrey, Tony Galento, Jack Gross and registered two wins over Roy "Ace" Clark.

Billy Adams, who also fought as Billy Maxwell, was a tall but thin white heavyweight that the Baron managed from about 1910 to 1917. Dougherty referred to him as one of the White Hopes, who could hopefully take the title away from Jack Johnson. After Johnson defeated Frank Moran defending his title, Dougherty voiced his opinion in the *Chester Times* on July 1, 1914.

"I never figured Moran as a fourth rater at best," said Jimmy Dougherty, considered one of the best judges of fighters in America. "I, like others, hoped that Moran could bring home the bacon, but I figured if he did so it would not be because he was the better man. I have a youngster, Willie Adams, that I will willingly bet can stop Moran inside of ten rounds and he does not weigh within twenty pounds of Moran's weight either.

"Moran would prove pie for Adams, whose speed, I say is today is even faster than Jack Johnson. Adams is also developing a punch that would do damage to the crop of white hopes, as it will be shown soon.

"I intend to force Adams to the top by simply clearing his path of the bunch of white hopes, and when he reaches the top he will be weighing near the 204 pound mark, and then if Johnson is still around I'll produce the man in Adams that will bring back the heavyweight crown to the white race.

"I know there are lots of persons who cannot figure Adams as the man to redeem the blunder of Jeffries, but if these very persons will stop to consider what a greatly improved lad Adams has turned out to be since I took him, a big, half nourished lad three years ago, they will realize that my talk is not an idle one.

"I am grooming Adams, a far better man than Moran ever hopes to be, to win back the title, and I'm going to bring home the bacon when I send Adams after the title. There will not be any grabbing of cheap coin or moving picture privileges. All I want is a chance to show what will then be the best white heavyweight in the world, Willie Adams."

Adams fought Jack McCarron, the $50,000 beauty managed by Jack O'Brien, Eddie Palmer, the Bearcat from New Orleans, and Dougherty even took him on a steamer to England in 1913 for a bout. He fought Kid Ashe, Peck Miller, Tommy Coleman, and Frank Clark of Pittsburg, but he never got the opportunity to challenge Johnson, because a year after Dougherty's boast, Johnson lost his crown to Jess Willard.

Eddie "Kid" Dorsey, who claimed to be the Colored Lightweight Champion of the World, was another one of Dougherty's black fighters. The Eddystone resident fought 59 bouts between 1911 and 1919. Many of his early fights were in Philadelphia and on January 25, 1916, he fought indoors at the Leader A.C. in Leiperville, promoted by the Baron's good friend Lew Bailey.

"Eddie Dorsey first arrived at Leiperville to box under the direction of James Dougherty on October 3, 1914," wrote boxing historian Chuck Hasson. "His first bout at Leiperville was on August 28, 1915; against Preston Brown of Philadelphia for the benefit of the James F. Dougherty Fire Company before over 1,000 fans. Dorsey was called the winner after a very close and lively encounter."

"Eddie Dorsey, the local colored champion, knocked out Willie Kline of Philadelphia at the Leader Club," reported the *Chester Times*. "With a quick left jab to the jaw, Dorsey floored his opponent, and he rolled for the count."

There was a change in the policy of the boxing club which was announced after the Dorsey bout. It seemed that any surplus money that was made from the show would be turned into a charity fund for the poor children of Chester, Eddystone and Leiperville.

Remember, this was a time in this rough and violent sport, where many towns and states actually outlawed boxing. Dougherty and his friend Lew Bailey wanted to show the community that some of the money raised would go back into the community to aid the poor. It was a good gesture on their part to the people who did not care for the sport and even wanted it banned.

"Little criticism has been heard over the receipts of the bouts," said Dougherty. "To hush all the talk of this nature, it was resolved to turn the affairs of the club over to a committee of citizens who have the interests of the sport-loving public at heart and allow them to conduct the affairs of the club."

Hasson said, "Dorsey left Leiperville in July of 1916, but kept in touch, reporting on his career, with Dougherty and his trainer Joe Brown, one of Dougherty's top teachers and trainers, by letters through the mail."

On September 9, 1917, Dorsey got the opportunity to fight Benny Leonard, who had captured the lightweight championship just four months earlier when he knocked out Freddie Welsh. Fighting one of the greatest boxers who ever laced up a pair of gloves was not an easy task for Dorsey, as he found himself on the canvas for the count in the second round of their bout in Buffalo, New York.

In 1919, after 59 bouts, Dorsey ended his career in the ring with a record of 30-23-4.

Billy Washington began his boxing career as a lightweight in New Orleans in 1915, and later made his way to Philadelphia where he became under the management of the Baron. As late as 1926, Washington was recognized among the top lightweights in the Philadelphia area.

In 1919, he defeated Johnny Brown, lightweight champion of British Honduras, in a title match. The fight, which had plenty of action, was fought in Belize, British Honduras.

Throughout his long ring career, Washington was known as an intensely aggressive fighter. This trait was once described by boxing writer Dick Kain as "Washington's constant determination and ability to wade in and force the fighting."

After his last bout in 1932, Washington stayed in Leiperville and trained fighters for Dougherty. He also worked with young fighters in the Leiperville area until his death in 1949 at the age of 56.

The *Chester Times* reported, "Until he was stricken suddenly, more than a month ago, with violent headaches, Washington maintained his interest in boxing. In recent years, in conjunction with the late Jimmy Dougherty, he trained juvenile fighters in a boxing school in Leiperville.

"And in August, 1948, he, the Baron, James J. Dougherty, assistant coordinator of recreation for the Department of Parks and Recreation of Delaware County, and some of their youthful pupils appeared on a national television hookup."

Leo Duncan, another boxer in the Dougherty camp, was a black light heavyweight who had over 50 bouts from 1929 to 1936. The *Chester Times* referred to him "as the classy, flashy Leiperville Negro who was exceedingly popular with the local fight fans."

Through most of the 1920's, Dougherty was still managing

Leonard Dixon, a heavyweight, was another one of the African-American fighters that seemed to gravitate towards Dougherty's management. Dixon fought much of his career in Philadelphia from 1929 to 1939.

fighters and promoting fight cards, and occasionally refereeing bouts, but by 1929, things were about to change for the Baron. A new law would prohibit him from managing and promoting, and if he wanted to continue to manage fighters, he would have to put a stop to his promoting business. Fortunately, he was able to keep the promotion business in the family when he chose his son Howard as the new promoter in the county. From that point on, Howard would be forever known as "The Boy Promoter".

- Chapter 9 -

The Boy Promoter

"Howard Dougherty is the youngest fight promoter in the country."

Chester Times

"In December, 1923, the state of Pennsylvania inaugurated a commission to regulate the sport of boxing," wrote Chuck Hasson, widely regarded as the ultimate expert on Philadelphia boxing history. "A few years later, they adopted a conflict of interest rule whereby a boxing promoter could not manage fighters. Baron Dougherty was particularly hit hard by this edict because he had a large stable of prominent boxers. The problem was solved, however, when he chose his son Howard to run the fight cards at the Leiperville Arena and also at the Chester Armory and St. Hedwigs."

Howard was not quite a novice when it came to the sport of boxing, as he was weaned on the sport. His apprenticeship with his father included helping to condition all the great fighters who came to the famous boxing training quarters on Chester Pike to prepare for an important bout.

Howard Dougherty is pictured here with his father pulling on his ears. Howard was always at his father's side and was weaned on boxing.

159

Also, when he drove George Godfrey across the country during his tour of taking on all comers, he cultivated contacts with the leading boxing figures from coast to coast.

"So when he began promoting, he quickly became a success importing top boxers from all over the country," wrote Hasson. "This is not to say that his father didn't exert some influence on him. Most fathers influence their sons to an extent, and the Baron expected some preferential treatment for his stable of fighters, and was a valued advisor for Howard. It kind of paralleled the set-up of the Duva clan's Main-Event promotional group with Lou Duva managing fighters and his son Dan in charge of the business end of the promotions."

However, even with the Dougherty's relationship, Howard was still his own man, and he eventually became a one man operation as the Baron became more involved in politics. Howard was also equally adept as a publicist, matchmaker, and hustler, as well as a promoter.

For the next twenty years, Howard would stage hundreds of top flight and world class boxing shows that featured many world champions and countless world ranked contenders. Even with the long shadow casted by his legendary father, Howard was still respected very highly throughout the boxing world.

Therefore, on July 2, 1929, Howard, only twenty-three years old, staged his first boxing show at the Delaware County Open Air Arena. The card consisted of five bouts with Leiperville's Billy Angelo meeting Gene Lester of Wilmington in the ten round main event. Leiperville's Gig Rooney fought Lew Zell of 69th Street in a six rounder in the first bout; while Chester's Joe Kushki tangled with Frankie Dunbar of Marcus Hook for six rounds. Also on the card was Spike Kenney of Clifton Heights against Marcus Hook's Joey Bradley. Finally, Essington's Joe Boris fought

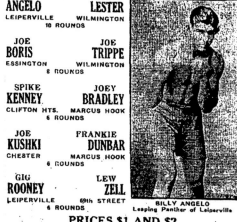

DELAWARE CO. OPEN AIR ARENA
LEIPERVILLE, PA.
ON CHESTER PIKE AT LEIPERVILLE
TONIGHT—GATES OPEN 6.15 P. M.—1ST BOUT 8.15 P. M.
PROMOTION—J. H. DOUGHERTY

BILLY **ANGELO**	GENE **LESTER**
LEIPERVILLE	WILMINGTON
10 ROUNDS	
JOE **BORIS**	JOE **TRIPPE**
ESSINGTON	WILMINGTON
8 ROUNDS	
SPIKE **KENNEY**	JOEY **BRADLEY**
CLIFTON HTS.	MARCUS HOOK
6 ROUNDS	
JOE **KUSHKI**	FRANKIE **DUNBAR**
CHESTER	MARCUS HOOK
6 ROUNDS	
GIG **ROONEY**	LEW **ZELL**
LEIPERVILLE	69th STREET
6 ROUNDS	

BILLY ANGELO
Leaping Panther of Leiperville

PRICES $1 AND $2
NO HIGHER
In case of rain the Show will be held the First Clear Night Following.
ONLY TICKET OFFICE
COLONIAL HOTEL, LEIPERVILLE, PA.
PHONE CHESTER 966

Howard Dougherty, the Boy Promoter, had his first boxing show in Leiperville on July 2, 1929. With the main event starring Leiperville's own Billy Angelo against Gene Lester of Wilmington, his debut show turned out to be a big success.

eight rounds with Joe Trippe of Wilmington before the main event.

The boxing poster made it very clear that the price for tickets was one and two dollars and no higher. It also stated that in case of rain, the show will be held the first clear night following the event. The gates opened at 6:15pm and the first bout began at about 8:15pm.

The *Chester Times* reported, "Howard Dougherty will stage his opening show at the new Delaware County Arena at Leiperville tonight, a show filled with action boys and one of the best fighting cards staged in this section of the state for some time."

Remember, in the early days, the Baron only had a gymnasium out back of the hotel. Then he had a ring built inside a tent, and now Howard had just completed constructing a boxing arena for his promotional debut that seated some 5,000 fans on wooden bleachers.

The *Times* continued, "The arena is all bedecked with flags commemorating the occasion of Howard's entrance into a new channel of the sport of which he has been a part since a very early age.

"But at this stage of the story, the weather steps in and things look rather cloudy for tonight. Still, you never can tell. Should it rain, then the show will be held on the first clear night following, observing the Sabbath of course."

"The Pennsylvania Boxing Commission will take charge of the show at 6 o'clock and from that time on the card will be under their jurisdiction."

Howard's first boxing show was a huge success as was Billy Angelo's main event win over Gene Lester, who he defeated with a TKO in the eighth round.

A couple of weeks later, Damon Runyon came to town to see Howard's fight house, which the writers at the Chester Times would sometimes call the Leiperville Arena.

"Damon Runyon, prominent sports writer of New York, was the guest of James F. Dougherty of Leiperville this morning," reported the *Chester Times*. "Runyon stopped off at Leiperville enroute to Rehoboth, Delaware.

"While here, he inspected the new Delaware County arena in the rear of the Colonial Hotel in Leiperville where Howard Dougherty, son of the 'Baron' conducts fight shows.

"Runyon left Leiperville this morning with Howard Dougherty to complete his trip to Rehoboth by motor. He will stop off at the Dougherty estate on his way back to New York this evening."

On July 30, 1929, Angelo again was the main event on Howard's fight card, and he did not disappoint the Delaware County fight fans.

John Webster of the *Philadelphia Inquirer* wrote, "The Dougherty's father and son Baron and Howard, the heir apparent to the Barony of Leiperville have sold boxing to the fistic friends of Delaware County, and if you don't think so last night's fights at the Delaware Arena should have been sufficiently convincing.

"I don't know how many fistic followers can find seats at the 'kid's arena', but there weren't many empty seats discernible from a ring-side seat when Billy Angelo, the greatest welterweight since Bobby Barrett, if you'll have the Baron's word for it, knocked Sylvan Bass of Baltimore silly in the third round of their ruckus to please the 3,000 fans who gathered at the arena that young Howard has erected."

Bill Burk, Sports Editor of the *Chester Times* wrote, "It was John Webster of the *Inquirer* that named Howard 'The Boy Promoter'."

The promotions seemed to be going great for Howard, and his first season was a success. His plan for the future, weather permitting, was to have a show every week or bi-weekly.

It wasn't long after his inaugural boxing season came to an end that the Stock Market crashed on October 29, 1929. The crash and the ensuing Depression just about ruined everyone financially.

However, as the 1930, outdoor boxing season approached, Howard was not about to let the state of the economy stop his plans of making some changes in the arena. He decided to alter the seating arrangements somewhat by arranging the ringside seats in sort of a wedge formation with a slight elevation. The stands were also painted and electricians made some changes in the wiring of the lighting system.

His first show was planned for May 27, 1930, with Billy Angelo, the Leiperville Panther, in the main event against Nate Goldman of Philadelphia. For his second season, Howard decided to stage his shows every week on Tuesday evenings.

One of the best bouts of that boxing season was a fight between Vince Dundee and Young Ketchell. It was being called one of the most thrilling bouts ever staged in Leiperville.

The *Chester Times* reported, "Quaint and quiet little Leiperville, where nothing ever happens, last night was the abode of one of the most torrid, blistering, sweltering welterweight battles that has ever been staged in this river-bordered section of the state.

"Nothing but the din and roar of motor traffic disturbs the town's serenity, but last night's crowd of men and women went wild, frenzied and cheered and yelled and stood in their seats as Young Johnny Ketchell, pride of Chester, off and on, and Vince Dundee, a sturdy Baltimore youth, slugged each other as men fight for their lives in Howard Dougherty's Open Air Arena.

"Dundee won the spectacular ring joust, but only after weathering Ketchell's fiercest assault, born of a stout heart and sturdy muscle and an unsatisfied will to win."

Being a boxing promoter is not always an easy job, and there are many things that can go wrong when preparing a fight card for the show. In July of that season, Herman Weiner, a heavyweight from Baltimore, was scheduled to fight Jack Gross of Salem, New Jersey when all of the sudden he disappeared.

"Weiner dropped from sight yesterday," reported the *Chester Times*. "He has not been seen or heard from since. Howard Dougherty, the promoter of boxing shows at Leiperville is up a tree.

"Has Weiner run out of the match?

"Has he been lured away?

"Will he carry out his contract and meet Gross?

"These are the questions the promoter asked himself this morning. There was no trace of Mr. Weiner.

"In the meantime, Dougherty is not going to take any chance on Weiner ruining his show. He has gone out and secured two heavyweights who are willing to tangle with Jack Gross tomorrow night.

"Today, he intended to report Weiner's disappearance to the Pennsylvania State Commission and also submit the name of the two heavyweights for their approval"

In August, Howard took a break from his hectic schedule to get married, but interestingly enough; the marriage was kept a secret from most people until April of the following year.

On April 18, 1931, the following appeared on the sports page of the *Chester Times*, "Howard Dougherty's wife is the former Miss Dorothy Moon of Wilmington, Delaware. He broke the news this week to his father, Jimmy Dougherty, noted sportsman and known throughout the country as the Baron of Leiperville. Howard's mother and the parents of the bride were in on the secret.

"The wedding took place on August 18, 1930, at the rectory of St. Madeline's Church in Ridley Park with Rev. James Gallagher officiating. This week the news leaked out, and since then the couple has been busy receiving the congratulations from their many friends.

"Howard Dougherty is the youngest fight promoter in the country. His bride was seen frequently in his company at the outdoor shows at Leiperville last summer."

One of the other obvious hazards of staging outdoor boxing shows was the weather. It was truly Howard's biggest worry when he was planning his boxing extravaganzas. In 1931, he had seven boxing shows that were rained out. Because of his bad luck with the weather, the *Chester Times* began to refer to him as Howard "Rainmaker" Dougherty.

The *Chester Times* reported humorously, "On learning that promoter Dougherty had listed a boxing show for next week, farmers about the county promptly announced a local holiday to celebrate the end of the dry spell, for it is almost a legend that a Leiperville leather-pushing attraction will cure the greatest droughts in history.

"If he has a better season next year, it looks as though 'Rainmaker' Dougherty may have to give up his position as official field wetter of the Famer's Association."

Sometimes putting on a boxing show could also be hazardous to your health. Howard actually got in a fight with another manager who had a fighter on his card.

"On one of my fight cards, Blinky Palermo had a fighter who he wanted paid before the bout," recalled Howard. "I told Blinky that all of the boxers on my fight cards get paid after their bouts. He tried to get rough with me, and we had a fist fight, which ended real soon when I knocked him down. Palermo thought he could push people around, but he didn't scare me."

Howard finally reached the national news when he became the subject of Damon Runyon's syndicated column in 1932. Having written about his father quite often, it was really the first time that the nationally acclaimed scribe had written about the Boy Promoter.

Runyon wrote, "In company with young Mr. Howard Dougherty, the Boy Promoter of Leiperville, I attended a presentation of fisticuffs in Wilmington, Delaware, the city of the bright sunshine.

"Young Mr. Howard Dougherty is the son of Mr. James F. Dougherty, the celebrated Baron of Leiperville, which is in Pennsylvania, twelve miles from Wilmington as the mallard flies. The Baron of Leiperville is the manager of George Godfrey, the renowned Black Shadow of Leiperville.

"Young Mr. Dougherty runs an open air arena in the summer time back of his parent's old hotel in Leiperville. Young Mr. Dougherty confided to me that he makes money any time his paw isn't around to give away all the tickets to his political pals in Leiperville.

"Young Mr. Dougherty draws his clients from Leiperville, Philadelphia, Chester, Marcus Hook, and even from Wilmington.

"For three years, up to about a year ago, young Mr. Dougherty courted a Wilmington girl, who is the new Mrs. Dougherty. Every night, young Mr. Dougherty had to drive from Leiperville to Wilmington and some nights it was pretty cold, too. Other nights it was hot.

"Anyway, young Mr. Dougherty got in the habit of coming to Wilmington and while his bride now lives on the Dougherty premises in Leiperville, young Mr. Dougherty hasn't yet been able entirely to break himself of the Wilmington habit, though he is now down to two nights per week.

"I cite this just to show you what habit will do to a fellow."

"The state of Delaware legalized boxing a couple of years ago. Before that, I recall seeing bootleg bouts of four rounds in Wilmington and other towns in the state and some pretty good bouts too."

That night, they saw a main event battle between Chester's Johnny Ketchell and Jimmy Smith of Philadelphia. Held at a low-ceilinged hall called the Auditorium, Smith took the decision from Ketchell.

Also at ringside with Runyon and Howard were Pete Tyrrell and Vince McMahon. Tyrrell was one of the great sports promoters from the Philadelphia area. He was an excellent boxing matchmaker and promoter who eventually became the general manager and president of the Arena in Philadelphia, where he founded the Ice Capades. Tyrrell brought ice hockey to the Arena with the Philadelphia Ramblers and was the first owner of an NBA team in Philadelphia when he established the Philadelphia Warriors, who captured the first NBA title in 1947. He was also one of eleven people who founded the NBA.

McMahon, a former boxing matchmaker at Madison Square Garden, was at that time the director of boxing at the Arena.

Runyon asked Howard, "Can you point out to me a DuPont at the fight, but he said he didn't think they go in for boxing to any extent."

Just like he did for the Baron some years before, Runyon was now helping to make Howard well known throughout the country through his syndicated column that appeared in over 200 newspapers from coast to coast.

In 1932, Howard also had his first wrestling promotion at the Leiperville Arena. On May 30, he put together a wrestling card that rivaled any shows that have been staged anywhere in the east.

The *Chester Times* description was as follows, "For his opening event, Howard spared no expense in getting together a program that will keep his patrons in a frenzy excitement every second of the way. One finish bout and three thirty minute bouts make up his first show.

"The feature event will present a real 'rasslin' natural in Nick Lutze, the ever popular Los Angeles artist, and John Spellman of Providence, Rhode Island. The promoter snared this duel away from the very noses of rival promoters from Philadelphia, Brooklyn and Boston. They will go to a finish."

"It wasn't a question of finances with me just so I was successful in landing the wrestling plum I sought," explained the usually quiet Howard. "I outbid the other promoters for this title just for the sake of proving to the customers that I intend to bring them the very best in the line of talent"

The *Times* continued, "The semi-final will present Jack Sherry of Chicago and Paul Finsky, the Russian terror; Karl Zbyszko of Poland and Boris Demitroff, the rugged Bulgarian come to grips in the second number; while Charley Hangen of Sweden and August Benkert of Germany will be the contestants in the opening number.

"A glance at the array of talent will provide a real battle in the League of Nations for it will be noted that Lutze is a German-American; Spellman is American; Sherry is Jewish and Finsky is Russian; Zbyszko is Polish; while Demitroff is Bulgarian and Hanson is a Swede and his opponent, Benkert, is a native born German.

"Promoter Dougherty will have popular prices of admission."

That same year, Howard made his debut promoting boxing indoors at the Four Horsemen Club located at State and Sproul Roads in Marple Township. Jess McMahon and Damon Runyon were both at ringside for his first show.

On May 29, 1933, the *Chester Times* headline read, "Dempsey to Officiate at Leiperville Tonight in Opening Outdoor Boxing."

"Howard Dougherty's opening show of the 1933 season consists of the always popular Popper Stopper of Chester against Wally Sears of Minersville," wrote the *Chester Times*. "The light heavyweights will go on in the windup battle for ten rounds with Jack Dempsey, former world's heavyweight champion appearing as an added attraction as a referee in this contest.

"Jack has been notified of his assignment to handle the bout by Robert J. Nelson, Philadelphia member of the State Athletic Commission, and he has acknowledged receipt of his notification and has advised the commissioner that he will be on hand to officiate.

"Dempsey will arrive in Leiperville sometime this afternoon. He will be taken on a sight-seeing tour and later will be the guest of Baron Jim Dougherty at a dinner. Dougherty, today, called attention to the fact that it will be Dempsey's first visit here since the time he trained at Leiperville before he was champion and says that the spot where he will referee is the place where he trained."

Popper Stopper, whose real name was James Richard Paul, knocked out Sears in the second round of the Dempsey refereed bout. Dempsey did not stay long in Leiperville after the fight because he was helping to promote the Max Baer-Max Schmeling fight in New York, and he was busy with the arrangements.

A few weeks later, Popper Stopper fought again in the main event at the Leiperville Arena against light heavyweight champion Maxie Rosenbloom. Howard was able to sign the New York playboy to a contract to fight the local Chester flash on a card that drew the largest crowd of the season for the Boy Promoter.

"The fight was far tougher than most of the crowd had expected," reported the *Chester Times*. "Popper was bewildered by Maxie's unorthodox tactics. Punches came from nowhere and landed everywhere, with the dusky boy's nose doing some handsome receiving for the most part. Popper was always dangerous with those long lanky arms of his and on several occasions stung the champ with stiff punches."

Rosenbloom won every round against the confident Popper. However, at the end of the bout, Rosenbloom had considerably more respect for the Chester product than he had before the fight.

"The boys put on a great show for Howard Dougherty's largest crowd of the season," reported the *Chester Times*. "Both fighters are clownish in their methods and Maxie seemed to get as much delight out of the going as did the fans. He tied the local threat in several difficult knots, and bewildered him with back-hand slaps, snake light thrusts, roundhouse rights and lefts that landed on the top of Stopper's head and flurries of promiscuous punches that had Stopper walking around in circles.

"Stopper's nose was in distress from the second round on. It bled freely. In the seventh round, Stopper caused Maxie's nose to bleed for the first time in the champion's past eleven years of fighting."

As the 1934 boxing season got underway, big plans were being made again to have Jack Dempsey referee another fight at the Leiperville Arena. This time, the former champion was scheduled to be the third man in the ring for the ten round bout between world middleweight champion Vince Dundee and Tommy Rios of Wilmington.

Dundee's title was not at stake for the Leiperville bout since Rios and the champion agreed to come in over the 160 pound weight.

The sports staff of the *Chester Times* remarked, "The Baron, who is one of Dempsey's closest friends, was one of the first to congratulate the famous former heavyweight champion upon the new addition to his family, a seven-and-one-half pound daughter, which was born to Mrs. Dempsey in New York on Saturday."

"I saw Jack in New York shortly after the baby was born," declared Dougherty, "and never have I seen a happier person. Jack was so excited that he smoked more than a dozen cigars during a talk with some newspapermen. He was passing out smokes and drinks as only a Dempsey can do.

"I'm going to give Jack a party Thursday before the fight that he won't forget for a long time to come in honor of his infant daughter. It is going to be one of those short and snappy affairs. Jack wants to get back to New York as soon as possible. He wants to stay near the bedside of his beautiful wife."

Dempsey and Dougherty were also booked to talk over old times with radio host Andy Stanton on WIP the night before the contest.

The *Times* reported, "It was at Leiperville that Dempsey prepared himself for some of his most important ring opponents when he ruined the heavyweight division. 'I always get a big kick out of visiting with Jimmy Dougherty.' Jack is quoted as having said in New York recently. 'I will never forget the many things the Baron did for me.'

"Every indication, according to promoter Howard Dougherty, one of the Baron's sons, points to the Dempsey-Dundee-Rios affair being a complete sell-out."

"I have received requests for tickets from all over the state," said Dougherty. "And I look for the match to attract a capacity crowd."

The Sports Shorts feature in the *Chester Times* remarked, "Dempsey's long friendship with the Baron has made him have an affectionate feeling for young Howard, who was a short paints kid when the Manassa mauler got his first start around these diggings many years ago."

Since the Stock Market Crash in 1929, Dempsey began fighting exhibitions, promoting, refereeing, and he still had some endorsements that helped him get through the financial crisis.

"I lost almost everything myself," said Dempsey to boxing trainer Ray Arcel. "I dropped three million dollars."

In 1930, he and Estelle Taylor divorced, and in a matter of a few years, Dempsey lost his championship career; his business partner, his wife, and his fortune.

Starting in 1931, he began fighting exhibitions, which he estimated at over 175 opponents in a three year period, sometimes as many as five a night.

There were many people who wanted to see Dempsey box just one more time, and Howard took advantage of his popularity by having him referee a few of his shows. He alone would bring out quite a crowd, especially in Leiperville where he had spent so much time during his early boxing days.

Howard Dougherty, with his arm around Jack Dempsey, visits Dempsey's Restaurant in New York with friends. Howard and Dempsey were lifelong friends.

Howard was anticipating a crowd of 6,000 to 7,000 but the rain which started about 4:00 pm and lasted for about an hour proved to discourage many who planned to attend the show. The skies threatened all night, but in spite of these obstacles, the Leiperville Arena still attracted over 2,500 fans.

Rios won the ten round decision from the champion even though Dempsey thought Dundee had won the fight. Dundee's manager Maxie Waxman went immediately to the dressing room to complain to Dempsey, but the former champion said, "It was too darn close and that decision wasn't robbery. After all, in a fight like that it can be called either way without taking anything from either boy."

Dempsey made a quick exit shortly after the bout. He was anxious to get back to his wife, Hannah Williams, and his newborn daughter.

In July, Howard tried his hand at wrestling again. On July 9, 1934, he staged a wrestling card that consisted of a headliner match between former light-heavyweight champion Joe Banaski and Fred "The Great" Mephisto of Germany. The rest of the card was full of outstanding wrestlers from all over the country. One such grabbler was Leo Walleck who had been a star halfback for Coach Howard Jones at the University of Southern California.

Midway through the 1935 boxing season, the headline in the *Chester Times* read, "Fight Game Faces Crisis at Leiperville Tuesday." The article that followed was not a good sign of things to come.

"The apathy of the fight fans shown during the last few years is not without rhyme or reason, but is based on the indifference of the fighters and fight promoters themselves," remarked the *Chester Times*. "The paying public could not be expected to rise up in arms when a game was allowed to go to pieces from the inside.

"The flossiest word from the fisticuff scribes could never get the fight fan to break his neck getting to the ringside, but a good card can always attract. For this reason, the show on Tuesday night out at Leiperville should not fail to please the public and should go a long way toward bringing the game back to the pinnacle it deserves.

"Jimmy Dougherty, Baron of Leiperville and father of promoter Howard Dougherty, was discussing the fine card arranged by his son for Tuesday night. He asked Pete Tyrell, the head of the Philadelphia Arena, what he thought of the show. 'Baron,' said Pete. 'If that show don't pack them in, the best thing for you to do is to get some gasoline, spread it around your arena and then light a match to it.'"

"We hardly believe it will be necessary to start any conflagration such as that, but we do think that the Baron has had ample cause for worry concerning his son's past few years of fistic promotion. Postponements because of rain have been the biggest bugaboo Howard has faced, but he has also been unfortunate in having several last minute substitutions, which never fail to antagonize the crowd, although being no fault of the promoter."

On June 27, 1935, the American Legion sponsored a card of professional boxing which was promoted by the John Wesley Cross Post No. 507 in Norwood. There were five bouts scheduled with the second fight of the night being of some interest to this writer. Frank Mela, my great uncle, was one of the fighters in that boxing show. Mela, who had an outstanding amateur career, was fighting professionally as a lightweight for the sixth time. He also was deaf, and had been quite a good all-around athlete at the Pennsylvania School for the Deaf.

"When each round ended," recalled Mela, "I couldn't hear the bell so they had to throw a towel into the ring so I knew the round was over."

His opponent that night was Joey Evans of Chester, and after six rounds the contest ended in a draw.

Mela, one of only a few deaf fighters in boxing history recalled, "I had one more pro fight after the Evans bout. I knocked out Eddie Slotto at Convention Hall in Atlantic City. I had gotten married, and my wife didn't want me fighting anymore, so I retired from the ring."

My great uncle retired with a record of 4-1-2, but he let me know that he really enjoyed his fight at the Open Air Arena in Leiperville. It was the only time he ever fought outdoors as a professional.

The 1936 professional boxing season was preceded by Frankie Carr's first Delaware County Amateur Tournament. Carr's Lloyd A.C. movement was for the betterment of the amateur ranks, which in turn would feed Howard future boxers for his pro shows.

The 1936 season would also bring wrestling back to the Open Air Arena.

Sports Shorts reported, "Howard Dougherty has hooked up with Ray Fabiani, the mad mat maestro of Philadelphia who gets his inspiration fiddling around with a violin and with first class heavyweight grunt and groan artists from the Land of the Behemoths."

Ray Fabiani was not only Philadelphia's top wrestling promoter but he was also nationally known. Fabiani worked with some of the top wrestling promoters on the east coast and would later promote the sport on television.

With a history of mostly successful wrestling and boxing promotions, things began to fall apart for Howard during the 1936 season. On July 24, 1936, the *Chester Times* headline read, "No Crowd; Fight Show Canceled."

The *Times* went on to say, "The death knell of professional boxing in Delaware County was sounded last night when promoter Howard Dougherty cancelled his card at Leiperville Arena and refunded ticket money to the crowd of less than 100 persons which trickled into the fight arena to witness a show which was to be headed by a windup between the undefeated Johnny Hutchinson and Joe Maffie.

"Dougherty held off the cancellation as long as possible, trying to get official sanction of the move and hoping, in the meanwhile, that enough fans would fill the seats to make expenses. When the crowd numbered about 80 at 9:15, Dougherty called off the show without being able to contact Jules Aaronson, boxing commission secretary.

"The move probably means that Dougherty's license will be revoked when he appears before the boxing commission this afternoon."

Dougherty would have to explain to the commission why he called off the fight because only a small amount of cash was taken at the gate.

The word out of Philadelphia was that Dougherty had to explain why he decided a fat pocketbook was a lot better than mounting debt and called off a fight card because only $200 was taken at the gates.

Anronson warned Howard that he couldn't cancel the show unless he paid off the officials.

Howard said, "I could not pay off the officials, and it looks as though I am through as a promoter anyhow. So I gave back the customers' money and turned out the lights."

Howard didn't put on any boxing or wrestling shows in 1937, but with the help of some old friends, he did get back into some promoting again the following year.

Those old friends who came to the rescue were Jack Dempsey and Doc Kearns. Kearns brought his heavyweight hopeful Jimmy Adamick to Leiperville in the early summer of 1938 to train for his bout with Al Ettore in Philadelphia.

Dempsey brought down his greatest heavyweight protégé Bill Boyd to meet Jake Friedman, an outstanding Jewish heavyweight from Baltimore.

The *Chester Times* Sport Shorts column remarked, "The return of Kearns and Dempsey has stimulated the boxing enthusiasm out at the pike arena and as of today it has almost returned to the beehive of activity that marked it's affairs in the golden era of the twenties.

"Dempsey may bring some of this good fortune to the boy promoter just as he hopes to get some for his fighter Bill Boyd. Bad breaks in the weather during the last three years have stymied Howard's attempts to restore boxing in its more lively status, but with Dempsey's Boyd meeting Friedman, good times may be here again."

Also during this time, Howard had formed a partnership with William Gunnis to promote boxing in Chester during the winter. They had both been working on plans for their first show when Gunnis was found unconscious on a street in Philadelphia, where he had been severely beaten and his skull was fractured. Gunnis was the son of the late Bobby Gunnis who was one of Philadelphia's greatest boxing promoters, working many fights with the legendary Herman Taylor until 1936 when he died right before the Joe Louis-Al Ettore bout. The young Gunnis had also been a University of Pennsylvania football player.

In 1939, there wasn't much going on in the way of boxing shows at the Leiperville Arena, but the arena was always a busy place for many of the world class boxers who needed a place to train for their fights in the Philadelphia area.

Tony "Two Ton" Galento, who had just fought Joe Louis for the heavyweight championship in June, trained at Leiperville for his fight with Lou Nova at Municipal Stadium on September 15, 1939.

The *Chester Times* reported, "With Tony Galento busy busting beaks in his training routine out at Leiperville, boxing enthusiasm in this area has increased immeasurably during

Tony Galento (left) poses with Billy Angelo (right) while Baron Dougherty looks on. Galento was training at the Baron's training quarters in Leiperville for his upcoming fight with Lou Nova.

the last few days. Galento was seen getting his hands taped prior to his workout at the arena.

"Jimmy Dougherty, famous fight manager and referee, was acting as host to Galento. Galento also promised that he would attend the amateur fights at Lloyd A.C. the night before he tangles with Lou Nova at Municipal Stadium."

"The admission to see Galento train was fifty cents, but no one paid because they didn't want to see him train," recalled Howard Dougherty, who tells a different story than the local sportswriters. "Galento wanted me to manage him during that time, but I really didn't want to."

That same year, light heavyweight champion Billy Conn trained at Delco's Open Air Arena for his upcoming bout with Gus Dorazio at Shibe Park. Crowds of people always came out to see Conn train. He even attracted many prominent people of the fight game.

The *Chester Times* stated, "Mike Jacobs, leading fight promoter of the country, took a flying trip over from New York yesterday to confer with his fellow-promoter, Herman Taylor in Philly, and the two notables ventured down to Baron Jimmy Dougherty's training quarters in Leiperville to watch Billy Conn work out in his preparation for the light heavyweight title defense at Shibe Park next week.

"Leiperville may be further honored today as Dougherty's close friend, Damon Runyon, is reported en route to the famous boxing headquarters to watch the graceful Conn ready for the rugged Gus Dorazio and swap a few more stories with the popular Baron.

"Large crowds have been watching Conn train. The boy does his training around 1:15 every day."

"My uncle, Joe Brennan, took me to the Colonial Hotel to watch Billy Conn train for his fight with Gus Dorazio at Shibe Park, " remembered Frank Boyle of Norwood. "My uncle had grown up with the Baron in Chester, and they hugged when they saw each other. I was nineteen years old and watched Conn work out with his brother Jackie in the ring at the back of the hotel."

Notables Visit Dougherty Camp

Mike Jacobs, leading fight promoter of the country, took a flying trip over from New York yesterday to confer with his fellow-promoter, Herman Taylor in Philly, and the two notables ventured down to Baron Jimmy Dougherty's training quarters in Leiperville to watch Billy Conn work out in his preparation for the light heavyweight title defense at Shibe Park next week.

Leiperville may be further honored today as Dougherty's close friend, Damon Runyon, is reported en route to the famous boxing headquarters to watch the graceful Conn ready for the rugged Gus Dorazio and swap a few more stories with the popular Baron.

Large crowds have been watching Conn train. The boy does is tasks around 1.15 every day.

Mike Jacobs and Herman Taylor, two of the greatest promoters in the country, visited Leiperville to watch Billy Conn train for his fight with Gus Dorazio at Shibe Park.

Longtime Leiperville resident, Vito Greto, not only got the chance to see Conn train at the Baron's headquarters but also received some special treatment from the champion.

"There was a ball field next to the Baron's ring," recalled Greto. "A bunch of us kids would pry open one of the boards which was part of the fence that surrounded the ring and bleachers. After we all got in, we would neatly put the board back in place."

"This one day, Billy Conn was training with his brother Jackie, and when he was finished, he grabbed me and put me on his shoulders and paraded me around the ring. Why he picked me out of about 12 kids, I will never know, but it was quite a thrill for a ten year old kid like me."

"I saw lot of great fighters down at the Baron's when I was a kid," continued Greto, who loved boxing and had always wanted to be a fighter. "Guys like Ike

174

Williams, Sugar Ray Robinson, Tony Galento, Bob Montgomery, and of course Billy Conn all trained there.

"One day George Dougherty, know relation to the Baron, brought the great Hack Wilson down to Dougherty's. It was about 1948, and I was 19 years old. Wilson was drunk and telling all of us guys never to take a drink. He kept saying it over and over again. He had a real drinking problem in his later years in the majors."

In 1940, Howard and the Baron decided to rent their arena to other promoters so that the promotion of boxing in Leiperville became someone else's headache. Howard, who had been so unlucky with staging boxing shows because of the rain and was even given the nickname of the Rainmaker, now had given that headache to someone else.

The first promoter to take advantage of the Leiperville Arena was nineteen year old Jimmy Toppi Jr. Toppi, who was being called the Boy Promoter like Howard had been. Toppi was the son of Jimmy Toppi Sr. and they both like the Baron and Howard before them, were very famous and prominent as a manager and promoter team.

The *Chester Times* description of Toppi was very similar to Howard's same association to the sport and his father, "Toppi Jr. comes to Leiperville at the tender age of 19, but he comes with a brainful of fistic lore, garnered by association with his Dad throughout the growing years. When other lads of his age were going to the movies, having dates, playing sports of all kinds, Toppi Jr. was haunting the gymnasiums, meeting the pugilists of this and that stable, and getting himself ready for a career like his father's."

"The last pro boxing show at Leiperville Arena was between Cocoa Kid and Ellis Stewart in the main event on August 19, 1947," wrote boxing historian Chuck Hasson. "The last amateur show was on September 27, 1945, a year when the Leiperville Arena was the host to nine amateur boxing shows."

The last scheduled amateur show was supposed to be in 1950, but after two rainouts they cancelled the card. Also in August of 1950, they tried to match featherweight champion Willie Pep against Willie Alexander for a non-title overweight bout, but the fight fell through and that ended Leiperville's association with boxing.

Those boxing shows at the Leiperville Arena through the 1940's were no longer promoted by Howard. As he got less involved in the sport of boxing, the Baron got more entangled in the world of politics, becoming a two-term County Commissioner and even taking a stab at the State Senate.

- Chapter 10 -

Dougherty the Politician

"It's not what you know, but who you know."

Jimmy "Baron" Dougherty

Up until 1902, Ridley Township was a Class Two township, but as the population increased, Ridley was incorporated as a Class One township, and Jimmy Dougherty was appointed as one of its five commissioners. However, even before that, the Baron had had his hand in politics, serving as the township's supervisor and tax collector in the 1890's.

To understand the political climate that Dougherty was a part of, you first must understand the political machine that was run by the McClure family and dominated the political life of the entire county.

Democratic Candidate
FOR
SHERIFF

James F. Dougherty

The Baron of Leiperville

I am in full accord with the policy of our President and our Governor and the New Deal platform of the Democratic Party.

Baron Dougherty had his hand in politics, serving as Ridley Township's supervisor, tax collector, commissioner, and also Delaware County Commissioner. Later, he ran for state senator and sheriff, claiming to be in full accord with the policies of F.D.R.

This Republican political machine was itself controlled by one of two men: William "Billy" McClure, from 1875 until his death in 1907; and John J. McClure, William's son, from 1907 until his death in 1965.

Politically, Dougherty enjoyed a very close working relationship with Billy McClure. McClure was very involved with a new era in Delaware County politics, the era of the "Liquor License Ring". According to author John McLarnon in his book, *Ruling Suburbia: A Biography of the McClure Machine of Delaware County*, "in 1874, McClure was issued a liquor license at his cigar store at Third and Kerlin Streets in Chester, and he would soon become the largest liquor wholesaler in all of Delaware County."

By the early 1900's, McClure had become a wealthy man.

"In addition to the tobacco, liquor, and hotel businesses, he was president of the Consumer's Ice and Coal Company and secretary-treasurer of the Chester Brewing Company, "wrote McLarnon. "He also sat on the boards of directors of the Chester Shipping Company, the Delaware County Subway Company, the Delaware County trust, and the Delaware County National Bank. In February 1890, he chartered his own social organization, the McClure Gun Club. Later in the decade he sponsored a successful team in the fiercely competitive Delaware County Baseball League."

By the turn of the century, Billy McClure totally ruled the City of Chester. He especially controlled the judge that handed out the liquor licenses, and he owned the Chester Brewery, the only brewery in the county. If you owned a tavern or hotel with a bar, you had to buy your beer and liquor from McClure.

McClure died in the spring of 1907 from typhoid fever but the political machine that he established did not die with him. His only surviving son, twenty-one year old John J. McClure would be the heir to his throne.

John, who was an outstanding athlete at Swarthmore Prep, was in his second year at Swarthmore College when his father died, and he took control of the Republican organization.

Dougherty always felt he helped John athletically because he stoutly insisted that he gave boxing lessons to McClure when he was a boy in need of exercise to aid in his development.

To put the importance of beer and alcohol in perspective, McLarnon wrote, "The Philadelphia Housing Authority described pre-war Chester as a city that had thirty-one policemen and forty-one saloons, so liquor interest dominated its politics."

When John took over this over powering political machine, Dougherty was just putting the finishing touches on his Colonial Hotel and needed to have a liquor license to serve beer and liquor. The Baron ran into opposition initially, and he gave his patrons free beer for a time, but John McClure came to the rescue, and in October of 1907, the Baron was issued a liquor license, and the money started pouring in at the Colonial Hotel on Chester Pike.

Besides buying his beer and liquor form McClure, Dougherty and other hotel and saloon owners were expected to contribute to the organization's campaign fund and make sure all of their patrons made it to the polls at least once on Election Day.

During prohibition, many felt that beer and liquor was finished as a source of political power.

John McClure, who Baron Dougherty gave boxing lessons to when he was a boy, took over the Republican political machine in Delaware County in 1907 after the death of his father, who Baron Dougherty had a close relationship with. (Keith Lockhart Collection)

"McClure continued to manufacture and distribute 2.75-beer, claiming that it was not prohibited under the terms of the Volstead Act," wrote McLarnon. "His Chester Brewing Company sent letters to bars and hotels throughout the county advising them to keep selling his beer. 'We're taking a chance,' the letter read, 'why can't you take a chance too?'"

After four years into prohibition, an investigative reporter for the New York Tribune visited five cities in Pennsylvania and found that the Keystone State was "as wet as the rainy season."

McLarnon wrote, "The 1,300 saloons in Philadelphia paid no attention to the 18th Amendment, and In Delaware County Judge Johnson issued seventy-two liquor licenses in December of 1922."

Many groups actually set up their own stills to produce liquor and some sold their homemade liquor to the bars and taverns in the area.

McLarnon explained one particular still, "They set up a 1,500-gallon plant for re-distilling denatured alcohol on the banks of Crum Creek in Ridley Township, and county employees, impatient with the delays in getting liquor delivered to their offices, set up their own still in the basement of the court house in Media."

So the Colonial Hotel like many other bars and taverns could stay in operation for a price, and be exempt from harassment by local police and forewarned of federal or state raids.

McClure, who was a State Senator by now, was the overseer of the wholesale liquor business in the county, and throughout Prohibition, business had been very good. Even though he sold the Chester Brewery in 1926, he still maintained a financial interest in the business and the brewery continued to produce beer.

McLarnon explained, "Chester policeman Howard Grubb told the court that on specified nights, kegs of illegal brew rolled out of the brewery under the watchful eye of police and constables on the McClure payroll. In order to insure against any unwanted interference, the beer was loaded by candlelight; and, through a connection in the Streets Department, the street-lights within a four-block radius were turned off. Eventually, the brewery operators ran a pipe to a junk yard across the street where the kegs were filled in a make-shift rack room. 'Then,' according to a convicted extortionist Harvey Sykes, 'they ran the loaded trucks through a hole in the fence and thence down an alley'."

Homemade stills were everywhere in the county. "Stella Rudinski operated a tiny still in Leiperville that barely supported herself and her three children," wrote McLarnon.

Over a period of time, the federal authorities were investigating the Rum Ring, as it was called. The Ring, run by McClure, was involved in the importing of Canadian whiskey and many other illegal liquor manufacturing.

"As well organized as the McClure liquor operations were, they paled in comparison to his protection racket," remarked McLarnon. "Every sort of moonshining, bootlegging, and speakeasies had to pay tribute to the organization or run the risk of being raided by police on the organization payroll. Anyone who refused to pay, or who got too far behind on his or her payments, was raided on McClure's direct orders."

When the investigation was complete, an indictment was handed down that included ninety-four men and two women, including several of the most prominent names in county politics.

"Before the two sides began their summations at the trial, federal prosecutor Chester Keyes offered a motion to nol pros (Latin for we will no longer prosecute) the indictments against three defendants," wrote historian McLarnon, "one of whom was nationally known boxing promoter and Ridley politician James

Dougherty, the Baron of Leiperville. Judge Welsh, an ex-boxer, agreed to the motion with a bizarre speech:

'You bear a reputation unequaled in the sporting world. It is second to none. You were always noted for clean sportsmanship, not only in this country, but in many foreign countries. The lovers of good clean sports throughout the United States will be as pleased to hear of this as you. The Court is personally happy to do this'."

After deliberation, the jurors found McClure and his seventy remaining co-defendants guilty as charged. McClure was sentenced to eighteen months in prison and a $10,000 fine, and the remaining defendants received lesser sentences. All those convicted appealed their verdicts, and during that time, prohibition finally came to an end.

"The Supreme Court directed the government to drop all investigations and discharge all pending prosecutions under the Volstead Act," explained McLarnon. "The conviction and sentencing of McClure and his fellow defendants was null and void."

McClure, who spent only about forty minutes in jail, was set free.

In 1939, Dougherty, who had already been a Ridley Township Commissioner, ran for County Commissioner, but this time as a Democrat. The law required minority representation on the commission, and McClure chose Dougherty, a lifelong Republican, to run on the democratic ticket.

It was an excellent choice for McClure because Dougherty was probably the most recognizable man in the county. The Baron, who enjoyed a close working relationship with William McClure, had also been in business during prohibition with John McClure and a fellow defendant in the Rum-Ring trial. The Baron could still be a formidable opponent to McClure in a local contest, and all things considered, he was a better man to have as an ally than an enemy.

JAMES F. DOUGHERTY
Candidate for County Commissioner
Delaware County
DEMOCRAT TICKET

In 1939, Dougherty ran for county commissioner, but this time as a Democrat. The law required minority representation on the commission, and McClure chose Dougherty. Many people felt he was still truly a republican so they referred to him as a McClure Democrat.

McLarnon explained it this way, "Under McClure's direction, several thousand party regulars split their ballot and cast only one vote for a Republican. The other went to Democrat James F. Dougherty.

"Approximately 12,000 Republicans cast one of their two votes for Dougherty. The final count showed the effect of McClure's tactics. Each of the two Republican candidates for county commission garnered about 53,000 votes, 6,000 less than every other Republican candidate for county office. Dougherty won nearly 26,000 votes, 14,000 more than the fourth-place finisher."

As the election approached for his second term as County Commissioner, Dougherty, who again was running as a Democrat, refused to endorse Vernon O'Rourke, the favorite to win the Democratic Party's congressional nomination.

McLarnon wrote, "Baron Dougherty, the self-proclaimed leader of the Jeffersonian Constitutional Democrats (otherwise known as the McClure Democrats), believed that O'Rourke, a Swarthmore College professor and leader of the Liberal Action Democrats, was a dangerous subversive.

"He's a Communist," said the Baron, "and would destroy our form of government."

Dougherty said he would support the republican incumbent.

"O'Rourke is no Democrat," Dougherty declared, "and I intend to go all over the county this November to electioneer against him."

The Baron always denied any ties to McClure. He even threatened to sue the *Philadelphia Record* when it claimed that he was a 'McClure stooge masquerading as a Democrat.'

"His differences with O'Rourke and the Liberal Action Democrats were ideological, he claimed, not political," explained McLarnon. "While he remained an admirer of FDR, he despised the liberals whose socialistic ideas of government the New Deal seemed to encourage. Later he would announce that, 'the Democratic party died with Roosevelt.'"

In Dougherty's second term as county commissioner, McClure tried to increase tax revenues by assessing industrial machinery separate from the property on which the machinery was located.

McLarnon wrote, "Baron Dougherty, the lone Democrat on the county commission, turned on McClure and warned his friends in the business community of a closed December meeting of the county commissioners at which an increase in commercial assessments was discussed.

"The plan never became law because it failed to win the approval of two of the three county commissioners. Dougherty vetoed the scheme. In return for the Baron's disloyalty, McClure threw his support to Al Crawford for minority commissioner in the next election.

"Baron Dougherty's disloyalty gave McClure the opportunity to reward Crawford, the loyal Democrat who agreed to be the sacrificial lamb in the 1945 judicial race. With McClure's backing, Crawford won the election to the county commission in November 1947.

"McClure retained his control of both the city and county governments, engineering the ouster of Judge Albert MacDade and minority commissioner James 'Baron' Dougherty in the process."

After making a failed attempt to run for a third term as county commissioner, Dougherty announced his candidacy for the US Senate which was occupied by Senator Joseph F. Guffey, who was the leader of the Democratic Party in Pennsylvania. He didn't get far with his plan and his candidacy never saw fruition.

He even sent an open letter to Senator Guffey and bitterly attacked him and his policies. He accused Guffey of trying to ruin the Democratic Party in Delaware County. Dougherty's letter which appeared in the *Chester Times* talked about his relationship with Guffey over a period of years and how the Senator was criticized for turning over local patronage to liberals and Republicans who never voted for FDR.

That same year, 1943, he wrote an open letter to the President warning him about his enemies. He spoke about the people who voted for him, including Republicans and how many of them were not loyal to him in the last election. In particular, Dougherty mentioned Wendell Willkie, who Roosevelt sent to North Africa and Russia on his behalf, and the first thing Willkie did was state how Russia was dissatisfied with the President's administration.

Willkie ran against Roosevelt as the Republican candidate in 1940 and lost, and initially he was against the president's New Deal policies. However, later he traveled the world in Roosevelt's behalf meeting and talking with many of the world's leaders. Dougherty did not like his liberal ways, and that was the essence of his letter to Roosevelt. That liberalism lost him support in the GOP and he dropped out of the 1944 race. He never did hold any political office.

He had been friends with William Sproul for many years, and in 1907, when the Dougherty Fire Company was organized in Leiperville, Sproul and Dougherty were members and bought the first hose carriage for the company. At that time, Dougherty was the first to say that one day Sproul will be governor of the Keystone State.

Sproul had graduated from Chester High School in 1887, and with honors from Swarthmore College in 1891. He was also a state Senator for over 20 years before the Republican Party nominated him for governor in 1918.

The Baron, with Casper Sharpless and Captain McCurdy, helped Sproul during his coming-out party at the Strathhaven Inn in Swarthmore.

"Dougherty was responsible for bringing Teddy Roosevelt here to visit Sproul's home," wrote Walter Schlichter of the *Philadelphia Inquirer.* "Teddy never heard tell of Sproul until Dougherty sold him to him as the man to lick Penrose and the Republican organization in Pennsylvania. Dougherty and Roosevelt had become friends in the old days when Teddy was Police Commissioner of New York City."

This picture was taken in the living room of Senator William Sproul's home on December 1, 1917. Sproul is standing in the center, and Baron Dougherty is sitting in front of him and a little to the left.

On January 20, 1919, Sproul resigned from the senate after twenty-two years and became the governor of Pennsylvania, the first and only governor of the Keystone State to hail from Delaware County.

A year later, Sproul decided to become a candidate for President of the United States. Dougherty, still upset about Sproul killing his boxing bill which would have allowed him to secure the deal for the Dempsey-Willard bout, was determined to block Sproul's chances for the nation's highest office.

Even though Sproul was governor, Dougherty elected his two men national delegates and defeated William I. Schaeffer and Miller of Chester County. He elected Sam Vauclain and Horace Beagle of Chester County and broke up the solid delegation and endorsement in Pennsylvania and gave Senator Penrose the first encouragement to break down Sproul from being President.

Dougherty not only attended the Republican Convention in Chicago, but went so far as to manufacture and distribute lapel buttons bearing a picture of Vauclain, which the Baron helped to distribute to the delegates at the convention.

"Dougherty had a private car to that convention in Chicago," recalled Schlichter. "He had Clem Condon as his press agent and set up a printing house in Chicago and had the Philadelphia Transcript printed there, comparing Vauclain with Lincoln and stating that he wanted a business man for President instead of a college man. This paper was circulated all during the convention.

"On Thursday night the powers of Wall Street pulled Vauclain out and made a compromise with Penrose's candidate, Warren G. Harding, and offered Sproul the Vice Presidency. Sproul refused it and turned it over to his friend and pal Calvin Coolidge. That is how near Delaware County came to having its first President in the history of the United States."

If Sproul had accepted the vice presidency, it is probable he would have become president of the country assuming Harding had still died in office. Instead, Calvin Coolidge stepped into that role.

In December, 1947, at a testimonial to Dougherty, Judge William Toal spoke highly of the Baron, "You have brought good government to Delaware County. You are known by the great of our country. You have devoted your life to the welfare of boys, uplifting sports. We've had the honor of having you as a commissioner for eight years. You've belonged to the minority party, but you have cooperated with the majority."

- Chapter 11 -

The Sequoia is Lost

"Now I can go out of the world the way I came into it, not owing anybody as much as 25 cents."

Jimmy "Baron" Dougherty

Jimmy Dougherty was always entertaining at his hotel and even at his mansion known as "Sequoia" on Chester Pike in Ridley Park.

One such party at Sequoia was for the legendary sportswriter Lou Jaffe, who in 1927, was getting married. The Baron, who was the host, invited fifty newspapermen form Philadelphia and other parts of the country.

The *Chester Times*, without a by-line, wrote, "Mr. Jaffe is about to take a high-dive as they say in boxing circles. Mr. Jaffe writes news about fighters for the *Evening Public Ledger*. After seeing fights for 35 or 40 years (nobody knows how old he is) he has decided to get into a big brawl himself. So he is going to get married this week."

Many of Jaffe's friends thought it would be appropriate to say farewell to him so Dougherty staged the farewell party. The Baron also had George Godfrey spar in his spacious backyard where he had a ring setup for training and exhibitions.

After several rounds of boxing, the newspapermen all went into the house for some more entertainment. Charles E. Bryan, who is an actor from Jersey City, did most of the entertaining.

Among those present were a who's who of sportswriters and other sports people of that time. They included: Jaffe, Frank MacCracken, Jimmy Isaminger, Eddie Pollock, Bill Heinholtz, Dick Kain, Harry Nason, George Wallace, Jimmy Gantz, Joe Cunningham, David Cohen of Wilmington, promoter Herman Taylor, Tommy Riley, famous referee, and Francis X. O'Conner, who was the master of ceremonies.

Also in attendance was: boxer Alex Hart, Gump DeLaney, Charlie Swift, Chuck Vorhis, Leo Riordan, Joe Dey, Seth Maxwell, former boxer Harry Lenny, Harry Neily of Chicago, Larry McCrossan, Harry Liberman, Tom Reynolds, Johnny O'Donnell and boxers Young Ketchell and George Godfrey.

In December, Dougherty would always host his annual Christmas dinner at the Colonial Hotel. This Yuletide annual event was started by the Baron in 1908 with a luncheon of ham and cabbage for the special guest of honor Sam Vauclain, president of the Baldwin Locomotive Works.

In one such Christmas dinner, Dougherty invited over 100 guests of the political and industrial world.

The *Chester Times* reported, "Yesterday, Jimmy Dougherty had the entire county judiciary, city, county and state officials, key men of industry in the 'billion dollar' war defense area from Essington to the Delaware State line; bankers, businessmen, British, Canadian and American officers and a representative of the Soviet government."

"Seating among the judiciary was Judge Samuel E. Shull of Stroudsburg. Alfred G. Hill, editor and publisher of the *Chester Times*, was introduced to the assembly."

These Christmas dinners usually consisted of industrialists, newspapermen and politicians from the area, and the Baron knew them all. There were years that his only reason for getting everyone together was so he could express his appreciation for favors rendered during that year.

At one such Christmas dinner during the war, William H. Harmon, president of the Willkie Clubs of Pennsylvania and vice president of the Baldwin Locomotive Works, debated with Dr. Luther B. Harr, state chairman of the Roosevelt campaign committee. John B. Kelly, the Philadelphia Democratic chairman, also got in on the discussion.

Dougherty received telegrams from two noted indivials who could not attend the festivities.

The *Chester Times* wrote, "A telegram was received from James A. Farley in New York, regretting his inability to attend, and Damon Runyon, noted sports, news and fiction writer, a frequent visitor to Leiperville, informed Dougherty by telegram that only an attack of grip prevented his attendance. Farley was praised by Boniface Dougherty as the man directly responsible for the repeal of the prohibition act."

The *Times* also reported that James A. Gallagher of Ridley Park entertained everyone with a series of rib-tickling anecdotes and witticisms.

The list of guests included: William Harmon and William Smock of Baldwin Locomotive; George L. Alston of General Steel; William Zimmerman and Conrad Schatte of Sun Oil; Albert Granger of Philadelphia Electric; Gideon M. Stull, representing the Ford interests; William Faison, president of Atlantic Steel; Delaware County National Bank's Joseph Pew, Jr.; Captain George Richardson, Philadelphia Detective Bureau;

Also on the list was a who's who of sportswriters from the Philadelphia area. They included: Perry Lewis and John Webster of the *Philadelphia Inquirer*; Bill Driscoll and Joseph Phelan of the *Philadelphia Record*; the *Evening Bulletin's* John Fried; Lou Jaffe and Ed Pollock of the *Evening Ledger*; Stoney McLynn, radio sports announcer and writer for the *Daily News*, and Herman Taylor, boxing promoter.

On November 20, 1947, Baron Dougherty had a luncheon at his hotel dedicated to "Captains of Industry and Sport". Five of those guests that appeared in this Chester Times photo included: l to r John Pew and Robert Haig of Sun Ship, Connie Mack of the Philadelphia Athletics, Dougherty, Judge Albert Dutton MacDade, and Sam Riddle, the owner of legendary horse Man O' War.

On November 20, 1947, Dougherty had another one of his lunches, this time it was dedicated to the "captains of industry and sport". The front page of the *Chester Times* the following day said it all with a picture of six of the guests which included Dougherty.

The caption read, "Remarkable figures in the world of industry and sports. The fabulous James F. 'Baron' Dougherty smiles as he faces the camera, Thursday, at the Colonial Hotel in Leiperville, on the occasion of another of his lunches to 'captains of industry'. At the right is Samuel D. Riddle, who ten days ago laid to rest his immortal race horse, Man O' War. To the left of the 'Baron' is the ageless Connie Mack of the Philadelphia Athletics. The two world-famous Sun Shipbuilders, John G. Pew and Robert Haig, are to the left of Connie, while Judge Albert Dutton MacDade is over the Baron's left shoulder. The average of the above sextette is about 80 years."

Having been a lifelong friend of Sam Riddle, Dougherty was given this painting of Riddle's legendary horse, Man O' War. Around the outside of the painting were numerous autographs of athletes and celebrities that the Baron knew and befriended.

Those individuals were honored, but it really turned out to be the Baron's Day. It was a kind of climax to a career added color to sports, politics and business in Delaware County and the nation.

"James F. Dougherty retires next month after serving two terms as commissioner of Delaware County," wrote Tony Zecca of the *Chester Times*. "The guests on Thursday were treated to a meal, not just a luncheon of ham and cabbage, the menu that launched the affairs in 1908. There were punch bowls and pitchers of beer, but the' Baron' took time to say that, if he had his way, there would be no liquor industry 'to take the hard earned money from poor working people.' And he was most bitter about the government's taxes on beverages.

"The guests all signed an illuminated scroll in honor of the 'Baron', and it was presented to him along with a purse of money, gift of his business friends.

"John G. Pew, Jr. made the presentation in which he lauded Baron Dougherty for his share in 'bringing mills and factories to Delaware County,' and thanked him for the annual luncheons which he called 'milestones in the program of a progressive and busy community.'"

George L. Alston, General Steel Corporation executive was the toastmaster at the luncheon. He introduced Tommy Richardson, president of the Eastern Baseball League and owner of the Williamsport Club, who kept everyone listening intently with his stories.

The Baron spoke next, and he was in rare form. He started off by saying that he was patterning his life after those sterling figures in the world of sport, his good friends Connie Mack and Sam Riddle.

He also touched on the highlights of his career and revealed that gamblers had offered him $200,000 to call the Gibbons-Dempsey fight a draw. He told how the gamblers had threatened to kidnap him in order to swing the fight their way.

Among the others present at the luncheon were the following: John G. Pew, Sr., and Robert Haig of Sun Ship; F. Farwell Long and Frank H. Griffin of Viscose; Sun Sip's Richard L. Burke; Joesph G. Shryock and John A. Mitchell of Belmont Iron; George L. Alston of General Steel; Herbert C. Gross of Philadelphia Electric; Charles E. Acker of Baldwin Locomotive; Raymond Mateer and Larcom Ober of Scott Paper; Ed McCadden of Pure Oil; Texaco's Charles G. Cramer; and Rex J. Self of Sinclair Refining.

In 1937, the Ridley Township High school football team finished the season undefeated and was given a banquet in the school's gymnasium. There were many speakers in attendance, the first being head Coach Jesse "Hal" Brewster. After a few more administrators and board members spoke, Dougherty, who had been invited to the banquet and referred to as "public citizen number one" of the township, got up to say a few words.

The *Chester Times* reported, "Baron Dougherty gave a rousing speech in which he declared that the youngsters were products of old Mother Ridley and as such carried out the great teachings of that community and followed in the footsteps of the other sons of the township who had made the high school a reality. Dougherty pointed out that Ridley Township was the oldest township in the county and a part of it was the first settled community in the days when the Swedes first landed on the Delaware River banks."

During these years, Dougherty continued to support local sports teams, such as the Leiperville baseball squad that played in the Delco Baseball League from 1934 to 1948. Managed by Vito Greto, the 1937 edition captured the league championship.

The Delco Baseball League, which has been around since 1908, is the oldest continuous semi-pro baseball league in the country. The league's official historian, Kyle Barrett, wrote, "The league has featured such outstanding talents as 'Home Run' Baker, and baseball executives like Connie Mack. Heck, even the fabled Babe Ruth almost played for the league's Upland entry."

In Robert W. Creamer's book entitled *Babe: The Legend Comes To Life*, he wrote, "Ruth sent a wire to Frank Miller in 1917, manager of the baseball team that played for the Chester Shipyards in Chester, Pennsylvania, just south of Philadelphia, asking what he would be paid if he left the Red Sox and joined the shipyard's team (the team was actually the Upland edition of the Delco League and Frank Miller was their manager). Miller immediately sent a representative to Baltimore to talk to Ruth, and they worked out terms for Babe to appear with the shipyard team when it played on the Fourth of July, two days later."

A *Chester Times* article that same year entitled, "Frank Miller Helped Ruth," explained how Upland's manager Frank Miller was looking for a pitcher to compete with former Philadelphia A's hurler Chief Bender, who had been signed with the Chester Club.

The *Times* article told a little different story on who met with Ruth and where their meeting took place. However, one thing is certain; Frank Miller tried to lure Babe Ruth away from the Boston Red Sox.

"Late last Thursday night," reported the *Times*, "Frank Miller stepped off the train in Boston armed with a satchel of John P. Crozer's yeallowbacks. One hour later, Miller was in private conference with Babe Ruth at his apartment in a residential suburb of Boston. The conference was arranged by telegraph.

"Miller asked Ruth what his salary was in the American League, and after Ruth submitted the figures, Miller said, 'I will give you the same, and you will only have to pitch once a week.'

"'Give me time to think,' replied Ruth. Ruth still loyal to manager Jack Barry got his manager on the telephone. The consequence was Johnson, President of the American league, was advised what was going on.

"Miller had returned to Upland, and got in conference with John P. Crozer and Albert R. Granger, president and vice president of the club. A few hours later, Ruth received a telegram stating that including the meeting about the American League salary, the Upland team would pay his wife's expenses here and pay whatever fine the American league imposed at the end of the season for his jumping to the millionaire circuit.

"Ruth took this telegram to manager Jack Barry and again Ban Johnson was advised. Late Saturday night, the American League head handed out Ruth's mild punishment.

"Ruth had been fined and suspended for one week by Johnson because of his flagrant attack on umpire 'Brick Owens'. However, the punishment was very lenient because after Miller's offer, Johnson got scared that Ruth would jump leagues, so he lightened the punishment.

"Upland's deal to land Babe Ruth never did come to fruition, but it did give the Delco Baseball League plenty of national exposure that began with Home Run Baker."

However, three years later, Ruth would find himself in Delaware County under some very unusual circumstances.

In 1920, his first season with the Yankees, he drove his big four-door touring sedan on a Yankee road trip to play the Athletics in Philadelphia and then to Washington to meet the Senators. When the game was over in Washington, he drove back to New York.

In the car with him was his wife Helen, a rookie outfielder named Frank Gleich, a second-string catcher named Fred Hofman, and Charley O'Leary, an old infielder who was now a coach under manager Huggins.

Creamer, Babe's biographer, wrote what happened next, "The trip was a jolly one, with songs, much laughter and occasional stops for sips of bootleg liquor. Babe was driving, which he did with exuberance and not too much attention to minor vagaries of the road. The narrow highway weaved and curved its way into Pennsylvania. It was night, perhaps two in the morning. Ruth was singing at the wheel. He was really letting it all out in the soft summer night.

"Just outside the hamlet of WaWa (Delaware County), near Philadelphia, the road curved sharply. Babe was driving much too fast and could not make the curve. He hit the brakes; the car skidded, spun off the road and turned over. O'Leary and Helen were thrown from the car, Helen onto relatively soft dirt at the side of the road, O'Leary onto its hard surface.

"Ruth squirmed out of the wreckage. Gleich and Hofmann were okay. Helen was bruised, her stockings almost torn off, but she was not otherwise hurt. O'Leary, lying on his back in the middle of the road, appeared to be unconscious, possibly dead.

"Except for a headache, he was all right and so were the others, although Ruth had banged his knee and was limping. The five of them walked half a mile down the road to a farmhouse, where they were able to spend the night."

They all made their way into Philadelphia the next day where they saw a newspaper headline that read, *Ruth Reported Killed In Car Crash*. They did get back to New York City where Ruth played for the Yankees the next day.

His stay in Delaware County was short, but those occasional stops for bootleg liquor (fortunately not at the Baron's tavern) almost put an end to his career and maybe even his life and the life of those with him.

There was no doubt that in his lifetime, Dougherty rubbed elbows with celebrities in all walks of life. He would entertain them lavishly, particularly the sportswriters. From sipping champagne with Queen Marie of Romania, to having dinner with Teddy Roosevelt in the White House, the Baron did it all.

"Everybody was there on Sunday afternoon," recalled Marie McGettigan, a high fashion model in Philadelphia who often mingled with the celebrities at the hotel. "Anthony Drexel Biddle, Mickey Cochrane, Damon Runyon, H.L. Mencken, Jack Dempsey and Estelle Taylor were all there. It wasn't a very high class place. It was like an old western hotel with a long, long bar alongside the railroad tracks. But all the celebrities were there. They all loved the Baron."

ZaSu Pitts, seen here acting with W. C. Fields, was a frequent guest at Dougherty's house in Ridley Park with her husband Thomas Gallery. Pitts' last role was as a switchboard operator in the Stanley Kramer comedy, "It's a Mad Mad Mad Mad World".

Elizabeth Dwyer, one of the Baron's daughters who was a clerk in the office of former Chester Police Chief Joseph Bail, remembered, "Actress ZaSu Pitts was among the celebrities at the housewarming my father had at the Big House in Ridley Park, as well as Grace Kelly's father, John B. Kelly Sr."

ZaSu Pitts was an American actress who starred in many silent dramas and comedies and later made the transition to comedy sound films. Her last role was as a switchboard operator in the Stanley Kramer comedy *It's A Mad, Mad, Mad, Mad World*. When she would make her trips to the hotel, she was married to a friend of the Baron's, Thomas Sarsfield Gallery, who was also an actor and later became a well-known Los Angeles boxing promoter and later a TV executive.

Gallery was primarily a silent film actor, and interestingly enough, he had a part in *One-Round Hogan*, the silent film in which George Godfrey wrote the screen story.

Dougherty had known Gallery since his days refereeing, promoting and managing his boxers on the west coast. Gallery had succeeded Tom Kennedy, another movie actor, as the matchmaker at the famous Hollywood Legion Stadium. Later, he would become the matchmaker at the Dreamland Arena in San Francisco and the Olympic Auditorium in Los Angeles.

In 1939, Gallery promoted a world heavyweight championship bout in Los Angeles between Champion Joe Louis and a veteran challenger Jack Roper. As expected, Louis stopped Roper in the first round, but the fight drew a large crowd.

After his days in the world of boxing, Gallery became a television executive.

Once in his visit to "Sequoia", he met Ann, the Baron's oldest child and commented on how beautiful she was. "She is even more beautiful than actress Mary Pickford," commented Gallery.

Even during the 1940's, Jack Dempsey continued to drop by the hotel to see the Baron and his many Leiperville fans.

Bill Burk, the sports editor of the *Chester Times*, wrote the following in 1944, "Well sir, you could have knocked the boys dead in the Colonial Hotel Thursday evening when who should come strolling in for a short beer but the one and only Jack Dempsey, now a Lieutenant Commander in Uncle Sam's Coast Guard.

"Here was a guy who had a joint of his own in New York that is called Dempsey's Punch Bowl and the cover charge is enough to buy the week's groceries for the family. Over there the mugs seeking autographs stand in line buying gin flips at a buck a throw until Lieutenant Commander Dempsey shows up and even then some of them never get to touch his coat let alone getting his signature.

"But the guy who put Leiperville on the map comes in with Dempsey and shouts, 'Boys, the drinks are on the house because this is none other than the one and only Jack Dempsey,' and sure enough they were and he was."

Thomas Gallery (right) greets boxer Tony Canzoneri and his manager Sam Goldman in 1931 in Los Angeles. Gallery, a Hollywood actor and husband of ZaSu Pitts, was also a boxing promoter and a good friend of the Baron's, where he was a frequent guest at his home and boxing headquarters.

They were all there to see the former champion: Vince Mallon, the old athlete and coach; Henry Fenza, who was the unofficial goodwill mayor of Chester Pike; PeeWee DeVico, Big Joe Fizzano and Reds Roma to name a few.

Just six months after his last luncheon, Dougherty, who had financial problems, put his estate on Chester Pike in Ridley Park up for auction. The auction entailed more than just the four-pillared mansion known as "Sequoia". It also included the adjoining garage with an upstairs apartment, three other houses and two good-sized lots nearby which was on 1,634 acres of land.

Piece by piece, the property went to the highest bidders.

Dougherty, who by this time was separated from his wife, was living upstairs at the Colonial Hotel and the mansion was now an apartment house accommodating a half dozen families. The adjoining garage with the upstairs apartment was now the home of the Baron's wife Mary, and her daughter Margaret and her husband Bill Stull. During the auction, Stull had won the bid for the garage combination at $7,850.

The Baron seemed happy when his son-in-law won the bid and whispered to a friend, "They've got a fine place to live for the rest of their lives."

The mansion went for $32,000 to Samuel Greenberg, a meat market proprietor from Crum Lynne. Dougherty showed his unhappiness with a deep frown, and he paced nervously among the real estate agents, neighbors and onlookers.

Dougherty had wanted to turn "Sequoia" over to the Delaware County Boy's Club for a sort of athletic shrine.

"But I outlived my budget," explained Dougherty.

Ronald Van Tine of the *Philadelphia Bulletin* wrote, "The Baron was heard saying that this is just giving the place away as he mounted the steps to the wide veranda where he used to greet the Stotesburys, Wrigleys, Pews and Gimbels, or the Benny Leonards, George Godfreys, and Philadelphia Jack O'Briens."

Louis Traiman, the auctioneer, led the crowd in the final piece of property, a three-story frame house at 20 Stewart Lane, the home of John Burnside, his wife and ten children.

The bidding started at $2,000 and wound up going for $5,000. The Baron was happy about this sale because the buyer was Burnside, who had been paying $60 a month rent.

When the auction concluded, Dougherty's properties brought in a total of $56,300.

When the Baron looked out over his auctioned property, he remarked, "Over there," pointing to a clump of weeds bordering on the railroad tracks "was where we were going to build the arena. Greatest ambition of my life, that was."

"Now I can go out of the world the way I came into it, not owing anybody as much as 25 cents," said Dougherty. "After I pay my debts, there won't be much left.

"But when I disappear down the valley of the dark shadows, nobody will be able to say, 'There goes the ….. who owes me ten bucks.'"

"Sequoia" was no longer the home of the Dougherty family, and now the hotel had become the Baron's resting place, but much of its glamour was gone. George Godfrey, Jack Johnson, Damon Runyon and many others from that Golden Era of sports had all passed away. Soon the Baron would join them, and it seemed that after the auction that time was getting much closer.

- Chapter 12 -

The Passing of a Legend

"My spirit is alive, but my body is at Clancy's Funeral Home."

Jimmy "Baron" Dougherty

In December of 1948, just six months after Dougherty auctioned off his mansion and other properties on Chester Pike, he was stricken with pneumonia while living at the Colonial Hotel. He was in the middle of preparing for his last fling at his annual Christmas Party when he became ill. He was in Taylor Hospital in Ridley Park for several weeks, but was released just in time for Christmas.

Early in 1949, the Baron suffered a stroke as he met with his attorney, Guy de Furia, in the law library at the Media Courthouse.

He was confined to Chester Hospital for more than a week, and then was released; apparently well on the road to recovery.

On July 5, 1949, the Baron had a second stroke, and again was hospitalized, this time in Taylor Hospital.

Eight days later, he returned to Taylor Hospital after he fell down the stairs in his home at the hotel during an early morning foray for something to eat.

Two months later, Dougherty returned to the Hotel where a nurse, Mary Ferry, and a maid, Ella Green, watched him constantly every day.

During this time, Dougherty would have some interesting visitors. One such visitor, who made the trip down from New York was Jack Dempsey and former lightweight fighter, Joe Benjamin. A picture of all three appeared in the *Philadelphia Sunday Bulletin*.

The caption read, "Dempsey gives an old pal a helping hand. Former world heavyweight champion Jack Dempsey and Joe Benjamin came down from New

On February 29, 1949, Jack Dempsey (left) and former boxer Joe Benjamin (right) came down from New York to visit Dougherty, who had just recently suffered a stroke. Dempsey is seen here massaging the Baron's partially paralyzed left arm with an electric vibrator.

York to visit Jimmy Dougherty, the Baron of Leiperville, who suffered a stroke recently. Dempsey is massaging the Baron's left arm, which was partially paralyzed, with an electric vibrator."

Another day, he had whispered to a *Chester Times* reporter, "The spirit is here, but the body's at Clancy's," in reference to the late John L. Clancy, who operated the funeral home at 8th and Upland Streets.

On the night of October 4, 1949, the Baron was not feeling real well, and he requested that his family come to his bedside. The next day, October 5, he passed at 10a.m. in the morning.

"Even death had a tough time disposing of the rugged 80-year old Baron," said sportswriter Tony Zecca. "Twice he came off the floor from recent strokes before taking the final count."

Gathered around his bed when he died were his wife, Mary Dougherty, his daughters, Dorothy McLaughlin of Ocean City, Margaret Stull, Elizabeth Dwyer and Mary Damico; and his three sons, Matt, Jimmy and Howard.

Howard remarked, "Despite the fact that he started slipping last night, he rested generally pretty comfortably."

Dougherty's death ironically came on the day of the biggest national sporting event of the year, the World Series. In that game, the first of the series, a dramatic ninth inning home run by Tommy Henrich, the New York Yankees' "Old Reliable," gave the Yankees a 1-0 victory over the Brooklyn Dodgers.

His interest in sports never flagging, he had made arrangements for a radio to be placed near his bedside, so even in his emaciated and weakened condition, he could listen to the opening game.

His obituary appeared in many newspapers, even *Ring Magazine*, the Bible of Boxing. In the December, 1949 issue, editor and publisher Nat Fleischer wrote,

"The death of James F. Dougherty, the 'Baron of Leiperville' brought to an end the career of one more prominent figure in the boxing world. The colorful 80 year old Pennsylvania sportsman, figured prominently for more than half a century in the news of the boxing and political world. Most of his life, he was in the spotlight as a promoter, manager and referee, but in his later years, he became quite a figure as a political rebel in his native state where he opposed Governor Sproul.

"At one time, he managed Harry and Eddie Lenny and George Godfrey, the giant Negro who fought Primo Carnera. Although he had trained Jack Dempsey for a time, he was selected as referee of the Gibbons-Dempsey fight at Shelby, Montana, on July 4, 1923.

"In 1946, he sought the nomination for United States Senator in opposition to the Pennsylvania boss, Joseph P. Guffey, but the court ordered his name stricken from the ballot because he had failed to have the proper petitions."

The day after his death, an impressive tribute was paid to the Baron when Judge William R. Toal, in Court no. 2 at Media Courthouse, requested a moment of silence in memory of Mr. Dougherty.

As court attaches, lawyers and persons in the huge room stood, Judge Toal said,

"Mr. Dougherty was a colorful, very unusual and, I might say, a great personality.

"Delaware County for years has been proud of the fact that the Baron was one of its native sons. With his passing has passed an era.

"He worked hard and developed himself. For years he had close contact with the great, and he was a real friend of man. Many, many times out of his pocket would come $5.00 for someone when it was most needed. He was a real friend of the down-and-outer. I know he would not have us be sorry for his death, because he always faced life courageously."

Dougherty's viewing was on Friday, October 7, at the Clancy Funeral Home after a Mass in St. Rose of Lima Church on Chester Pike in Eddystone. The burial was the following day at St. Michael's Cemetery.

"It was the biggest demonstration in my 30 years in the funeral business," said John L. Clancy, owner of the funeral home at 9th and Upland Streets.

Chester Times writer Orrin C. Evans reported, "The citizens, high and lowly crossing racial and religious lines, began forming lines out 9th street and down Upland Street long before the doors to the chapel in which lay in death Leiperville's leading citizen were due to open at 7:00p.m.

"There were, of course, men by the hundreds. But, also, there were women. Old women, young women, pretty girls, the matronly woman of middle age and children whispering in awed tones as the line tortuously inched up to the wide-flung double doors leading into the chapel.

"Many of them were poor; their clothes showed it. They moved slowly, oh so slowly into the chapel, two, three, and often four a breast.

Coming out of Baron Dougherty's viewing are: l to r Earl "Rodeo Morton Pool V.B.A. "Smith, Tippy Martin, Bobby Barrett, and Herman Taylor.

"And as they filed through the quiet funeral chapel, a still swelling crowd lined the sidewalk, waiting. By 11:20 p.m., there were still heavy clusters outside, trying to gain admittance to the funeral parlors. In deference to them, Clancy ordered the doors closed. Already they had remained open one hour and 20 minutes beyond the scheduled time."

More than 4,000 people looked for the last time at Jimmy Dougherty. A few of them, notably some of the older residents of Leiperville, looked at a man they had known intimately from childhood.

The list of honorary pallbearers was a who's who in sports, business and civic circles. Jack Dempsey and James Farley led the special list. Also on that list was Doc Kearns, Dempsey's former manager and a lifelong friend of Dougherty's.

"I was terribly shocked to learn of the death of the Baron," said Dempsey. "He was one of my first friends back in the days when I was trying to get a break in the fight game. I'd be at his funeral no matter where I'd be."

Farley, the former postmaster general, was enroute from Europe with members of his family when he was notified of Dougherty's death. He was going to try and be there if his ship arrived in time.

In addition to Dempsey and Farley, the following served as honorary pallbearers: George L. Alston, Sam D. Riddle, Auditor General Weldon B. Heyburn, Senator Elmer Wene of New Jersey; John G. Pew, Connie Mack, Sugar Ray Robinson, John J. McClure, Jack Farrell, Herman Taylor, C. William Kraft, Charles E. Acker, Casper Sharpless, Albert Crawford Jr., John Doherty, Clarence L. Conner, William D. Mooney, Alfred G. Hill and Joseph E. Dougherty.

Also included as honorary pallbearers were: Stoney McLinn, Judges Harold L. Ervin, William R. Toal, Henry G. Sweney, Arthur P. Bretherick and E. LeRoy vanRoden of Delaware County, and Judges Eugene Bonniwell and Herbert E. Millen of Philadelphia Municipal Court.

Other honorary pallbearers included: John Dolan, Robert McBride, Cameron Donato, Pete Tyrell, Harry Toppi, Leon Rains, Mickey Walker, Jack Freed, John Webster, Orrin C. Evans, Lanse McCurley, William D. Mason, Vito Greto, Alphonso Cename and Charles Price.

The active pallbearers were: George Souers of Norwood; Woodlyn's Vincent Mallon; Bobby Barrett of Clifton Heights; Sun Hill's Jack Feeley; William Martin of Woodlyn; and Media's Raymond Dawson.

Many who attended the funeral were quoted in the Chester Times about their relationship to the Baron.

Herman "Muggsy" Taylor, Philadelphia's greatest fight promoter, said, "I knew him since I was a kid 13 years old. I never admired anyone like him. I had a great affection for him, and truly loved him."

Herman Taylor, who actually promoted boxing longer than anyone (1912 to 1975), was a good friend of Dougherty's. He also was a close friend of Nucky Johnson, who ran Atlantic City and is the main character of HBO's popular series entitled, "Boardwalk Empire". In Grace D'Amato's book, *Chance Of A Lifetime*, she claims that before Nucky departed for prison in 1941, he had dinner with a handful of friends which included Herman Taylor.

Phillip Glassman, former manager of Lew Tendler and one-time fight and wrestling promoter in Philadelphia, said, "He was a boost to the boxing business. All the sporting people will miss him."

"I was indeed sorry to learn of the death of James F. Dougherty," said Judge Harold L. Ervin, president judge of the Common Pleas Court of Delaware County,

"While I could not always agree with the position he took in public matters, I could not help but admire the strong fighting qualities which he so frequently exhibited. For many years, he was an outstanding figure in the life of Delaware County, and he will be long remembered by enemy and friend alike."

"The Baron was a man who really had the common touch," recalled Jack Farrell, who was a hotel owner in Philadelphia and associated with Dougherty in fight promotions and baseball enterprises. "He never got too big to be ready to offer a helping hand to the underdog. He was a hard-hitting opponent, and a very clever man, both in the field of sports and in politics. He'll leave a big gap in Delaware County."

"He definitely was one of the best friends sports ever had," said Stony McLinn, veteran Philadelphia sportswriter and sports announcer. "He always was an asset to the boxing game, square and honest. What he did for the kids in his area no one ever will know. He had friends throughout the country, yes, throughout the world."

Clarence L. Conner, executive manager of the Chester Municipal Authority, former president of the Delaware County Commissioners during one of two terms served by Dougherty, was shocked at the death of his former colleague.

"I served four years as county commissioner with Mr. Dougherty, and I found him to be at all times sincere in his effort to serve the people of the county during that time. He was very cooperative with me, and I mourn his loss to the community."

The Baron's bar was never empty, and he was so personable and big hearted that he would literally give you the shirt off his back. All his life, he was a champion of the needy and the down-and-out people of our society.

"That was his trouble," said Vince Mallon, who was an outstanding athlete and later became a Justice of the Peace in Ridley Township. "He was always buying food for this family, or sending a ton of coal to that family. He was a promoter who never stayed on the job at the hotel. He could have been a millionaire."

"He was a real friend of the down-and-outer," said Judge William R. Toal. "Many, many times out of his pocket would come $5.00 for someone when it was most needed."

Dougherty once said, "I've paid off hundreds of notes I'd signed for no-good bums all over the country who didn't meet their obligations."

He had quite a liking to animals, especially dogs. A few years before his death, the Baron was saddened by the death of his pet terrier, Mickey, named for his friend and former boxer Mickey Walker.

Dedicating his 1946 Christmas card message to Mickey, the Baron wrote, "Mickey died last March but in memory he will live on forever as the truest friend man ever had. Life, as it was for Mickey, is for all of us uncertain. We who are left on this earth should be thankful. Sometimes we think we have suffering and hardship too heavy to bear. But we must remind ourselves of the millions of others whose burdens are heavier than our own. And so in this Holy Season, let us offer up our thanks to God."

During Christmas of 1946, Baron Dougherty sent out Christmas cards with this picture of himself with his dog Mickey, named after his friend and former boxer, Mickey Walker. Mickey had passed away in March and the Baron dedicated his holiday message to Mickey.

He also liked to do things for the kids. It was an annual occurrence for him to gather hundreds of youngsters and take them on picnic outings to Willow Grove or some other park.

One newspaper headline from August, 1922 read, "Leiperville Kids' Annual Outing: Jimmy Dougherty entertains 2,000 Leiperville kids as his guests at Fairmont Park in Philadelphia."

The Baron was always helping someone and was even partly responsible for establishing boxing in the world of higher education.

Walter Schlichter wrote, "Dougherty was one of the early crusaders with Philadelphia Jack O'Brien, Major Tony Biddle and Danny Hutchison to put boxing on a higher plane in the world of sports and they were responsible for putting George Decker as boxing instructor in the University of Pennsylvania. Soon, other colleges took up boxing."

Samuel M. Vauclain is seen here on the left with Jack Dempsey at one of Dougherty's outings for the kids at Fairmount Park in 1922.

Dougherty knew Decker quite well because Decker had fought two of his fighters (1903-1904), Harry and Eddie Lenny. His career lasted from 1903 to 1913, where he met such fighters as: Young Erne, Frank Klaus, Leo Houck and Jack O'Brien.

In 1919, Decker, with the help of Dougherty, Biddle and Hutchison, was hired to not only be the boxing instructor at Penn, but to also establish a collegiate boxing team. That team, coached by Decker, met Penn State that same year in the first collegiate boxing match.

By 1921, boxing had become so popular at Penn, that more than 400 students were interested and being instructed by the veteran coach.

Dougherty was always giving fighters and former fighters a helping hand. Whether it was getting them employment at his establishment or through all the individuals he knew in industry, the Baron was always there for a rundown fighter.

As some writers had mentioned, Dougherty always went out of his way to help the black fighters of that time.

"My grandfather was way ahead of his time when it came to race relations," said James Dougherty II, a nationally known lawyer and grandson of the Baron. "He was always helping out black fighters."

"My father was always lending money to black fighters who needed it," recalled Howard. "I remember a few times when the Baron lent money to Jack Johnson.

Johnson borrowed money from my father one Sunday when we were cleaning up the bar. He stopped by on his way down south. Johnson died not long after that."

Mary Damico, the Baron's daughter, remembered, "My father would always let Jack Jonson sleep over in our house on Chester Pike in Ridley Park. It would upset my mother, but my father did what he wanted."

Remember, this was a time in America when the white population considered Johnson too uppity for a black man. Most whites saw him as a perpetual threat and very arrogant, amoral and a danger to the order of things in America.

Many decades later, black professional athletes were still being segregated on away trips with their teams and some couldn't even eat in restaurants with their white teammates.

However, in the period before Johnson captured the title (1904-08) and during the Roaring 1920's, one of the most hated black men in America spent the night and felt very comfortable in the Baron's home.

Another black boxer who the Baron befriended and helped was Joe Gans, the lightweight champion of the world. Gans, known as the "Old Master", became the first American-born black world champion in any sport when he kayoed Frank Erne in 1902. He held the lightweight title from 1902 until 1908 and had close to 200 fights with 100 of them coming from the knockout category. Many boxing historians consider Gans to be one of the greatest fighters of all time, pound-for-pound.

Dougherty had known Gans since the turn of the century, and Gans had trained for some of his fights in Leiperville and Chester. He also knew Gans' trainer Al Herford, and Herford spent time at the Chester Training quarters and at Leiperville.

In a 1944 interview with Bill Burk, who was the sports editor of the *Chester Times*, Dougherty said, "I built that Leiperville ring especially for the Herford crowd, and Joe Gans was their star. I even boxed with Gans on many occasions.

"Joe and I trained two Negro youngsters, and we toured the U.S. in a boxing and dancing set known as Dougherty's Piccaninnies."

In 1938, Dougherty and Gans were the subject of Damon Runyon's column, "The Brighter Side". Runyon told of Gans' visit to see the Baron in 1905 before making his trip to the west coast.

"Joe Gans was one of the few geniuses of the ring," wrote Runyon. "He was such a geniuses that in his time prize fighting could truly be called boxing. He

207

made it a game of skill not just a test of slugging power. He was not only the greatest Negro fighter that ever lived, but no white man ever surpassed him in knowledge of boxing.

"He was in the hands of crafty manipulators, and even when he was still lightweight champion and his great skill was generally recognized, he fell into disrepute and drifted to the village of Leiperville in Delaware County, Pennsylvania, where he had often trained for his fights.

"There he looked up a man named James Dougherty, noted in prizefighting circles as 'The Baron of Leiperville,' and he told Dougherty he was pretty sick but if could get money enough to reach Chicago, a newspaper friend there would give him railroad fare to the Pacific coast, where he might get some matches.

"Dougherty took Gans to his own family physician and had him examined and afterwards the physician called Dougherty aside and said, 'Didn't you tell me this man was some sort of an athlete?'

"'That's right,' said Dougherty. 'He is a boxer, the lightweight champion of the world.'

"'Impossible!' said the physician. 'Why he is not only in advanced stages of tuberculosis, but he has other serious ailments. He should be in bed.'

"However, Dougherty sent Gans to Chicago and from there the fighter went to the coast to put in some of the greatest battles of his career, including the famous 42-round fight in Goldfield, Nevada, when he won from Battling Nelson on a foul and kept his lightweight title."

Tuberculosis was nothing to fool with. Even the White House was not safe as President Harrison's wife Caroline Harrison had died of tuberculosis at the White House in October of 1892.

Gans had had a falling out with Al Herford, his manager and made the trip without him. But for Gans to fight forty-two rounds in the heat and in the advanced stages of tuberculosis seems impossible. The doctor who examined Gans before the fight found him in perfect shape.

Two things we know for sure. First, Gans had some form of tuberculosis when he defended his title against Nelson. Dougherty's personal physician attested to that.

Second, Gans trusted the Baron, and knew he could borrow money from him. Without Dougherty's loan, Gans may never have gotten to Chicago and eventually the west coast.

Joe Gans is pictured with his hands on his hips at the weigh-in for his historic bout with Battling Nelson (left with arms folded) in 1906. Dougherty, a close friend of Gans, gave him money to help him get to the west coast to take part in Tex Rickard's first great fight promotion in Gold-field, Nevada.

Before he eventually died of tuberculosis in 1910, Gans returned to his hometown of Baltimore with the $11,000 he received for winning the Nelson bout and built the Goldfield Hotel, which opened in 1907, the same year as the Baron's Colonial Hotel opening. The Goldfield was a jazz club and precursor to the Cotton Club in New York. Jack Johnson visited Gans' establishment quite often during that time, and was inspired to build his own bar and restaurant in New York, which later became known as the Cotton Club. It was at the Goldfield where Gans gave musician Eubie Blake his first big opportunity making $55.00 a week playing the piano.

Gans was also used by Ernest Hemingway as a character in his 1916 short story, "A Matter of Colour". This early story set the stage for Hemingway's famous 1927 parable, "*The Killers*".

Joe Damico, a very successful lawyer in Delaware County and the grandson of the Baron, once as a young child got to meet one of the truly great boxers of all time at the Leiperville training quarters.

"I was probably six or seven years old," remembered Damico, " and my mother dropped me off at my grandfather's training quarters to carry the water bucket for one of the boxers training that day behind the hotel. When my mother came to pick me up, she asked the fighter's name that I worked with. I told her his name was Sugar."

Little did Damico know at the time, that he was the water boy for a future world champion and one of the greatest fighters of all time, Sugar Ray Robinson.

In an interview with Bill Burk in 1944, Dougherty recalled, "I first saw Sugar in the amateurs and later at my training quarters, and I broke one of the rules of the boxing commission when I trotted him out at a Leiperville show to tell the fans that here is a boy who is as good right now as Joe Gans, one of the great lightweights; Benny Leonard, Lew Tendler, Freddy Welsh and Joe Bernstein, when they were at their best."

He then explained to Burk why Robinson is so good.

"He has that something none of the rest had excepting Gans," explained Dougherty, "and that is the foot movement and the knack of balancing his body without being thrown out of position to hit. That comes from proper training in the beginning an asset that few present day fighters have, mainly because the teachers don't know these things themselves.

"It was the first fundamental for Professor McClain, Jack O'Brien, Mike Donovan, and Billy Edwards. They taught foot movement before allowing you to put up your hands.

"Joe Gans was a great buck and wing dancer, and I am told that Robinson studied dancing under Bill Robinson as a boy. The Sugar could have been the lightweight champ and will be the welter and middleweight when and if he gets the opportunities. He may go down in history as the Sam Langford of his class, because I doubt if they'll ever fight him."

Dougherty's predictions were quite accurate, because two years later in 1946, Robinson captured the welterweight title, and a year after that, he won the middleweight championship.

Robinson fought many times in Philadelphia during the early part of his professional career. In 1944, he was training at Dougherty's for a fight with Richard Ragnel at Convention Hall that was being promoted by Herman Taylor.

A few years before his death, the Baron, who had been out of the boxing game for quite some time, revealed to Damon Runyon that he had an outstanding heavyweight prospect that he felt could become a world champion. Runyon even wrote about it in one of his last columns on January 18, 1946.

Runyon wrote, "The Baron said he is a great big kid, and he thinks he is a coming heavyweight champion of the world for sure."

"The Baron has got a big box of live house flies, and he has a fellow letting these flies out of the box one at a time and the kid has to stand there and grab at the flies with his left hand. That's to teach him a fast left hand. You know you have to grab fast to catch a live fly with one hand."

Dougherty never mentioned the kid's name, but there is a good chance that it was Leiperville's own Harry Kurlish. A photograph was found some years ago that showed Kurlish in boxing garb and a fighter's stance. On the photo was written to Kurlish, "To your pal, Baron Dougherty, August 17, 1947, Champion of the World in 1950."

In an interview with Kurlish some years later, he explained to me that when he entered Ridley Township High School, he began training at the ring in Leiperville.

"Dougherty felt that I had some promise as a fighter and had me train and spar with the 'Arizona Kid. The Arizona Kid was from Media, and he trained fighters for the Baron. The story was that he had just missed becoming the middleweight champion.

"I use to work-out with him three times a week, and we would go fifteen rounds. He really worked me hard and got me ready for my first fight and a possible ring career."

Pictured here is Baron Dougherty shaking hands with Harry Kurlish, who he thought could become a world champion. Damon Runyon even wrote about his prospect in one of his columns, but the Baron would not mention his name. Still in his school at Ridley Township and a football player, Kurlish stopped boxing after his coach Phil Marion discovered what he was up to.

Unfortunately, that ring career never came to fruition because in 1947, Kurlish stopped boxing to concentrate on football at Ridley. Legendary coach Phil Marion found out about his boxing interest and was extremely upset. That season, Kurlish was going to be Marion's starting fullback.

Kurlish, whose brother Bill had been an All-American at the University of Pennsylvania, would be selected to the All-Delco and All-Suburban teams a year later. The Baron's dream of a possible world champion would never be.

After the passing of the Baron, his oldest son Jimmy and Howard ran the hotel and bar until 1954 when the Colonial hit on hard times. Litigation and law suits clouded the ownership, and finally on October 20, 1954, the title to the old landmark passed from the Dougherty family and into the hands of another sporting figure, Billy Ritchie.

Ritchie, a former lightweight boxer of the 1920's and early 1930's, had once sold newspapers as a kid in front of the hotel. He also fought at the Open Air Arena in the back of the hotel, one time appearing on the same card with Maxie Rosenbloom and Popper Stopper.

"Well, I had fought here and spent time here," said Ritchie. "I was running a bar in Chester, and I heard this place was available. It wasn't publicized, but I heard it through the grapevine.

"So I bought it. I had the place done over. Now I live here to."

After those extensive alterations, Ritchie re-opened as a modern bar and restaurant.

In 1966, Ritchie was interviewed by the *Philadelphia Inquirer*, and he recalled, "Boxing had quite an effect on youngsters in Leiperville. Because boxing dominated the area, many Leiperville youths learned to fight.

Billie Ritchie, who was a good lightweight boxer in the 1920's and had also sold newspapers as a kid in front of the Baron's Colonial Hotel, bought the establishment in 1954 from the Dougherty family. (Chuck Hasson Collection)

"There is a legend that Leiperville boys were so eager to test their prowess on their peers from neighboring Eddystone that young Eddystone residents would take immense detours rather than walk through Leiperville."

"You know it wasn't just fighters and fight fans that came to the Colonial," continued Ritchie. "After a big victory by Man O' War, Sam Riddle would hold a victory celebration here. And the top Delaware County politicians used to meet here."

Bill Feeley, who grew up in Leiperville and spent a lot of time at the bar, was also quoted in the Inquirer article, "The Baron always had three or four fighters, and he would take care of a lot of top ones when they were in the East. He also promoted a lot of big fights in Philadelphia besides promoting here.

Dempsey was a great friend of the Baron. He even dropped in after his honeymoon."

"Damon Runyon was here a lot," continued Feeley. "He was always bringing fighters down. He'd stay a week or two, hanging around the bar. The last time he was married, he even dropped in here on his honeymoon."

After twenty years, Billie Ritchie sold his restaurant and bar in 1974 to Nick Ford from Springfield, and shortly after, there was a fire that destroyed the place.

Some years before, the name Leiperville was replaced by the town's new name, Crum Lynne; and now, after the fire, there was nothing left to indicate that the Colonial Hotel ever existed. Only the remaining photographs are proof of the legendary hotel's existence.

Runyon and Jack Johnson both passed away in 1946, and George Godfrey died a year later. Now the Baron was gone and so was the "Golden Era" of Leiperville, an era of greatness that no community in Delaware County has ever equaled.

The late *Daily Times* sports writer Matt Zabitka wrote, "Back in the 1920's and 1930's, the little community of Leiperville, bisected by Chester Pike and sandwiched in by Eddystone, Woodlyn and Ridley Park, was famous for boxing, Baldwin Locomotive Works and bootleg booze.

"With the late Baron Dougherty in the saddle as the rajah, the town flourished as a boxing Mecca. The greats of the day, the near-greats and the has-beens flocked to the tiny burg whose chief citadel was the Colonial Hotel and the ramshackle 5,000-seat arena at the rear of the inn.

"Maxie Rosenbloom fought in that rickety ring. So did George Godfrey, Popper Stopper, Kid Chocolate, Billy Angelo, Billy Ritchie, and scores of other big name gladiators.

"Jack Dempsey trained there. So did Tony Galento and Billy Conn, and famous writers like Damon Runyon and Red Smith were frequent visitors.

"It was truly Leiperville's 'Golden Era'."

And without the Baron, there would have been no "Golden Era".

James F. Dougherty was the most colorful sports personality Delaware County has ever known in the 20th Century. He made a real name for himself during the Roaring 20's, which was billed as the Golden Age of Sports in America, and he is a true legend in every sense of the word and must never be forgotten.

Bibliography

Aycock, Colleen and Mark Scott. *Tex Rickard: Boxing's Greatest Promoter*. North Carolina and London: McFarland & Company, 2012.

Clark, Tom. *The World Of Damon Runyon*. New York: Harper and Row, 1978.

Corum, Bill. *Off And Running*. New York: Henry Holt and Company, 1959.

Creamer, W. Robert. *Babe: The Legend Comes To Life*. New York: Simon and Schuster, 1974.

D'Amato Anselmo, Grace. *Chance Of A Lifetime: Nucky Johnson, Skinny D'amato And How Atlantic City Became The Naughty Queen Of Resorts*. New Jersey: Down the Shore Publishing, 2001.

Fleischer, Nat. *Black Dynamite: Volume V*. New York: The Ring, 1947.

Johnson, James" Body". *The Fight That Won't Stay Dead*. Shelby, Montana: Promoter Publishing Company, 1989.

Johnston, J.J. and Cogswell, Don. *Uncrowned Champions*. Self-published, 2011.

Kahn, Roger. *A Flame Of Pure Fire: Jack Dempsey And The Roaring* 20's. New York: Harcourt Brace & Company, 1999.

Kearns, Doc and Oscar Fraley. *The Million Dollar Gate*. New York: The MacMillan Company, 1966.

Kelly, Jason. *Shelby's Folly: Jack Dempsey, Doc Kearns, And The Shakedown Of A Montana Boomtown*. Lincoln and London: University of Nebraska Press, 2010.

Lockhart, Keith. *The History Of Ridley Township*. Ridley Township Tercentennial, 1987.

McLarnon, John. *Ruling Suburbia: A Biography Of The Mcclure Machine Of Delaware County*. Ann Arbor, Michigan: Bell & Howell Company, 1999.

Moyle, Clay. *Billy Miske: The St. Paul Thunderbolt*. Iowa City: KO Publications, 2011.

Moyle, Clay. *Sam Langford: Boxing's Greatest Uncrowned Champion*. Seattle: Bennett & Hastings Publishing, 2006.

Roberts, Randy. *Jack Dempsey: The Manassa Mauler*. New York: Grove Press, 1979.

Schulberg, Budd. *Moving Pictures: Memories Of A Hollywood Prince*. New York: Stein and day Publishers, 1981.

Ward, C. Geoffrey. *Unforgivable Blackness: The Rise And Fall Of Jack Johnson*. New York: Alfred A. Knopf, 2004.

Newspapers

Albuquerque Morning Journal

Chester Times

Great Falls Tribune

Los Angeles Herald

Los Angeles Times

New York Herald Tribune

New York Times

Philadelphia Record

Philadelphia Inquirer

Philadelphia Daily News

Philadelphia Public Ledger

Philadelphia North American

Philadelphia Bulletin

The Police Gazette

Portland News

The San Francisco Call

San Francisco Chronicle

Yonkers Herald